42 TODAY

42 TODAY

Jackie Robinson and His Legacy

Foreword by Ken Burns, Sarah Burns, and David McMahon

Edited by Michael G. Long

Afterword by Kevin Merida

A WASHNGTON MEWS BOOK

NEW YORK UNIVERSITY PRESS

New York

WASHINGTON MEWS BOOKS

An Imprint of

NEW YORK UNIVERSITY PRESS
New York
www.nyupress.org

References to Internet websites (URLs) were accurate at the time of writing. Neither the author nor New York University Press is responsible for URLs that may have expired or changed since the manuscript was prepared.

Library of Congress Cataloging-in-Publication Data
Names: Long, Michael G., editor.
Title: 42 today : Jackie Robinson and his legacy / foreword by Ken
Burns, Sarah Burns, and David McMahon ; edited by Michael G. Long ;
afterword by Kevin Merida.
Other titles: Forty-two today
Description: New York : New York University Press, 2021. |
Series: Washington mews books | Includes bibliographical references and index.
Identifiers: LCCN 2020015026 (print) | LCCN 2020015027 (ebook) |
ISBN 9781479805624 (cloth) | ISBN 9781479805631 (ebook) |
ISBN 9781479805617 (ebook)
Subjects: LCSH: Robinson, Jackie, 1919–1972. | Robinson, Jackie, 1919–1972—
Influence. | African American baseball players—Biography. | Discrimination in
sports—United States—History—20th century. | United States—Race relations—
History—20th century.
Classification: LCC GV865.R6 A15 2021 (print) | LCC GV865.R6 (ebook) | DDC
796.357092 [B]—dc23
LC record available at https://lccn.loc.gov/2020015026
LC ebook record available at https://lccn.loc.gov/2020015027

New York University Press books are printed on acid-free paper, and their binding materials are chosen for strength and durability. We strive to use environmentally responsible suppliers and materials to the greatest extent possible in publishing our books.

Manufactured in the United States of America

Book designed and typeset by Charles B. Hames

10 9 8 7 6 5 4 3 2 1

Also available as an ebook

To Rachel Robinson

I have devoted and dedicated my life to service.

* JACKIE ROBINSON

CONTENTS

PART III. CIVIL RIGHTS AND POLITICS

PART IV. THE WIDE WORLD OF SPORTS

FOREWORD

Taking Jackie Robinson Seriously

KEN BURNS, SARAH BURNS, AND DAVID MCMAHON

On April 15, 1947, Jackie Robinson sent a seismic wave across America with his barrier-breaking first game in Major League Baseball. It was arguably the most significant progress in civil rights since Reconstruction.

That summer, Robinson captivated fans with his electrifying blend of speed and power, while meeting the withering barrage of hate he faced on and off the field with quiet restraint. His success made him the most famous black man in America and paved the way for other talented black players to join him in the integrated big leagues. It's a well-told story, one that in the decades since Robinson's pioneering first season has become almost mythological and taken on a sentimentality that has blinded us to his true nature and minimized the noxious racism that hardly retreated in his heroic wake. Too often we have remembered him as an unthreatening martyr who "turned the other cheek," dependent on a helping hand from well-meaning whites. It's a safe and simple narrative that provides white America convenient cover and does a disservice to an uncompromising patriot. It also distracts us from a dark reality: the oppressive conditions Robinson faced across his fifty-three years—casual and structural—remain as present in society today as they were then.

The silent stoicism that marked Jack Roosevelt Robinson's initial year with the Brooklyn Dodgers ran contrary to his character. Stubborn, intelligent, with a fiery temper and full of deeply held convictions, Robinson had rarely missed an opportunity to speak out against the prejudice and injustice he saw nearly everywhere. Growing up in depression-era Pasadena, California, he faced down racist neighbors and refused to sit in the segregated section at the movie theater or leave a Woolworth lunch counter until he was served. Once he was arrested for singing a song that a police officer found offensive. Another time, while just a bystander to an argument, an officer rushed in and pulled a gun on Robinson before knowing who was to blame. As a second lieutenant in the U.S. Army during the Second World War, he faced a court-martial after refusing an order from a white civilian bus driver to move to the back of a military bus at Fort Hood, Texas—ten years before Rosa Parks's own bold act of defiance in Montgomery, Alabama.

Brooklyn's general manager, Branch Rickey, a high-minded opportunist, knew of Robinson's scrapes with the law and his early discharge from the U.S. Army before signing him to the Dodgers. In these incidents, Rickey saw a man of considerable character who, though strong-willed and defiant, would care enough about succeeding that he would, for a time, suppress his natural impulse to fight back—and during his first few seasons, Robinson mostly did. But once his place in the game was secure, it was no longer necessary for Robinson to keep quiet. As President Barack Obama later observed, Jackie Robinson "had purchased the right to speak his mind many times over."[1]

Throughout his remaining playing days, Robinson used his enormous fame to bring attention to the countless ways in which his world was patently unjust. He criticized umpires who he believed were treating him unfairly, demanded that hotels provide equal access to him and his black teammates, and accused the New York Yankees of prejudice for failing to promote any black players to their team. When, during a midgame birthday celebration for the team's Kentucky-born shortstop Pee Wee Reese, the grounds crew raised a Confederate flag over Ebbets Field, Robinson fumed. "Who would ever let Jim Crow back in the ballpark?" he asked resentful teammates, who were enjoying the festivities.[2] The press, many of whom had once praised him for his self-control, took exception to his outspokenness, calling him ungrateful and urging him to be a baseball player, not a crusader. Bill Keefe, sports editor of the *New Orleans Times-Picayune*, declared that "no ten of the *most rabid segregationists* accomplished as much as *Robinson* did in *widening the breach between* the white people and Negroes."[3]

"If you showed anything that suggested dignity and the sense that you believed in equality, you were immediately undesirable," said Harry Belafonte, referring to Robinson. "There's always going to be a price to pay for any rebel sound that challenges oppression."[4] This of course remains true to this day. In 2016, San Francisco 49ers quarterback Colin Kaepernick chose not to stand for the national anthem in protest of police brutality against African Americans. His actions were denounced by star quarterback Drew Brees as disrespectful and criticized by the National Football League as unpatriotic, and President Donald Trump described his dissent as grounds for firing. A free agent the following season, Kaepernick went unsigned and three years later remained out of the league in spite of his earlier success and widely acknowledged talents.

Toward the end of his career, when Jackie Robinson and his wife Rachel sought to buy a larger house to accommodate their growing family, they were met with resistance. Touring homes in New York City's northern suburbs, they were glared at by neighbors, denied access by owners, and in one case, after making an offer, told it was off the market. The effect of such racially restrictive agreements among homeowners, brokers, and community associations—even though in some cases ruled unconstitutional decades earlier—continues to keep neighborhoods segregated and limits the housing opportunities of people of color.

After baseball, Robinson wrote hundreds of newspaper columns about inequality and injustice and raised money for the NAACP and Southern Christian Leadership Conference. When Martin Luther

King Jr. asked Robinson to help boost morale among civil rights workers in Georgia or Alabama, Jackie took the next available flight. He also sparred with Malcolm X over the direction of the civil rights movement and later seemed to some out of touch in forcefully dismissing the arguments of younger, more militant activists who had grown frustrated with the slow pace of change, including Muhammad Ali. But Robinson continued to make his voice heard.

He stumped for politicians who he believed would best support the interests of African Americans, including Richard Nixon, a decision he later regretted. At the 1964 Republican National Convention, Robinson attended as a special delegate, rallying a tiny band of African Americans, who were abandoned when the party lurched sharply to the right. The eventual nominee was Barry Goldwater, who had voted against the Civil Rights Act of 1964 and whose supporters included the John Birch Society and the Ku Klux Klan. At a rally outside the convention, Robinson thundered his disapproval. "I am an American Negro first, before I am a member of any party," he told the audience. "We will not stand silently for any major party nominating a man who in my opinion is a bigot and a man who will attempt to prevent us from moving forward."[5] That fall, Lyndon Johnson trounced Barry Goldwater at the polls. More than fifty years later, the party of Lincoln continued to find support among far-right organizations standing for white supremacy. In 2017, when hate groups gathered in Charlottesville, Virginia, to rally against the removal of a monument to Confederate commander Robert E. Lee, President Donald Trump, a Republican, declined to condemn the marchers after their gathering resulted in deadly violence.

If we are serious about the kind of meaningful change Jackie Robinson campaigned for both on and off the field, and before, as well as long after his monumental major league debut, we should remember him in full, celebrate his outspokenness, and acknowledge that many of the obstacles he faced as a black man in America remain fixed, blocking the path to first-class citizenship for African Americans.

INTRODUCTION

That Day

MICHAEL G. LONG

"A life is not important except in the impact it has on others." These are the familiar words engraved on Jackie Robinson's tombstone in Cypress Hills Cemetery in Brooklyn, not far from where he began his public campaign to redeem the racist soul of America. Robinson's signature, with its soft curves and loops, appears below the chiseled words, authorizing the wisdom as his own. There's no citation on the headstone, of course, but the statement comes from the epilogue to *I Never Had It Made*, Robinson's final book, a searing account of his life on and beyond the baseball diamond.[1]

In this same book are those other memorable words, quoted so many times after NFL quarterback Colin Kaepernick took a knee during the national anthem: "I cannot stand and sing the anthem. I cannot salute the flag; I know that I am a black man in a white world."[2]

Published in 1972, *I Never Had It Made* offers remarkable insight into the frustrations Robinson felt near the end of his life. With diabetes ravaging his body, he was benched, far from the center of action, when he learned about Richard Nixon's attack on busing for the purpose of desegregating public schools, about Republican plans to slash warfare, and about the brutal response to the uprising at Attica Prison. These were not easy days for someone long accustomed to creating opportunities and forcing results, from a stolen home plate in the World Series to the opening of a bank in Harlem.

Robinson's voice in *I Never Had It Made* often reveals fury and frustration, disgust and disappointment, and anger and annoyance. Because Alfred Duckett wrote the text—the book lists the author as "Jackie Robinson as told to Alfred Duckett"—it's unclear whether the tone throughout is Robinson's or Duckett's, though perhaps it belongs to both men, steeped, as they were, in the white backlash of the Nixon era.

It would come as no surprise if the book's fury, especially over the flag, was solely Robinson's. In a July 1969 interview with the *New York Times*, the American icon sounded a similar note. "I wouldn't fly the flag on the Fourth of July or any other day," he said. "When I see a car with a flag pasted on it, I figure the guy behind the wheel isn't my friend."[3]

Robinson was chairman of the Freedom National Bank in Harlem at this point, and he believed that the flag had become captive to the conservative movement, with its emphasis on law and order, its opposition to ongoing demands from the civil rights movement, and its support for the Vietnam War. Robinson was not a vocal opponent of the war, but he scoffed at the notion that love of country should translate into uncritical support for the policies of the new president, Richard Nixon.

Robinson's scorching comments about the flag, in 1969 and in his final book, seem in sharp contrast to the patriotism he displayed in his testimony against Paul Robeson at a 1949 hearing of the House Un-American Activities Committee or in his praise of democracy in a fawning 1956 letter to President Eisenhower or even in his defense against Malcolm X's mocking of America in 1963. But Robinson's patriotism, formed in the crucible of Jim Crow America, including a racist Fort Riley in Kansas during World War II, was always a volatile mix of praise and criticism, with an extra heavy dose of the latter.

Rachel Robinson was not a fan when she read her husband's comments about the national anthem in *I Never Had It Made*; nor was she pleased to learn that more than a few writers cited her husband's words in an effort to defend and legitimize Kaepernick's protest. When asked whether Jack—she called him Jack rather than Jackie—would approve of Kaepernick's knee taking, she said she didn't think he would, though she quickly added that she could not speak for her deceased husband.

Although Rachel's opinion might raise a few eyebrows, given Jack's own statement about not standing for the national anthem, it's in direct line with her longtime efforts to shape her husband's legacy in a way that shows him as more than the man who appears in *I Never Had It Made.*

Rachel has focused particularly on countering claims that her husband was angry on and off the field. After the release of the film 42, she stated that those who think of Jack as angry on the baseball diamond are flat-out wrong. "Sometimes people attribute Jack's actions to anger," she said. "When he played, he was assertive. But all too often people equate assertiveness on the part of black males as anger and aggression, and that wasn't Jack."[4] She made a similar point in the Ken Burns film *Jackie Robinson*: "He was not an angry black man. He was an athlete who wanted to win."[5] And in 1997, long before the release of either film, she said, "As people discuss Jack, it's often as a martyr. They overlook the joys he had, the exhilaration of winning, the joys of his children and his home."[6]

This book challenges Rachel's claim that Jack wasn't angry, and it does not correct the lack of attention to his joyful side. Rachel herself has already done exactly that in *Jackie Robinson: An Intimate Portrait*—a delightful book that includes stories and reflections that reveal the joyful side of Robinson's life as a husband, father, friend, athlete, and activist. Sharon Robinson offers a similar perspective in *Stealing Home: An Intimate Family Portrait by the Daughter of Jackie Robinson.* Sharon's other books, many of them published by Scholastic, as well as her numerous public comments, have consistently characterized Jackie as a generous father to his children and a favorite father in the family's former neighborhood in Stamford, Connecticut. Like Rachel, Sharon does not suggest Jackie was the perfect father—he had trouble especially when dealing with Jackie Jr.—but her belief that her father created a legacy of love is unwavering.

This book does, however, support Rachel's other primary goal when advancing her husband's legacy: to depict Jack as more than the black man who shattered the color barrier in Major League Baseball in 1947. The esteemed contributors to this volume—filmmakers, writers, journalists, scholars, and activists—add depth and nuance to the Jackie Robinson that our culture has unjustly frozen in 1947: the silent warrior who courageously used nonviolence, the nice young man who turned the other cheek, the polite player whose easy smile has graced countless children's books ever since.

Although our book does indeed address the legacy of the silent warrior as well as the ways that Robinson transformed Major League Baseball, it does so in a way that deconstructs the self-congratulatory myth that the smiling, easygoing, nonthreatening Jackie Robinson of 1947 is concrete evidence that we have largely overcome "America's original sin."

We also dive deep into Robinson's overlooked legacy in civil rights, politics, and the wider sports world. By exploring his legacy in all its complexity, we show Jackie Robinson not as the one-dimensional figure highlighted in so many annual tributes to his sacrifice in 1947, but as a complicated man who left multiple legacies, on and off the field, that defy easy characterization. Robinson lived such a large life, moving in and out of so many fields, that it would be wrongheaded to force all of his contributions into something called "*the* Jackie Robinson legacy."

Legacies are never easy to describe with accuracy and certainty. They're like moral character—best viewed from many different angles, in historical context, and over a long period. Like studies of character, explorations of legacies also lead to a culminating question: Is there anything that ties the different parts together? In this case, is there a unifying element in the various legacies that Robinson left us? Although the answer to this question will emerge throughout this book, Robinson's own reflections in the epilogue to *I Never Had It Made* hint at the answer:

> Life owes me nothing. Baseball owes me nothing. But I cannot, as an individual, rejoice in the good things I have been permitted to work for and learn while the humblest of my brothers is down in a deep hole hollering for help and not being heard.
>
> That is why I have devoted and dedicated my life to service. I don't like to be in debt. And I owe. . . . I still feel I owe till every man can rent and lease and buy according to his money and desires; until every child can have an equal opportunity in youth and manhood; until hunger is not only immoral but illegal; until hatred is recognized as a disease, a scourge, an epidemic, and treated as such; until racism and sexism and narcotics are conquered and until every man can vote and any man can be elected if he qualifies—until that day Jackie Robinson and no one else can say he has it made.[7]

Robinson's fervent commitment to serving "the humblest"—those who lacked the privilege he enjoyed, especially poor black people—is the one thread that ties together the many moving parts of his large life. If this becomes clear in the pages ahead, so too will the unfortunate fact that Robinson's life of service has not yet yielded the results he so aggressively fought for and desperately craved.

Robinson devoted himself to a life of service whose goal was, as he put it, "that day"—a time and place free of poverty, discrimination, and hatred, and full of equal opportunity and enfranchisement. Robinson's "that day," like Martin Luther King Jr.'s "beloved community," was nowhere in sight during his lifetime, and neither is it now: the legacy of Jackie Robinson, like King's, remains unfulfilled.

Perhaps more troubling to the optimists among us is that we have no reason to suggest that Robinson, like the ever-hopeful King, believed that "that day" would really arrive in human history. Robinson's eschatology was not nearly as optimistic as King's.

Nevertheless, you who enter these pages need not abandon all hope, if for no other reason than that an abundance of evidence, presented in this book, reveals that Robinson acted as if "that day" was still worthy of relentless pursuit, even if it was not realizable in human history. At last, then, the legacy of Jackie Robinson remains unfulfilled, and perhaps it will always be so, but it's still an urgent invitation, or better yet a demand, to pursue the impossible anyway, even unto death.

* * *

Note to the reader: There is a rough chronological order to this book, even though the writings are organized topically, making it possible for you to read them out of order without the threat of missing a coherent biographical narrative. If you wish to read a substantive overview of Robinson's life as you begin this book, you can find one in Peter Dreier's chapter on Robinson's legacy in the wide world of sports. Unlike the other chapters, Dreier's offers a detailed account of Robinson's life.

PART I

FOUNDATIONS

At Ebbets Field in 1957, a year after he retired from baseball. National Baseball Hall of Fame Library.

1

THE OWNER

HOWARD BRYANT

One of the great mysteries of the Jackie Robinson story is where *it* came from: his uncompromising sense of equality; his belief that no one was inherently better than anyone else, and certainly black people were not inferior to anyone; his insistence that he and all of the black people like him were entitled to the rights and courtesies of full citizenship; his insistence on ownership—of his person, of his environment, of his share of the American dream; his position that black people were not making a request to be considered, but were assuming access to an inalienable necessity. One doesn't ask permission to breathe.

The old stories of his early encounters with racism and his willingness to fight are well documented, from the time he countered the young white girl in Pasadena who called him a nigger by calling her a cracker, only to have her checkmate him with a rhyme (*soda cracker's good to eat, nigger's only good to beat*) to the time with the Kansas City Monarchs when he pulled the hose out of the gas tank from a merchant who would take their money but wouldn't let the members of the black ballclub use the men's room. Each reinforced the Robinson traits that would become his hallmark, but less certain was what created it, who instilled it, and how and why it remained when so often others who possessed the same instincts were left on the roadside, permanently broken.

The world Robinson entered was not welcoming to black service or sacrifice abroad. He was born in January 1919, just two and a half months after the armistice. Black American GIs had done their part in World War I, and for their blood black people were expected to return to their place, subservient to whites, unexpected to aspire, and discouraged to consider it an option. Violence was the primary weapon for the discouragement, used to police black aspirations, physically in the present by threat of murder, psychologically in the future by making black people ask if self-determination was worth their lives.

When Robinson was six months old, in July 1919, seventeen-year-old Eugene Williams was stoned by Chicago whites for swimming in a segregated area of Lake Michigan and drowned after being hit. When police refused to arrest the perpetrators, black people protested. After they protested, white Chicagoans killed and burned black homes on the South Side. The Chicago Riots of 1919 the history books would call it, and twenty-three blacks and fifteen whites were killed in a week.

There was Chicago. And Omaha. And Washington, DC. And Knoxville. Incidents varying the same theme: hostile white response to the black presence, for jobs, housing, opportunity. Robinson was in diapers during Red Summer. The summer of 1919, marked by blood, blood shed by blacks killed for aspiring, for doing when Robinson couldn't yet walk what he would embody once he could. Whites returned home from World War I to a competitive job market and an influx of blacks. Economic anxiety provided an incubator for racism—and murder.

Two years later, whites infamously raided the Greenwood district in Tulsa, known as Black Wall Street. It was not a riot, where two sides resorted to armed conflict, or an insurrection by the people put down by the state. This was a massacre, where whites shot and killed hundreds and burned black aspiration—buildings and flesh—to the ground. By the time Robinson was fourteen, in 1933, the National Football League had made its unofficial ban of black players official, joining baseball as another professional sport unavailable to black athletes. Surrounding Robinson was a specific form of American terrorism with a specific aim: to demoralize a people who had believed they were not given the handout of citizenship but had earned it through loyalty and blood. America was talking to its black people, telling them the American ideal of betterment through hard work, assimilation, did not apply to them—and they were determined to prove it, using arson, terrorism, and murder as primary tools.

The strong figures in his life—his mother Mallie, his sister Willa Mae, his brothers Frank and Mack, his mentor Reverend Karl Downs, and of course his wife Rachel—built in Robinson a strong man, and had his mandate of urgency of owning a piece of the elusive ideal been shared by his country, considered an asset even, perhaps the Robinson family influence would have better explained his foundation. Perhaps it would have even been celebrated as the kindling of his rebelliousness, providing an admirable model for others facing the psychological intimidation and the physical evidence of maimed and killed bodies.

But the mandate was not shared by his country. The country wanted him to be patient, a "credit to his race," accepting of glacial change as progress. And it was here where the Jackie Robinson narrative would be appropriated, rerouted, detoured along a different, accommodating pathway. He would become synonymous with not ownership, which is taken with pageantry, but *advancement*, which is granted. He would be recast as one small but outsized piece in the long struggle toward freedom, in the martyr's path, where the reward of his sacrifice would be enjoyed not by him but by some unknown generation at some undetermined period in the future.

Advancement is the historical path of black people and the preferred narrative of whites, who are afforded a wide berth. They can be deliberate. They can be patient. They need not sacrifice in the short term provided they agree to a covenant of fairness to be delivered at an unspecified date—as long as it's not today. And they can dole out the platitudes about Robinson's dignity for they are not threatened with the sharing that comes with ownership, the partnership with power. Robinson and his wife living with a black family on the outskirts of town in spring training was framed as a sacrifice, pitied as an injustice, but not an offense to be immediately remedied. When Robinson integrated eating facilities at the Chase Hotel in St. Louis by taking Rachel to the dining room, refusing the hotel's directives that he and his wife eat their meals in their room as a condition of allowing him to stay with his own team, the historical framing of that moment placed Robinson as defiant. It placed the moment as triumphant, another subtle step toward equality. It was a victory for advancement.

Ownership is quite different, for it takes the keys to the house of self-determination in real time, without asking, and does not offer points for compromise or patience. Either one is an American or one is not an American, and if one is an American, other Americans are not to be commended for the grand gesture of treating an American as one. When Robinson once played an exhibition in the South, the black fans cheered when they were allowed to sit in the grandstand instead of in the bleachers, the usual "colored seats." Robinson was infuriated. "Don't cheer those goddam bastards. Keep your fucking mouths shut. You got it coming. . . . Don't cheer."[1] Being refunded one's own money is not a commendable act but an obviously unremarkable one, unless the cultural subtext is that certain people do not deserve to have what is already theirs.

America wanted advancement. Robinson wanted ownership, and whenever it became clear that advancement, *with all deliberate speed*, would be the preferred route, it was a blow, and their insistence on advancement exposed Robinson to the impatience and anger of his fellow black people, who as the years went by began to blame him for not asking for enough, for the naïveté of asking at all.

Telegraphs to Presidents Eisenhower and Kennedy, sent from his touring of the Deep South, portended the refusal to be lawful on the parts of whites, and their willingness to kill to maintain their racial hierarchy, and were met with caution, which meant that the president of the United States was willing to sacrifice black lives, no one knew who or when or how many, all because America hadn't yet advanced enough.

Robinson would die before seeing baseball hire a black manager, and it would be seventeen years after his death before baseball would have two black managers working at the same time. The response to the Robinson query was always the same. There were plenty of quality black people who could manage, but it wasn't *time* yet. America needed to keep advancing.

Eventually, even the greatest fighters, against the darkening, impossible odds, begin to weary. Punches that once shattered their targets now lose their sting, while the blows they absorb now inflict greater damage, challenging their thresholds of resolve and pain. The dual effect saps them.

The periods of the Jackie Robinson story that have received the least attention have been overlooked not due to them being the least important, but because they are the most difficult to square with the fantasy of the hero narrative, both his and that of his time. When he was a symbol of advancement, safe, unthreatening, he was a hero. When he demanded ownership, unconditional, without permission, he was angry, bitter, agitating.

The dots between Robinson's heroism and disillusionment never quite connected, and the reason, of course, is that Robinson was never satisfied with mere advancement, even as others applauded his dignity. He did not live with boundless optimism for the future and eventually displayed a certain punched-out nakedness to his disillusionment. His belief in ownership never waned, but his confidence that it was something he could personally experience did.

As the end drew closer, and it became clear that advancement was as good as it was going to get, he let the America that considered him an ally know that it had failed his people and he would not participate in the charade. And these dots did not connect because the people who needed to hear this part of the story had stopped listening. "I cannot stand and sing the anthem. I cannot stand for the flag. I know that I am a black man in a white world."[2] The most attentive, the ones who could relate, listened, and they continued to listen even after he was gone, but the rest took the legend, as they did with King, and they molded and shaped it into a convenient and comfortingly dishonest blanket that has kept them warm, using his pain to sustain their myth.

Had they followed the story to the end, they would have discovered a poignancy and the true call to action from the boy who fought for his place with his words and his fists, the younger man who carried an Army rifle and promise of a better America, to the young but older man who after a lifetime of needing convincing that America could not live up to its promise finally dropped his gloves and listened.

2

A METHODIST LIFE

RANDAL MAURICE JELKS

Jackie Robinson was a Methodist. However, what exactly did that mean? Robinson's mother Mallie was a devoted and prayerful Christian woman who shepherded her family through an arduous migration from Cairo, Georgia, to Pasadena, California. This journey of faith, for sure, was no less grueling than the one that the ancient Hebrews had undertaken when escaping through the desert from the clutches of the fabled biblical Pharaonic Egypt. Only this time the Moses of the story was a woman, Mallie Robinson, who with the aid of a half brother led her five children—Edgar, Frank, Jack, Mack, and Willie Mae—across the country, seeking more freedom from U.S. apartheid so that they could earn a living, gain an education, and live as respected citizens. Mallie's decision was an act of faith. It was one that influenced all the Robinson children. Each would imbibe her deep sense of faith in some form or fashion, especially Jack Roosevelt Robinson, otherwise known as Jackie Robinson.

Upon her arrival in Pasadena, Mallie would find fellowship at Scott Methodist Church. The church was named after of one of the first African American bishops in the Methodist Church, Isaiah Benjamin Scott. The highly accomplished minister served as a missionary bishop in Liberia, as the first African American president of Wiley College in Marshall, Texas, and as a state commissioner at the Chicago World's Fair in 1893 and the Atlanta Exposition two years later.[1]

The Pasadena church's name and connectivity within the Methodist Episcopal Church meant that the congregants aspired to a kind of Christian experience that was beyond the boundaries of the racial status assigned to its members in 1903. The church was founded as the legalized status of African Americans was diminished both legally and culturally to second-class citizenry. De facto and prescribed legalities conscribed life for all African Americans, including ones living in California, at the turn of the nineteenth century to the twentieth. As lovely as Pasadena's physical geography is, racial harassment was par for the course when Scott Methodist Church was formed.[2] Like other black churches, Scott was an institutional haven for African American denizens of the city.[3] Although the greater world sought to punish African American communities, the collective faith practiced inside of these churches allowed its members to dream beyond everyday racism and wage struggles on behalf of their human dignity. When Mallie Robinson and her children joined Scott Church, they became a part of a community, fellowship, and network bigger than themselves. These connections helped to form the aspirations and worldview of the Robinsons and their fellow congregants.

The migration, resettlement, and construction of a new life were all expressions of Mallie's deep faith. As Jackie Robinson biographer Arnold Rampersad rightly observes, Mallie's faith was omnipresent: "Family was vital to Mallie, but God was supreme. For her, as she tried to make her children see, God was a living, breathing presence all about her, and she seeded her language with worshipful allusions to the divine. 'God watches what you do,' she would insist; 'you must reap what you sow, so sow well!' . . . 'Prayer,' she often told her children, 'is belief.'"[4] Mallie's belief is further confirmed by Michael Long and Chris Lamb in *Jackie Robinson: A Spiritual Biography*.[5] However, what the authors miss in their descriptions is that Robinson's faith development cannot be captured by a narrative focusing on one extraordinary individual's beliefs. It is equally a story about the institutional parameters that provided the context for the development of individual convictions. Because religious faiths always have institutional contexts, it is important to set Robinson's individual beliefs inside the context of church teachings (doctrines), clerical impact, and denominational history.

The Methodist Church began in eighteenth-century England under the auspices of John Wesley, an Anglican priest. The Anglican Church was the official church of England, and its history was part of the spread of Protestantism that began with Martin Luther's theological disputations with the Roman Catholic Church in the city of Wittenberg, Germany. Of course, the Anglican Church's beginnings had nothing to do with a theological disputation and everything to do with marriage and male succession to the throne. It had been formed by King Henry VIII under the Tudor dynasty. By the mid-eighteenth century, when John Wesley began to contemplate his ministry to the English urban poor and the slowly emerging proletariat, the Anglican Church was fully ensconced as the cultural arbiter of British society.

In 1738, Wesley described a Christian mystical experience: "I felt my heart strangely warmed. I felt I did trust in Christ, Christ alone, for salvation; and an assurance was given me that he had taken away my sins." This spiritual transformation led Wesley to believe that personal faith could instantly transform human behavior. Faith was efficacious for him in the same way that prayer was for Mallie Robinson.

By 1739, Wesley was preaching outdoors to the emerging English working classes. Camp meetings and tent revivals would be the forerunner of today's stadium rallies in the arsenal of rising global evangelicalism.[6] Wesley also formed local groups for prayer and Bible study. His shaping of how working-class men and women thought about their collective identities was equal to that of the Chartist movement, Marxism, or socialism. Wesley helped to shape a Christian identity amid a rising new social class identity.

While still belonging to the Anglican Church, Wesley emphasized teachings that stressed personal salvation in four basic tenets: all need to be saved (the doctrine of original sin), all can be saved (universal salvation), all can know they are saved (assurance), and all can be saved completely (Christian perfection).[7] These doctrines gave Wesley's followers an assurance of salvation and the idea that God was not some distant ruler in the sky but a God who, through their relationship to Christ, cared for their existence. This faith conviction had racial implications. To be a Methodist was to be engaged in a pursuit of biblical holiness. God gave human beings the ability to make changes within themselves by pursuing Christ's teachings, and those changes, if pursued vigorously, would lead to society becoming wholesome or, in other words, holier.

After Wesley's death, Methodists in England would leave the Anglican Church and form their own separate entity. Methodism then spread throughout the British Empire. One of its greatest impacts would be in the British colonies in the Caribbean and through the southern portion of its colonies in North America.[8] Methodists initially enshrined freedom and abolitionism as part of their tenets of holiness. However, they would soon compromise on the latter issue because of slavery's decisive capital power in the southern colonies.

By 1794, many formerly enslaved African Americans in Philadelphia began their own Methodist movement with a mass protest at St. George's Methodist Episcopal Church over their sacred rights and racial equality among members of the church.[9] This protest was officially led by Richard Allen and Absalom Jones, but it was also unofficially organized through a network of Methodist women.[10] The protest foreshadowed the formation of the African Methodist Episcopal Church as an independent denomination. But even when enslaved African Americans were not visible institutionally, they used meeting structures within Methodism to create a system of their own faithfulness.[11] In the meantime, Methodists as a whole contended with contentious internecine rivalries over the issue of slavery in 1844. This theological crisis over the most extreme exploitation of human labor as a means to wealth questioned everything that John Wesley held dear.[12] And we cannot forget that the forebears of Jackie Robinson in Georgia were the brutalized laborers of this iron-fisted capitalist system of exploitation. The Methodist Church in the United States thus remained in division over the issue for ninety-five years.

This history is important for understanding Jackie Robinson. Whether he knew it or not, his faith was shaped by debates about socially embedded ideas and beliefs in Methodism. These debates became the sources of Robinson's moral beliefs about the social conditions around him. For example, in his autobiography Robinson describes how he felt theologically alienated in adolescence. Despite having faith, his family was overwhelmed with the structural conditions of the Great Depression, which appeared to him to render faith as foolishness. He could not reconcile himself intellectually to the social exclusion factored into the most personal of daily encounters. In the eyes of an urban adolescent male, he could not reconcile his own feelings of being excluded and impoverished. The streets were more exciting and more truthful than the people in the church.

This alienation among young black men was a norm that extended back to the years of U.S. enslavement itself. It was the Achilles' heel of black churches steeped in a piety that changing one's heart was key to changing society. Impoverishment was itself a singular and painful alienation and reminder of social exclusivity. In addition, new forms of entertainment—arcades, bars, dance halls, motion pictures, and radio programs—provided new social outlets that challenged the pieties of mothers like Robinson's. And this new challenge presented a crisis for black churches over questions of masculinity. Churches were highly gendered, with male clergy running the institution in a space where women and children made up the vast majority of the membership. By the time Robinson was an adolescent, the notion of being a good family meant having good churchgoing parents. Males had a godly duty to be good fathers. In Robinson's case, his father, Jerry Robinson, had abandoned the family when Jackie was an infant, and so there was no role model of fatherly piety in Jackie's home. In fact, Mallie's children were all painfully aware of the absence of their father.

Churches like Scott Methodist encouraged familial piety as a way to build biblical holiness; they also created aspirational values as to how family life was to be enacted. Through church teachings, nuclear families became the bourgeois norm of what a family should look like. However, in black communities, legalized segregation, sharecropping, and the Great Depression told another story, one about families in distress.[13] In Robinson's story, running the streets appeared more visceral and engaging than attending church. What Jackie went through, however, was a growing crisis within many black denominations over its male youth.[14]

This brings us back to Scott Methodist Church and the issue of denominational structure. In the post-Emancipation era, black people who aligned with the Methodist Episcopal Church were partners in creating a variety of regional educational institutions, especially colleges. Wiley College was founded in 1873 in Marshall, Texas, and Samuel Huston College in Austin, Texas, opened its doors in 1900. These institutions became the training ground for an emerging leadership class within the denomination as well as in a societal struggle to make the United States an inclusive democracy.

When the Methodist bishop appointed Reverend Karl Everette Downs to Scott Church in 1938, it was of singular importance, as Jackie Robinson noted.[15] Downs was from a clergy household; his father was a Methodist minister. Downs was also from the era when the black Social Gospel was being promoted by clergy and scholars such as Benjamin Mays and Joseph W. Nicholson, whose groundbreaking book, *The Negro's Church*, took the temperature of black churches in the Depression. Their survey showed the activism and the self-defeating behaviors of black congregations and set the tenor for black theologians in claiming the mantle of church-based activism and spirituality—what has been dubbed the Social Gospel, a progressive movement that began with New York City pastor and theologian Walter Rauschenbusch.[16]

Downs brought a zeal to Scott Church, and the church's motto under his leadership read "A Crusading Body Seeking to Establish a Divine Society."[17] The church, he believed, was there to build a just society. Additionally, he was a well-trained pastor who understood that his parishioners faced the triple burdens of exclusion by gender, race, and social class in the very minutia of their lives. Under his leadership, Scott Church became a haven where congregants could build strength and power for confronting the humiliation and crucifixion they faced on a daily basis. For Robinson, this is what made the church relevant.

Further, Robinson discovered that he could share his own personal predicaments and struggles with his thoughtful new pastor. Robinson was especially torn by his mother's menial work and his own inability to support her financially. This, though it is not stated, deeply affected his sense of manhood as he thought about his athleticism and his desire to support his mother. Because of Downs's pastoral counseling, as Rampersad notes, Robinson began to experience a "measure of emotional and spiritual poise such as he had never known."[18] Downs's counsel, coupled with his ability to organize constructive youth programming, encouraged Jackie to see the church as a community servant.

The two remained friends and associates after Robinson left his childhood home. When Downs left Scott Church to become president of Sam Huston College, he successfully invited Robinson to join the school's coaching staff. It would be Downs who would serve as liaison between Robinson and another Methodist, Branch Rickey. Sadly, Downs died at the age of thirty-five in 1948, not long after Robinson's breakthrough summer of 1947.

Reverend Karl Downs played a formative role in Robinson's faith development. National Baseball Hall of Fame and Museum.

If Downs made an impression on Robinson, so did his wife-to-be, Rachel Isum. She was also a Methodist, a member of the venerable tradition of the African Methodist Episcopal Church begun under the leadership of Richard Allen.[19] In fact, her home congregation—Bethel AME Church in Los Angeles—was named after Mother Bethel Church in Philadelphia, which Allen and others established after they left St. George's Methodist Episcopal Church.

The AME Church was one of the greatest institutions that African Americans created and supported during the nineteenth century. Daniel Payne, one of the church's more illustrious bishops, helped to found Wilberforce College in Ohio, the first historically black college in the country run by African Americans.[20] When Emancipation came, the AME Church spread all across the country and into the U.S. South.

From its inception, the denomination called for black folks to lift up their own from impoverished conditions. The AME Church shared general Methodist rectitude, but from its birth in 1816 it empowered black folks without the generosity of white aid. As fragile as the organization was, it believed in the strength and power of black communities long before the arrival of Black Power sloganeering. By the turn of the twentieth century, according to historian and sociologist W. E. B. Du Bois, the AME Church was one of the more sophisticated denominations among the Negro churches.[21] The spiritual power of the church lay in its claim that black people could find biblical holiness independent of white control.

Rachel Isum's Methodism, outside the purview of white Methodism, exuded self-determination, self-sufficiency, and black independence. These beliefs, grounded in the history of the AME Church, also served Jackie Robinson. Through Rachel, Jackie came to see that he could control his own fate and determine his own identity. This conviction was AME spirituality in a nutshell. Rachel's influence on Robinson's faith and religiosity was tremendous, and it remains undervalued.

When Branch Rickey, president and general manager of the Brooklyn Dodgers, began holding conversations about Robinson coming up to the major leagues, he wanted someone who could exercise discipline. Rickey used his Methodist network to discover that Robinson, a world-class athlete, could handle the scorn that would be heaped upon him as he crossed the color barrier in what was then America's favorite pastime. Although this aspect of Robinson and Rickey's relationship is important, we need to be careful not to be pietistic about or romanticize it. Rickey was a baseball owner; his Methodism did not affect his corporate calculations.

Robinson and Rickey might have shared denominational affiliation and spiritual affinities, but that affiliation did not trump the fact that Rickey was one of the owners of the Brooklyn Dodgers.

Players in Robinson's day were subjects of the owners; they were not free agents. That oppressive reality would not begin to change until 1969, when Curt Flood mounted a legal challenge to Major League Baseball's "reserve clause."[22] But in Robinson's era, owners owned their players. Rickey, as an owner, had a decisive advantage over Robinson. What Rickey needed Robinson to do was to make a profit by filling the stands. Robinson's extraordinary prowess and his religiously undergirded middle-class norms and propriety were a match made in heaven for Rickey to publicize and market.

While it helped that both men were influenced by Methodism, this did not mean their business negotiations over pay were not difficult or contentious for Robinson. Rickey was an unwavering capitalist, and his Methodism did not supplant his desire to make more money than simply breaking even. He wished to profit off his initial investment. Robinson's Methodism was virtually incidental; he wanted to fill the stands.

When Robinson retired from baseball, he pursued business opportunities. He also chose to align himself with the Republican Party. Black Americans still had a considerable investment in the party at that time, even though the majority of working-class black Americans had abandoned the Republican Party by 1936, voting overwhelmingly for Franklin Roosevelt. Robinson believed that the GOP was pro–small business and that it stood for lower taxes and the right of every person to be free of coercion. However, the party had long since abandoned black voters, particularly in the 1930s. It was no longer the party of Lincoln.[23]

We can only speculate about Methodism as a determinant of Robinson's political views. However, it is worth highlighting the individualism of Methodism throughout history. When pursuing moral perfection, Methodists typically thought about being good individuals. They did not usually consider the corporate body or the corporate forces that shape and change the course of an individual's life. The practice of Methodism was largely about the individual being open and willing to see the light of Christ. Though charitable to fellow human beings, Methodists often missed the point that in fact there are corporate forces and organized power working against the freedoms of individuals.

It would shake Robinson to the core that his party would follow Barry Goldwater as the 1964 Republican nominee for president. Goldwater aligned with southern Democrats in attempting to strike civil rights legislation. A fierce proponent of individual freedom, Goldwater told audiences he cast his vote in the name of liberty. This was a shock to Robinson and challenged him to dig deeper spiritually, to confront the dangerous legacy of individualism, and to serve his community and the wider culture and society.

Unfortunately for all of us, Jackie Robinson died in 1972. His diabetes left him stricken and then slowly shut down his body. He died as a man of deep faith, willing to express his deepest moral convictions with the same aggression he displayed when playing baseball. More importantly, he carried to his grave the spiritual goals that Reverend Karl Downs had encouraged him to adopt:

> To be able to recognize God as the vital force in life.
> To develop one's own self to the best of one's ability.
> Not only to stay out of evil—but to try to get into good.
> To seek to help others without thinking so much of what we
>   will get out of it, but what we are putting into it.[24]

These were words that strangely warmed the heart, to paraphrase John Wesley. Robinson lived a strong and faithful life, just as his mother had prayed for. He kept the faith.

PART II

BASEBALL

3

JACKIE ROBINSON BALL

GEORGE VECSEY

This happened a couple of decades ago when my young son and I were sitting in the mostly deserted stands at Shea Stadium, during one of the Mets' regular wretched decades.

A Mets baserunner stumbled into some horrendous mental error and got himself tagged out equidistant from first and second. It's in the Mets' DNA.

A couple of (empty) rows away, two older (black) guys turned to each other, and one said, "Jackie Robinson wouldn't have done that."

I chortled, and told the fan, "You got that right," and for the next few innings we carried on a running conversation, via our bond in Jackie Robinson as the symbol, the touchstone, the epitome of aggressive baseball smarts.

Jackie Robinson transformed baseball, his fourth best sport, soon after arriving with the Brooklyn Dodgers in 1947. The skills and the inner drive were all his, but they also came from the separate style of black baseball.

To this day, when a runner breaks from third base, he carries the image of Jackie Robinson, with number 42 on his uniform, trying to distract pitcher and catcher. The hard slide, now marginalized by recent safety rules, has Robinson's image superimposed on it. Whether fans know it, think about it, Jack Roosevelt Robinson upgraded the game.

Nowadays, Robinson serves as an icon, a name out of history, honored once a year on April 15, the anniversary of his debut in

1947: his number 42, retired throughout baseball, is worn by every player, as confusing as that is.

Robinson is honored with the foundation that bears his name, which does good works, offers scholarships, hosts forums, and the like. His daughter, Sharon Robinson, is the visible icon, and his widow, the estimable Rachel Robinson, the most beautiful nonagenarian in history, has been the link to her husband.

(A decade or so ago, the Jackie Robinson Foundation held a conference. In the reception, videos of Jackie Robinson's four sports— basketball, track and field, baseball, and football—were being shown. We whooped as Robinson made some hipper-dipper football moves through the defense. As a bunch of us chatted, Joe Morgan, the Hall of Fame second baseman, referred to Mrs. Robinson as the Queen Mother. I have used that title for her ever since.)

Jackie Robinson is useful for feel-good lessons in religion, scholarship, citizenship. In the living, breathing, ethos of the game, he is a presence, whether the players know it or not.

Robinson crystallized his drive as a four-sport star at UCLA, then as a proud Army officer who would not sit in the back of a bus for anybody, and after a brief stint (.414 batting average) in the Negro Leagues in 1945, as a willing student of baseball. It must be noted that he was accepted and mentored by a few minor league teammates like Al Campanis and George Shuba, white guys from Up North.

It took Robinson a while in the majors to unleash his innerdisciplined fury. Enos Slaughter managed to rake Robinson's instep with his spikes when Robinson was trying to learn first base in 1947. ("He can't fight you," Hugh Casey, the Dodger pitcher, out of the Deep South, said to Slaughter. "But I can.")

Soon enough, Robinson would loosen his aggressions—upgrading the American game. In addition to integration, enlightened aggression is his other legacy.

The physicality, the intimidation, came from within, but also from without. The Negro Leagues were a separate entity, not bound by the codas of the so-called major leagues. (How "major" were those leagues without Josh Gibson, Cool Papa Bell, Oscar Charleston, Buck Leonard, and Satchel Paige in their prime?)

Left to their own devices, the Negro League players were able to improvise, hustle, expand their arsenal, under bad lights, on bumpy fields. Hidden-ball tricks, near balks, doctored baseballs, hard slides. Robinson was a college boy, a novice at this game, but he learned fast. He made only a brief stop in the Negro Leagues, with the Kansas City Monarchs in 1945, but he learned the scuffling ways of black ball—anything to get an edge.

When he finally let go in the "major leagues," Robinson tossed his thickening running-back body at the knees of opponents who were trying to hold on to the throw. He dove to the ground to snare the line drive that could have finished the Dodgers in the 1951 pennant race.

Look at the end of that season—Bobby Thomson's homer off Ralph Branca to decide the historic playoff. Look at the Giants celebrating. Look at Branca beginning the long, sad trek to the clubhouse behind deep center field. But look at pigeon-toed number 42, hands on hips, staring at home plate to make sure Thomson actually touched it. Never give up. That was Jackie Robinson's on-field lesson.

He had his spiritual descendants, young players with equal talents and equal fire: Frank Robinson, no relation, bowling over infielders; Vada Pinson, his Cincinnati teammate; Roberto Clemente, the first Latino superstar who dared to flash his own fire. Willie Mays, who did not need fury or physicality because he had his own style, was free to play with abandon.

The first professional sons of Jackie Robinson were in the National League, Jackie Robinson's league. The Yankees dominated what my first newspaper boss called the "Brother-in-Law League," and Robinson's spirit was spread around the National League and was passed down. Frank Robinson and Vada Pinson exemplified it to a cheeky white kid named Pete Rose, who was a great competitor

Watching the end of the 1951 pennant race against the New York Giants. National Baseball Hall of Fame Library.

for so long, before he went rogue with the gambling. Rose passed along the fire to Hal McRae, who later became one of the first hard-sliders in the Brother-in-Law League.

Robinson never stole more than thirty-seven bases in one season (1949, his third, when he was relatively young, relatively thin, relatively healthy). But he certified the hard-sliding base runner, leading to spiritual heirs like Maury Wills, Lou Brock, Rickey Henderson, Tim Raines, Joe Morgan, Vince Coleman. (Coleman was once asked by a reporter to comment on some aspect of Robinson's career, and apparently said, "Don't know no Jackie Robinson, man." Much was made of Coleman's apparent ignorance, but I suspect he was merely trying to blow off the reporter, as quickly as possible. At any rate, I hope.)

I don't go to the ballpark much these days. Getting old. Don't like the hordes of "fans" taking selfies, hate the noise blaring from the loudspeakers, can't take the four-hour games.

Baseball is pilloried for not having many black players, and therefore very few black fans in attendance, but I give Major League Baseball a bit of a pass on that. Jackie Robinson's two other team sports—football and basketball—have long since attracted black athletes at a young age, for the challenges, the competition, the crowds at games, college scholarships, a way up and out. Then there is soccer, the next frontier. Imagine young, sleek Jackie Robinson as a striker for Real Madrid or Liverpool or Juventus. Baseball does not overtly reject black players or black fans. It's free enterprise, competition, the American way.

Besides, baseball is a different game these days. The analytics crowd has been unleashed, hitters have been deputized to swing from their butts, in hope of sending doctored baseballs on a "launch arc" into the stands. There is no shame to striking out. Baseball is aiming for the highlights on the tube—look at Sluggo putting another one into the seats.

But once in a while, particularly in the postseason, when quickie series dictate a mostly forgotten desperation, a runner gets to third base with a vital run. He remembers, oh, this is how it is done, and he makes a herky-jerky move down the line, possibly to distract the pitcher, anything to win, baby.

Sometimes, without permission from the analytics crowd, old-timey baseball breaks out. When some latter-day hustler slides hard, dances off third base, I think of those older black men sitting near me and my son on that torpid day in Shea Stadium.

"National League ball." That's what some of us call it. Jackie Robinson ball.

4

TELLING IT THE RIGHT WAY

JONATHAN EIG

Ever heard of Johnny Van Cuyk?

The left-handed pitcher from Little Chute, Wisconsin, was a late-season addition to the Brooklyn Dodgers' roster in 1947. He was a hard-throwing lefty, twenty-six years old. In his rookie season he appeared in only two games, allowing five hits and two earned runs in three and a third innings of work. He hung around with the Dodgers for two more seasons.

I mention Van Cuyk because in 1947 he was the only man on the Dodgers' roster with a uniform number higher than Jackie Robinson's 42. Van Cuyk wore 43. Harry Taylor wore 41. Erv Pálica wore 40. I'll save you the trouble of looking it up: Robinson is the only one of the four to make the Hall of Fame.

Why was Robinson lumped with Van Cuyk, Taylor, and Palica? Was he not the most exciting and important rookie in all of baseball at the start of the season? The Dodgers could have given Robinson number 2. They could have given him 4, which went to another rookie, Duke Snider. But Robinson got 42, and when he got his number, he didn't find his uniform hanging in a locker as his other teammates did; he found it on a spike in the wall. He'd get a locker later, presumably, if he stuck with the team.

Today, 42 is the most celebrated number in baseball, the only number in the majors retired by every team. Every player in the league wears it April 15, and no one wears it the rest of the year.

If baseball is a religion, as some devotees might argue, 42 is holy. Writer Will Leitch ranked it baseball's best number, one spot ahead of its reverse, 24, the number worn by Willie Mays, Rickey Henderson, and Ken Griffey Jr.

The magic of 42 requires context. It is not numero uno simply because Jack Roosevelt Robinson wore it his whole career or because it's been retired (we always want what we cannot have) or because Hollywood used the number as the title of the 2013 Jackie Robinson biopic or because Nate Thurmond wore it in the NBA. Forty-two matters because it's part of Robinson's story of overcoming incredibly long odds. The number 42, when we seek to understand it, is the kind of detail that puts meat on the too-often dry bones of history.

The problem with history, of course, is that we don't know it's history until it's over. And once it's over we know how it ends. The stories grow familiar until they become cliché. Jackie Robinson broke baseball's color line. He was brave. He turned the other cheek when taunted. We all know the story. We've all seen the movie.

But what if you were Jackie Robinson, or his wife Rachel, and you didn't know how it was going to end? What if failure *was* an option?

I didn't know much about Robinson's story when I first had an idea to write a book about him. To be honest, it wasn't really my idea. A reader of my Lou Gehrig biography emailed me with the suggestion that I write a book about the friendship between Robinson and Dodger shortstop Pee Wee Reese. According to this man's email and according to the often-told legend, Reese deserved much of the credit for Robinson's acceptance in 1947. Many of the Dodgers opposed integration. Some of them signed a petition saying they wouldn't play with a Negro. There were rumors that the Dodgers were trying to organize a league-wide walkout. They were willing to sacrifice one of the sweetest versions of the American dream—a big league baseball career—rather than accept a black man as a

teammate. But according to the legend, Pee Wee Reese, a Kentuck-
ian and captain of the team, changed his teammates' attitudes. One
story goes that Reese, while playing in Cincinnati, walked across
the ballfield and put an arm around Robinson to silence hecklers
who were attacking Robinson with crude racial epithets. He's not
a Negro, Pee Wee seemed to say with his gesture, according to this
version of events, he's a Dodger.

My initial reaction was that a book on Reese and Robinson
would probably be too sappy. But just to learn more about their
relationship, I phoned Rachel Robinson. As I asked her about that
1947 season and the relationship between her husband and Pee Wee
Reese, I sensed frustration in her voice. Answers came curtly. I cast
about wildly, trying to find a question she liked. She didn't like any
of them. Finally, I gave up.

"Mrs. Robinson," I said. "I'm sorry for wasting your time. Did I
do something wrong?"

"Well, yes," she said. "You assumed that Jack made it because Pee
Wee helped. I'm tired of people assuming that he needed the help of
a white man to succeed."[1]

I swallowed hard and said nothing.

She went on. In 1947, she said, she and Jack (she always called
him Jack) did not have the support of Pee Wee Reese or anyone else
on the team, at least not at first. Robinson's white teammates were
waiting to see if he would fail before they put any skin in the game.
If he didn't make the team, if the petition worked, if opposing teams
refused to play, if he got hurt, if he couldn't hit or field his position,
if the Dodgers slumped and white media blamed Jack for dividing
the clubhouse, he'd be sent packing, and the white players could go
back to their old way of doing things. That's why Jack and Rachel
and their baby didn't even rent an apartment—they stayed in a hotel
and then switched to a rented room in Bedford-Stuyvesant, sharing
a bathroom and a kitchen with the complete stranger who was their
landlord. Jack didn't have any friends on the Dodgers in 1947, and

Pee Wee Reese did not initially welcome Robinson as a teammate. National Baseball Hall of Fame Library.

neither did Rachel. Not in 1947, anyway. This was an experiment. Most experiments fail. That's why so few ballplayers wanted to risk getting close to Robinson and why their wives didn't want to get close to Rachel. That and the fact that some of them were avowed white supremacists.

When Mrs. Robinson paused, I meekly asked: What about the moment in Cincinnati when Pee Wee put his arm around Jackie and silenced the hecklers?

It never happened, she said. At least not in 1947.

But there are children's books about that moment. There's a statue depicting the embrace in Brooklyn. You attended the unveiling, and the base of the statue is engraved with the date when this embrace supposedly occurred.

Never happened, Rachel said.

Why did you attend the unveiling?

She sighed as if to say it was complicated; I would never understand.

But I tried to understand. I spent the next two years interviewing every living member of the 1947 Dodgers, everyone I could find who lived on the Robinsons' block in Bed-Stuy, everyone I could find who watched the Robinson experiment up close. I knocked on the door of the apartment where the Robinsons lived and measured the floor space in their tiny room, trying to comprehend how two adults and a child had possibly made it their home.

One of my favorite interviews was with Gil Jonas. Jonas was seventeen years old, a student at Lafayette High in Brooklyn, where he worked for the school newspaper. Gil had never had a meaningful conversation with a black person, but when his sister's boyfriend said he could introduce Gil to Jackie Robinson, Gil, like any baseball-loving American boy, jumped at the chance. The interview was arranged for the day that Robinson and his family moved from the McAlpin Hotel to their Bed-Stuy apartment. Gil sat beside Robinson on the stoop and asked him how the Dodgers looked for 1947. Could they beat the Cardinals? What about the Yankees? How was Robinson making the adjustment to first base, his new position?

Later, when Jonas went to see the Dodgers play at Ebbets Field, he heard white men calling Robinson horrible things. "I didn't know people could be that cruel," he said.[2] It was only then that it occurred to him that he had failed to ask Robinson the right questions. It had never occurred to him that Robinson was much more than another ballplayer. Nevertheless, Jonas learned. The next year, when he went to Stanford University, he started a chapter of the National Association for the Advancement of Colored People, led a drive to integrate the campus, and went out on a date the following year with the university's first female African American student.

That was Jackie Robinson's influence, and it was felt in big ways and small ways all over America in 1947. Sometimes you can see history right in front of your eyes if you pay attention. White Dodger fans integrated their factory floors in 1947—not all of them, of course, but at least a few. White competitors of the Dodgers began scouting black players, trying to keep up with the competition—not all of them, of course, but some of them. White politicians began making promises to tear down the walls of segregation—not all of them, of course, but some of them, including President Truman.

Would it have mattered if Robinson had worn number 2, or number 4? Would it have mattered if his uniform had been waiting for him in a locker rather than on a hook in the wall? Would it have mattered if the Dodgers had arranged more suitable accommodations for Jack and Rachel? Would it have mattered if he'd been treated like the star college athlete and blue-chip prospect that he was?

Well, it would have been kinder, certainly. It would have been respectful. It would have sent the message that the Dodgers were going all in, that Robinson was here to stay, that baseball was integrated, and that anyone who didn't like it could suck a resin bag. But that was not the world in which Robinson lived. In 1947, there was no such thing as a civil rights movement. Martin Luther King Jr. was still a teenage kid thinking about becoming a doctor or a lawyer. As Bobby Bragan, a backup catcher on the 1947 Dodgers, told me, he and his friends and family in Alabama were staunch white supremacists. They believed absolutely that Negro people were inherently inferior to white people, that it was a matter of science. All season long in 1947 he puzzled over how he was going to go home to Alabama and explain that he rode the bench while a Negro played every day.

By wearing number 42, by accepting without complaint being shifted to an infield position he had never played, by taking the abuse of fans and opposing players, by playing through death threats, by never reacting violently to violent encounters on the bases or to balls thrown at his head, Robinson took on the burdens, the assaults, and the insults that were a part of everyday life for African Americans. As Martin Luther King Jr. would say years later,

"Whenever men and women straighten their backs up, they are going somewhere, because a man can't ride your back unless it is bent."[3]

Jackie Robinson straightened his back in such a visible way that no one could miss it, day after day, through spring, summer, and fall, in front of 4.1 million paying fans. He became the biggest attraction in baseball since Babe Ruth. Railroad companies scheduled special runs to get black fans from their rural homes to the ballpark. "Jackie's nimble, Jackie's quick," wrote Wendell Smith, "Jackie's making turnstiles click."[4]

Given his obvious importance, one might conclude that the Dodgers were insulting Robinson by assigning him the number 42. Or perhaps one might conclude that they were challenging him. Or one might conclude that the clubhouse manager assigning uniform numbers didn't give a damn and wasn't about to risk his job by assigning a plum number to a black man.

But Robinson understood. He noticed and remembered every slight. He swallowed the insults and turned them to muscle. He knew that much of white society, including many of his teammates, wanted to see him fail, and he was determined not to give them that satisfaction. He knew, because he read it in the black press, that his people were counting on him to succeed. The *Boston Chronicle* ran this banner headline: "Triumph of Whole Race Seen in Jackie's Debut in Major-League Ball."

After my initial conversation with Mrs. Robinson, I saw how wrong I had been to consider writing about the Robinson-Reese relationship, and I became more interested in the Robinson-Robinson relationship, the one between Rachel and Jack. Grudgingly, Mrs. Robinson consented to meet with me and to take part in a series of interviews. She helped me understand, as only she could, how easily this experiment might have failed and how 42 might have remained one of the least desirable numbers in baseball.

Rachel told me she didn't know much about baseball when she married Jack. She had watched him play basketball and football at

UCLA, but baseball had never been his principal sport, and only in 1947 did she begin to understand the nuances of the game. It was during that season, as she sat in the grandstand with their infant son on her lap, that she realized that Jack wasn't playing the same way as his white teammates. He was taking bigger leads off the bases, taking wider turns on singles, stealing home. She wondered why. There were other speedy players on the team who could have done the same, or tried.

It slowly dawned on her that Jack was bringing some of the Negro League style to white baseball and that his aggressive base running was an expression of his strength and courage, that he would not go along with the expectations of white fans or coaches, that he would play with his back straight, his head high, and a cloud of dust behind him. He was sending a message. Rachel loved him for that.

In the years ahead, civil rights battles would be fought in the courts and in the streets and at the ballot box, the victories all too often offset by violent backlash. The backlash continues today.

It might seem like small consolation in today's divided America that for one day each year, April 15, baseball players all wear 42. But it doesn't have to be small if we tell the story the right way and remember when 42 represented a challenge, when Jack Roosevelt Robinson accepted that challenge, when he rose up against insults, rose up against hate, and played for all of us to win.

5

A CHAMPION OF NONVIOLENCE?

MARK KURLANSKY

Edward O. Wilson, the distinguished biologist who declares himself a pacifist, assured me that human beings are "hardwired for violence." Not to leave me too discouraged, he pointed out that ants, his expertise, are even worse. He opined that the world would last for only minutes if ants could get nuclear weapons. He also pointed out that humans do not always have to follow their wiring. After all, they are doubtless not wired to wear clothes, eat with forks, or carry out numerous other practices that we consider civilized. They are certainly not hardwired for monogamous marriages.

And so when it is pointed out, and it often is, that nonviolence was not in Jackie Robinson's nature, this is not a pivotal point. It was not in Mohandas Gandhi's nature or Martin Luther King's. Nonviolence, as Robinson was to learn on baseball diamonds, takes tremendous discipline and self-control. It is unfortunate that these men tend to be regarded as saints. As George Orwell wrote in his critique of Gandhi, "Sainthood is also a thing that human beings must avoid."[1] To make saints out of Gandhi and King, or even Robinson, is to miss what is most valuable about their legacies. These were pragmatic men who had concrete goals and reasoned that nonviolence was the political tool to achieve them.

My favorite Gandhi quote is this: "Whether mankind will consciously follow the law of love, I do not know. But that need not perturb us. The law will work just as the law of gravitation will work whether we accept it or no."[2] It was a pragmatic rather than a moral argument. It works.

Robinson was always in the spotlight because he was an extraordinary athlete—famous as a track and football star at UCLA and, with little experience, the man who not only integrated Major League Baseball but played it with a rare verve and excitement. And because all this happened at just the right time in history, this star athlete became a prominent civil rights figure. He was, as David Halberstam put it, "History's Man."[3]

And yet he instinctively refused to fit neatly in the roles offered him. He was a Nixon supporter, a Rockefeller Republican, a supporter of the Vietnam War, and he always refused to be considered a nonviolent activist.

The nonviolent civil rights movement began during World War II, started by a group of pacifists who went to prison for opposing the war. Some were black, such as James Farmer and Bayard Rustin, and some white, such as George Houser and David Dellinger. They formed CORE, the Congress of Racial Equality, in Chicago in 1942. They had as an advisor a student of Gandhi, Krishnalal Shridharani. But there were other influences. Bayard Rustin was a Quaker raised in the moral arguments of nonviolence. Another Quaker, Richard Gregg, a lawyer, ran across the writings of Gandhi in the 1920s and, after studying them, traveled to India and studied on Gandhi's ashram for seven months. When he returned to the United States in 1929, he became the leading spokesman of Gandhism in America. His 1934 book, *The Power of Nonviolence*, was read by young activists. This book also emphasized the pragmatic argument that nonviolence works.

Martin Luther King was introduced to the idea of nonviolent resistance in 1949 as a student at Crozer Theological Seminary. He attended a lecture on nonviolence by one of its leading advocates, A. J. Muste, Bayard Rustin's mentor. King argued vehemently against Muste's ideas, saying that the only solution to segregation was armed revolution. This was a more violent argument than Robinson ever espoused, and yet no one talks of King's violent past the way they do Robinson's. Of course, it was all theoretical. Neither one ever engaged in violence except, in Robinson's case, for a few youthful fist fights. It is often reported that he was in a street gang in his boyhood in Pasadena, but this "Pepper Street Gang" of Mexicans, blacks, and Asians, though they had frequent encounters with the police, was not a very dangerous group by today's standards. They stole fruit from stores and snatched golf balls from the local course and tried to sell them back to the owners.

Later in 1949, King attended a lecture at Howard University by the school's president, Mordecai Johnson, on Gandhi's ideas, and he began to change his thinking. It is interesting to note that by the time King began to embrace Gandhism, India had gained independence, and Gandhi had been martyred. This may have been King's understanding of the process.

* * *

The important facts of Jackie Robinson's life were all about coincidences of history and the times he happened to live in. This is what gave him the opportunities of greatness, but it is widely recognized that it was his strength of character that made these events work.

That Branch Rickey, the general manager of the Brooklyn Dodgers organization, decided to pursue the integration of baseball at the exact moment when Gandhi's movement was at its height and the idea of nonviolent resistance was just taking hold in the black liberation struggle in the United States, and that Rickey would employ the techniques of nonviolence in bringing Robinson into Major League Baseball, make it nearly irresistible to claim that the Dodgers had taken on nonviolence and that Jackie Robinson was a great exponent of the tactic. But even Robinson was clear that he was not a nonviolent warrior and that all this was a coincidence.

It is not clear what Rickey's motives were, but he never tried to connect himself with the civil rights movement. Rickey was a right-wing, Bible-thumping Republican moralist. He was the son of a lay Baptist minister. In 1942 he left his post with the St. Louis Cardinals to become general manager of the Brooklyn Dodgers. St. Louis was a southern town with deep racist sentiments. But Brooklyn, in the Northeast with a large black population, presented other possibilities. He often spoke on his conviction that segregation was wrong. But he was a complicated figure with a list of motives. To begin with, during World War II, much of the top talent in baseball was taken away by the war and the quality of major league play notably declined. But some of the finest players in the game were playing in the Negro Leagues. By integrating baseball, the quality of major league play could be substantially improved. Major league play was Rickey's interest. Part of his plan for integration was to weaken the Negro Leagues and the Latin American League—Cuba, Panama, Mexico, Venezuela, and the Dominican Republic—whose integrated teams had considerable standing. This was why the first thing he did with his newly integrated team was take them to Cuba and Panama—to show off the new major leagues.

There has been considerable discussion about why Rickey picked Robinson to be the first black player. He was certainly not the best, and some questioned if he was good enough, although that argument quickly disappeared. He was not an experienced player. At twenty-six, the age when most players come into their prime, he had had only one year of experience in professional baseball. Rickey looked at numerous players, and all of them had better credentials and more experience. Catcher Roy Campanella, whom Rickey signed but did not bring up first, was a much bigger name, a Negro League star.

Given the weakness of Robinson's position, it has always been assumed that Rickey decided that Robinson was the man with the strength of character to take on the demands that would be facing him. If that is true, it is a very interesting choice. Campanella had a much milder disposition. In fact, when they were teammates on the Dodgers, there were often disagreements because Campanella thought Robinson was too difficult and Robinson thought Campanella was too mild. Jackie was always known as outspoken, "fiery"; some said he had a "chip on his shoulder," others said he just wouldn't stand for abuse. After he became famous for his nonviolent approach to baseball, stories started coming out about his earlier violence, but most of these are unverified. Some say that when playing for the Kansas City Monarchs the year before Rickey signed him he knocked unconscious a man in Alabama who tried to stop him from using a men's room. This may or may not be true.

So had Rickey made the decision that it would be more effective for the public to watch the fiery Negro restraining himself than the mild-mannered one shrugging it off? There is nothing in Rickey's statements, interviews, or papers that really answers this question.

Rickey and Robinson had in common that they both had come up in integrated sports, Rickey as the baseball coach at Ohio Wesleyan University and Robinson as a track and football star at UCLA. Rickey may have liked having a player who was accustomed to playing with white athletes.

By the time Rickey sat down to talk with Robinson, he had a very clear program that he called his "noble experiment."[4] The program sounded a lot like classic nonviolence. No matter what teammates, opposing players, or fans did and said, Robinson was not to react. To prepare him for this, Rickey played the role of various racists. This was how the civil rights movement would train its volunteers ten years later. Rickey told Robinson that he was "looking for a player with the guts not to fight back."[5]

But there was an important difference. In the civil rights movement, actions would be taken, and when attacked, the activists were not to resist. But in Rickey's program, Robinson was to do nothing. Although Robinson was to later say he was not cut out for King's brand of nonviolence, it was actually what came naturally to him. It was resistance. Robinson was actually the original nonviolent warrior.

Martin Luther King once described Robinson as "a sit-inner before sit-ins and a freedom rider before Freedom Rides."[6] And this was true because Robinson was naturally defiant. But he did not have the organized discipline of a nonviolent activist and did not present himself as wishing no harm to his adversaries.

In 1942, while serving in the Army, Robinson refused to move to the back of a bus. He was court-martialed for refusing a direct order but was acquitted. The only other known freedom ride of that era was also in 1942 when Bayard Rustin, traveling alone from Louisville to Nashville, refused to move to the back of the bus. He was dragged off and, without any attempt to physically defend himself, took a severe beating while trying to explain his point of view to his assailants. It seems likely that at the time neither Rustin nor Robinson knew of the other's resistance. But Rustin may have known of Robinson's since he was a famous college athlete and his trial received some attention.

But the Robinson freedom ride was not the classic nonviolent tactic of Rustin or the later Rosa Parks. Lieutenant Robinson reportedly explained to a superior officer, "Captain, any Private, you or any General calls me a nigger and I'll break them in two."[7] Insubordination to a superior officer became one of the court-martial charges.

Rickey did not want any resistance like a freedom ride. He never spoke of nonviolent activism, may have never heard of Rustin, Farmer, Muste, or Gregg. He, no doubt, had heard the Gandhi story, but there is no indication that he was inspired by it.

He may have been partly instructed by the experiences of Jewish slugger Hank Greenberg, who endured anti-Semitic taunts throughout his career in the 1930s. A giant of a man for his generation, Greenberg confronted some of his adversaries once, even following a player into the opposing locker room and challenging him to a fight. But nothing he tried ever worked until he learned to ignore the abuse. Rickey was not close to Greenberg, and there is no record of

Robinson was not an absolute pacifist. *Look* magazine / National Baseball Hall of Fame Library.

Rickey holding him up as an example. Greenberg was close to Bill Veeck, who at the same time was trying to integrate the Cleveland Indians. Greenberg was on his staff, and the Indians pursued the same tactic. Greenberg certainly understood what Robinson was doing. In 1947, Robinson's first year as a player and Greenberg's last, when the Dodgers were playing Pittsburgh and Robinson was silently enduring endless racist harangues, he ended up on first base. First baseman Greenberg said, "Stick in there. You're doing fine."[8]

Rickey and Robinson had in common that they were both re-
ligious Christians, and so they spoke of turning the other cheek.
Rickey did not discuss the writings of Gandhi or Muste or Gregg.
These were activists using nonviolence as a means of attack. What
Rickey wanted was true pacifism—no action whatsoever. It was in a
sense political activism. Robinson's presence was integrating Major
League Baseball. But Robinson was to take no stance beyond that.
And so what he handed Robinson was a book that was very popu-
lar among Christians at the time, *Life of Christ*, by Italian author
Giovanni Papini.

This vaguely anti-Semitic book shows Jesus born into a world of
crude and uncaring Jews who were not interested in his message.
To be fair, according to Papini, the Romans were monsters, and
even the stable where Jesus was born was filthy. Jesus lived in a
miserable world.

According to Papini, the great teaching of Jesus had been "diluted by Talmudic casuistries." The teaching is simply "Love all men
near and far."[9] It is also worth noting, since Robinson was famously
hot-tempered, that according to Papini, Jesus warned against anger,
saying it "must be smothered at the first spark, afterward it is too
late." And then Papini relayed the most "stupefying" of Jesus's revolutionary teachings, "Ye have heard that it hath been said, an eye for
an eye and a tooth for a tooth. But I say unto you, that ye resist not
evil. But whatever might smite thee on thy right cheek, turn to him
the other also."[10]

Papini said that there were three choices when confronted with
violence: revenge, flight, and turning the other cheek. The first was
barbarous, the second strengthened the enemy. Papini acknowledged
that turning the other cheek is "repugnant to human nature"—E. O.
Wilson's point.[11] And then he used Gandhi's argument, that it works.
It is the only way to curtail violence.

This was the book Branch Rickey gave to Jackie Robinson to
read before suiting up to begin his major league career.

It can be argued whether Rickey's approach had a tinge of racism or he was just aware of the blatant racism of the general population. He seemed to think Negroes—Robinson and his black fans as well—were children to be carefully managed. No one would have dreamed of telling Hank Greenberg, who endured vehement anti-Semitisms, or Joe DiMaggio, who faced anti-Italian attacks and was once praised in *Life* magazine for not smelling of garlic, how they should act. No one would have dreamed of instructing Jewish or Italian fans on proper behavior.

But Rickey seemed to think Negroes were a bit wild and tended to act up, and that the men were angry and dangerous. He would tell them how they should act. Rickey actually went to African American leaders in Brooklyn and urged them not to celebrate or cheer too much for Robinson. He told the African American community in Brooklyn not to "strut." There were to be no parades or celebrations. "We don't want Negroes in the stands gambling, drunk, fighting, being arrested," he said. White racists had argued against integrating baseball because that was the way black fans would act, completely ignoring decades of successful Negro League Baseball. Rickey told black leaders it was important that the integration of baseball not be presented as "a triumph of race over race." In other words, don't offend the white people. Black communities organized committees to keep black fans subdued in Brooklyn and other ballparks under the slogan "Don't spoil Jackie's chances," which sounds very much like Rickey-speak.[12]

And then there was the issue of the angry black man. This strange counter logic goes back to slavery. You could not trust a slave who was angry. Through the years, whites have been acutely aware that black people have been mistreated. Beware of the ones who were angry about it. Logic never extended to the obvious other side that the black man who wasn't angry about it must be an idiot. Remember Barack Obama first running for president. One of the greatest hurdles was convincing white people that he wasn't angry.

Robinson recalled his first thoughts at Rickey's proposition. "I was twenty-six years old, and all my life back to the age of eight when a little neighbor girl called me a nigger—I had believed in payback, retaliation."[13] But Rickey convinced him, and Robinson, who never knew his real father, did not resent the older man's patronizing attitude and said he was "the father I never had."[14]

Jackie Robinson was an unmistakably angry man. He played by Rickey's rules and kept himself under control, but you could not miss the anger. It was even in the way he played baseball—his ferocity, taunting the pitcher from the base, constantly stealing bases, even stealing home. His fierce, competitive spirit made him one of the most exciting players in the history of baseball.

Maybe this was Rickey's plan. Maybe it was more exciting to watch a player who looked like he was about to explode always keep himself in check than a mild-mannered Roy Campanella. Larry Doby, the first black player in the American League, was a fine player for the Cleveland Indians and endured as much abuse as Robinson, but never achieved Robinson's fame. Perhaps it was because, although he was an emotional player, fans did not sense a volatile chemistry beneath the surface.

"Hey nigger, why don't you go back to the cotton field where you belong," the Phillies shouted when playing at Ebbets Field. "They're waiting for you in the jungle, black boy."[15]

Robinson, who in his youth had exploded at lesser slights, who did not believe such insults should go unanswered, ignored them. It could be argued that he was embracing the nonviolent activism of the civil rights movement, but this was almost a decade earlier and Robinson made clear that what he was doing was following "Mr. Rickey's" instructions. Mr. Rickey had listened to the public saying they would not attend integrated games because the crowd would be raucous and fights would break out on the field. He believed that if he could make sure that didn't happen, game attendance would hugely increase, drawing the fans from the Negro Leagues and the white fans who wanted better baseball. Though he often framed it as a moral cause, it was a commercial decision. Attendance in Ebbets Field increased 400 percent in Jackie Robinson's first season.

Robinson never denied that what he was doing was very different from what he was thinking. He was not King or Gandhi claiming that he was learning to love his adversary. King's statement, "Do what you will and we will still love you," was never fully embraced by Robinson.[16] Robinson later confessed that he longed to drop his bat, march over to the opposing dugout from where the remarks were coming, "grab one of those white sons of bitches, and smash his teeth in with my despised black fist."[17] Of course Robinson was an athlete, a physical man. Besides, some nonviolent activists may have had similar thoughts, but it was against the rules of their program to admit it. There were quite a few loaded shotguns in nonviolent southern homes ready to defend against an attack by the KKK.

Robinson always admitted that he felt no love for these racist adversaries. He wrote later in life, "I never would have made a good soldier in Martin's army. My reflexes are not conditioned to accept nonviolence in the face of violence-provoking attacks. My immediate instinct under the threat of physical attack to me or those I love is instant defense and total retaliation."[18]

Though Robinson became a close friend and supporter of King, he never had any delusion that they were cut of the same cloth or that he, Robinson, could ever have fought in the ranks of nonviolence in the South. He wrote, "Personally I am not, and don't know how I could ever be, nonviolent. If anyone punches me or otherwise physically assaults me, you can bet your bottom dollar that I will try to give him back as good as he sent."[19]

Robinson would have never taken the beating Bayard Rustin did in his Freedom Ride, nor the beating John Lewis and many others received on the Edmund Pettus Bridge in March 1965.

The turn-the-other-cheek behavior for which Robinson became famous was pursued for only three years of Robinson's life. He did it when Rickey took him to the minor league Royals and for two years on the Dodgers. Then Rickey concluded that he had succeeded and told Robinson he was free "to be yourself now."[20] Himself was not a raging man of violence, physically attacking adversaries, but Robinson no longer took insults and argued ferociously with anyone who he felt was denying him his dignity. He bitterly criticized Campanella for not doing more to stand up for himself.

Those three years of turning the other cheek were an extreme act of self-discipline. Robinson later wrote that it caused him periods of depression. Sportswriter Maury Allen interviewed African American pitcher Joe Black, who said of Robinson and his death from ill health at only age fifty-three, "He was a combative person by nature and that restraint went against his personality. He had to hold a lot in and it angered him terribly. Holding that much anger can really hurt a man, and I think all that name-calling in those years killed him. I really do think that."[21]

Starting in 1949, Robinson was an outspoken critic of racism in baseball, spiking opposing players as he slid into bases as payback for the same having been done to him, railing against umpires for unfair treatment so rigorously that teammates had to calm him down, denouncing teams like the Yankees for being slow to integrate, and, a point that is still salient, decrying the lack of black managers. The real Jackie Robinson from 1949 until his retirement and beyond was not as popular as the perfect nonviolent hero of 1945–47, but he earned respect and, more important, felt free to be who he was. And that was exactly what Robinson intended. He wrote in his autobiography that when a white umpire told him that he had liked the old Jackie Robinson better, he answered, "I am not concerned about your liking or disliking me. All I ask is that you respect me as a human being."[22] *New York Daily News* sportswriter Dick Young wrote of Robinson, "He made enemies. He had a talent for it. He has the tact of a child because he has the moral purity of a child."[23]

Branch Rickey had no illusions about who Robinson was. What was important was that he stuck with the program for the three years Rickey needed it. In 1963, Rickey described Robinson as "direct, aggressive, the kind that stands up when he is faced with injustice and will hit you right in the snoot."[24] This was not the Jackie Robinson of legend.

Some were disappointed and didn't like the real Jackie Robinson. Others loved him. But many people, once they saw who he really was, were filled with admiration for the strength he showed in the performance he put on for those three years, what he could do for the cause if he had to.

On the other hand, in the 1960s, when the split came between nonviolence and Black Power, Robinson was clearly on the side of nonviolence. It was the old pragmatic argument. He believed it worked and that the opposite approach being promoted, particularly by Malcolm X, did not. He admitted that in his youth he might have been attracted to the Black Panthers if he had the opportunity. But his thinking had changed, though he was still drawn to the Panther message of self-defense.

In 1960 he wrote, "It was a lot harder to turn the other cheek and refuse to fight back then than it would have been to exercise a normal reaction. But it works because sooner or later it brings a sense of shame to those who attack you. And that sense of shame is often the beginning of progress."[25] So he had learned the strategy of nonviolent activism. It works.

Robinson spent the rest of his life as an activist for black rights whether as an executive for Chock full o'Nuts, an important African American employer, a board member and leading spokesman and fundraiser for the NAACP, an active supporter of King's organization, or a fundraiser for the Student Nonviolent Coordinating Committee (SNCC). He established an African American bank, the Freedom National Bank, and supported other African American–owned companies. He had a weekly radio broadcast on race issues, and he was a celebrity marcher at many protests. He became a civil rights leader.

He was a tireless champion, and he always leaned toward King and the nonviolent movement even though, as he wrote once in his column, he did not see "how I could ever be nonviolent."[26] Though he sometimes agreed with Malcolm X, particularly on the lack of progress toward equality, he saw in the Black Power movement an encouragement of violence and hatred that he did not think was helpful. After all, Robinson was a walking symbol of integration, it was what he believed in, and the idea that blacks should be separate from whites was not appealing to him. He accused Malcolm X of hating white people, and while Robinson could not love his racist adversaries like a true nonviolence advocate was supposed to, he did not hate white people, had always lived around them, and was comfortable with them.

This is not to say that he was willing to feign friendship with those he perceived as enemies. When Barry Goldwater suggested they sit down together so Robinson could explain civil rights to him, Robinson quoted Louis Armstrong who was once asked to explain jazz. "If you have to ask," Armstrong answered, "you wouldn't understand."[27]

Nor was Robinson an advocate for the broader strategy of nonviolence. He did not reject war and in fact supported the Vietnam War and criticized King for opposing it.

But Robinson did truly abhor violence and denounced the assassination of Malcolm X as "black hands being raised against brothers."[28] He always saw violence as disastrous for the black cause. And though he was extremely militant and often criticized other black leaders such as Roy Wilkins and Whitney Young for being too soft, he never veered from the conviction that nonviolence was the only pathway to success.

He wrote, "We are adamant: we intend to use every means at our disposal to smash segregation and discrimination wherever it appears."[29] And this sounds much like the famous declaration of Malcolm X that rights would be gotten "by any means necessary." It was in fact very different because Malcolm X was saying that he would not rule out violence, and Robinson made clear that he did rule it out as an acceptable tactic.

In 1962 he wrote a letter to President John Kennedy in which he stated, "We do not believe in violence as a solution to the problems of the negro in this country." But he also added a warning: "But with all due respect to the preachments of Dr. Martin Luther King, we do not believe that the Negro is going to continue to turn the other cheek when his children are denied schooling, his family denied bread and butter, when he is denied the right to vote, to strike for advancement, to live where his desire urges him and his pocket book entitles him."[30] In other words, Robinson was not willing to turn violent, but he did warn that others might turn to violence without progress.

We need not portray Robinson as a champion of nonviolence. As Orwell said of Gandhi, he should not fall into the trap of being made a saint. Jesse Jackson's comparison of Robinson to Jesus does not seem appropriate. Like all of us, he was a flawed human being. He had a bad temper and enough bitterness to title his autobiography *I Never Had It Made*. He was not a violent man but could not fully embrace nonviolence. But he was a man who spent his life trying to advance his people and to use the fame he earned from phenomenal natural athletic ability to further a cause to which he was relentlessly committed.

6

THE WHITE MEDIA MISSED IT

CHRIS LAMB

Hector Racine, president of the Montreal Royals, the Brooklyn Dodgers' AAA team, told a packed conference room on October 23, 1945, that the team had signed Jackie Robinson of the Kansas City Monarchs of the Negro Leagues. Camera bulbs flashed and reporters moved quickly to the front of the room, where Racine and Robinson were sitting, while others rushed to call their newspapers and radio stations.[1]

Racine told the reporters that his team had signed Robinson because he was "a good ballplayer," and because it was a "point of fairness." Blacks, Racine said, had earned their right to play in the national pastime by fighting—and in some cases dying—for their country during World War II. Robinson's roster spot was not guaranteed. He would have to earn his Montreal uniform during spring training in Florida, Racine said. When reporters asked Robinson for a comment, he described himself as a "guinea pig in baseball's racial experiment."[2]

The announcement ended the color line in what was called "organized professional baseball" and forever changed baseball, sports, and American society.

To the black press and its readers, the announcement signaled the beginning of what they hoped would be a new day for fairness and equality. White sportswriters wondered what all the fuss was about. Black sportswriters, who condemned bigotry and, in many cases, fought for the integration of baseball, gave the story context so their readers could appreciate its significance and connect it to the larger issue of racial discrimination in society. White sportswriters kept their distance and said little beyond what Racine and Brooklyn Dodgers president Branch Rickey told them.

The newspaper coverage of Robinson's signing helped shape his legacy in the media in the more than seven decades that have followed.

To black America, Robinson changed what it was like to be a black American. He was a hero who was willing to sacrifice his life for the cause of racial equality and equal justice. Robinson was a larger-than-life civil rights leader, a "sit-inner before the sit-ins and a freedom rider before the Freedom Rides," as Martin Luther King Jr. described him.

To white America, Robinson was a black baseball player.

Sid Feder of the Associated Press reported within hours of the announcement that Robinson had been a star athlete at UCLA and that his signing had come after a three-year, $25,000 search by Rickey. Feder incorrectly reported that Robinson was the first black player in what was called "organized baseball." In fact, dozens had played in organized baseball at the end of the nineteenth century, including a few in the major leagues, until team owners agreed to prohibit black players.[3]

In a story the next day, AP reporter Jack Hand asked Rickey, who had not been at the press conference, if his decision to sign Robinson had been influenced by politics. Rickey was emphatic in his denial. "No pressure groups had anything to do with it," Rickey said. "In fact, I signed him in spite of such groups rather than because of them."[4]

This statement was repeated in stories throughout the country. But it was not true.

Rickey co-opted the integration story, ignoring the contributions of black and communist sportswriters and progressive politicians who had demanded and agitated for the integration of baseball for more than a decade. White sportswriters and columnists accepted what Rickey told them and passed this version on to their readers, leaving them to believe that it had been Rickey—and only Rickey—who ended segregated baseball.[5]

Robinson's breaking of Major League Baseball's color barrier is the most significant sports story in America in terms of its consequences for society. Jules Tygiel, author of the extraordinary *Baseball's Great Experiment*, wrote that the integration of baseball depended on the courage of Robinson and Rickey.[6]

Tygiel was absolutely correct. But the campaign by black and communist sportswriters to integrate baseball had little or nothing to do with either Robinson or Rickey. This part of the story went unreported in the mainstream press.

White sportswriters, particularly in New York, knew that political progressives had clamored for the integration of baseball because the city was the epicenter of the movement, but those journalists said nothing about this when Montreal announced it had signed Robinson. Sportswriters relied for the details of the story on Rickey, who said that he had signed Robinson because it was, as Racine had put it, "a point of fairness," and because it was a matter of faith. "I cannot face my God much longer knowing that His black creatures are held separate and distinct in the game that has given me all I can call my own," Rickey told reporters.[7]

The sixty-three-year-old Rickey had been involved in baseball most of his life and had rarely—at least publicly—expressed interest in ending segregation in baseball until he signed Robinson. If Rickey was taking orders from God, why did it take him so long to answer the Almighty's call? In addition, Rickey was well aware that others had been persistently removing the color barrier brick by brick.

Baseball could not have maintained the color line as long as it did without the aid and comfort of white mainstream sportswriters, who participated in what sportswriter Joe Bostic of Harlem's

People's Voice called a "conspiracy of silence" with team owners to keep baseball segregated. The Baseball Writers' Association of America, like team owners, had a color line. It excluded blacks from membership. Without a press card, black sportswriters were prohibited from press boxes, dugouts, baseball fields, and dressing rooms.[8]

Baseball writers were far more comfortable dressing up in blackface and speaking in black dialect during their skits at their annual banquet than in writing about racism. They used racial pejoratives and stereotypes in print and in conversation. Shirley Povich, who was one of the relatively few mainstream sportswriters who advocated for blacks in baseball, was asked why so few white sportswriters called for the end of the color line. "I'm afraid the sportswriters were like the club owners," he said. "They thought separate was better."[9]

White sportswriters made no attempt to put the Robinson story in historical or sociological context. Sportswriters rarely interviewed Robinson. They relied for their quotes about Robinson on Rickey or one of his associates or one of the black or communist sportswriters who interviewed Robinson. In some cases, they simply made up their quotes. To white sportswriters, it was as if the issue wasn't that Robinson had a different skin color; it was as if he spoke a different language.

Whatever the case, white sportswriters missed the most significant sports story in the history of baseball, and so did their readers.

* * *

On February 5, 1933, the New York Baseball Writers' Association met for their annual dinner, where they heard speeches and testimonials about the great game of baseball and took turns cracking themselves up with songs and skits. The high point of the evening, as it was every year, was a minstrel show, where sportswriters in blackface delighted the crowd of hundreds of white league executives, players, politicians, judges, and business leaders.[10]

Heywood Broun, the progressive columnist of the *World-Telegram*, took the occasion to respond to a recent editorial in the *Daily News* that called for the end of the color line in baseball. In his speech, Broun said he saw "no reason" why blacks should be kept out of the major leagues and then spoke at some length about why teams should sign black players. "If baseball is really the national game let the club owners go out and prove it," he said.[11]

Perhaps every sportswriter and columnist in New York City heard Broun's speech. Only Jimmy Powers of the *Daily News*, who praised Broun's suggestion, mentioned it in print. The *Sporting News*, the so-called "Bible of Baseball," also ignored Broun's appeal. The *Pittsburgh Courier* and the *Chicago Defender*, which had the highest circulation of any black newspapers in America, praised Broun and Powers and called for team owners to sign black players.[12]

Black newspapers recognized this critical juncture in the crusade for racial equality in baseball, and in the United States, and shared that story with their readers. Wendell Smith, Sam Lacy, and other sportswriters took up the issue in their columns, where they praised Negro League ballplayers, chronicled the hopes and frustrations of their readers, and challenged the claims of the baseball establishment. Black sportswriters wrote Major League Baseball commissioner Kenesaw Mountain Landis and league presidents and knocked on the doors of team owners, asking them to give tryouts to black players who they said would improve their teams.[13]

In early 1939, Wendell Smith asked National League president Ford Frick why there were no blacks in baseball. Frick said the fault for the color line rested with the racial attitudes of ballplayers and fans and not with owners and other baseball executives, who, he said, were willing to sign black players. He told Smith baseball couldn't sign blacks until players supported it.

Smith decided to interview ballplayers to see if this was true. Smith, as a black man, could not get a press card, which would have allowed him access to dugouts and dressing rooms. Over the next several weeks Smith interviewed dozens of ballplayers and managers in the hotel where visiting teams stayed when they came to Pittsburgh to play the Pirates. Nearly all of those interviewed, including Dizzy Dean, Gabby Hartnett, Carl Hubbell, Ernie Lombardi, Mel Ott, and Leo Durocher, said they had no objections to blacks in the major leagues, and many said adding black players to their rosters would improve their teams. Smith included the responses in a series of articles.[14]

The *Courier* and other black newspapers had little readership and/or political influence outside black America. This wasn't the case with the *Daily Worker*, a newspaper published by the United States Communist Party in New York City, which communists used to convince like-minded people to join their cause. Unlike black journalists, the communists had political influence among social progressives in the New York State Legislature and on the New York City Council.[15]

Communism increased in the 1930s as a result of the Great Depression, which many Americans, particularly those on the political left, viewed as a failure of capitalism. Communists tried to recruit black Americans, who were oppressed by the white establishment and were therefore open to a political system that included them. If the communists could integrate baseball, they believed they could win over the hearts and minds of black Americans.[16]

The *Daily Worker* began its campaign to end segregation in baseball on August 13, 1936, in response to Jesse Owens's bravura performance at the Berlin Olympics, where the black sprinter won four gold medals to counter German chancellor Adolf Hitler's theory of a master race. In the coming decade, *Worker* sportswriters wrote hundreds of columns and articles on the issue of segregated baseball. They collected hundreds of thousands of names on petitions demanding the integration of baseball and sent them to Commissioner Landis. Communists challenged owners to sign black players, criticized mainstream sportswriters for their silence, and shamed the baseball establishment into defending itself against racism. Baseball executives and mainstream sportswriters called the communists "agitators" and "social-minded drum beaters," which, of course, was true.[17]

In 1942, Pittsburgh Pirates owner William Benswanger told the *Worker* his team would give a tryout to Negro Leaguers. Even though Benswanger reneged on the promise, the announcement gave much-needed publicity to the campaign to integrate baseball. J. G. Taylor Spink, editor of the *Sporting News*, wrote an editorial with the headline "No Good from Raising Race Issue." He argued that black players did not want to play in the major leagues and that mixing blacks and whites on the field would result in race riots in the stands.[18] Neither of these arguments was factual.

Activists increased their pressure to integrate baseball during World War II, when the quality of play in the major leagues deteriorated as ballplayers left to join the armed service. Progressive politicians, including U.S. congressman Vito Marcantonio of Brooklyn, New York, state legislators, and New York City Council members, were among those calling for major league teams to sign black players.[19]

In early 1945, the New York Legislature approved the Quinn-Ives Act, making it the first state to ban racial discrimination in the workplace. Rickey, who had begun secretly scouting the Negro Leagues for players to sign, was at spring training when he read that Governor Tom Dewey was expected to sign the bill into law.

"They can't stop me now," he told his wife.[20]

Joe Bostic brought two aging Negro Leaguers to Brooklyn's wartime spring training in Bear Mountain, New York, and demanded that Rickey give them tryouts. Rickey reluctantly agreed. After giving the players a full tryout, he said the players were too old to sign to a contract. A few days earlier, a Boston politician pressured the Red Sox to give tryouts to three talented young Negro League players: Jackie Robinson, Sam Jethroe, and Marvin Williams. The Red

Sox had high school pitchers throw batting practice, and team officials reportedly sat in the stands yelling "get those niggers off the field."[21]

Mayor Fiorello La Guardia, facing pressure from the political left, created a committee to end Jim Crow in baseball. Rickey, who was a member of the committee, secretly signed Robinson and hoped to sign other blacks. La Guardia told Rickey he was going to announce on radio on October 18, 1945, that the committee was making progress on integrating baseball. Rickey asked the mayor to postpone his announcement. He did not want anyone to think he signed Robinson because of politics.[22]

When Montreal announced it had signed Robinson, black newspapers responded as if it was the moon landing. The *Chicago Defender* wrote that the signing of Robinson was more than just an opportunity for the ballplayer, it was an opportunity for all blacks. If baseball could be integrated, so too could schools, theaters, businesses, and swimming pools. The *New York Amsterdam News* called the news "a drop of water in the drought that keeps faith alive in American institutions." *New York Age* editor Ludlow Werner wrote that a lot of Americans hoped Robinson would fail. "The white race will judge the Negro race by everything he does," Werner said. "And Lord help him with his fellow Negroes if he should fail them."[23]

The *Pittsburgh Courier* filled its newspaper with photographs and articles, including two on the front page—one by Wendell Smith and the other with Robinson's byline, though it was ghostwritten by Smith. The *Baltimore Afro-American* included a long interview with Robinson on page 1 that quoted the ballplayer as saying, "I feel that all the little colored kids playing sandlot baseball have their professional futures wrapped up somehow in me."[24]

Mainstream newspapers responded with big headlines but said little of substance beneath them. There were few columns or editorials about what the signing of Robinson meant to black America or to America for that matter. Little was said about racial discrimination in America or about the reasons for the color line or about those who had fought for integration.

Few sportswriters openly opposed the signing of Robinson on the basis of his skin color, or they would have risked violating the principles of equality and opportunity that Americans proclaimed separated themselves from Nazi Germany, which America and its allies had just defeated in World War II. By saying nothing or as little as possible about Robinson's race, historian William Simons said, "one could thus impede integration without appearing to challenge the liberal consensus."[25]

Sportswriters found ways to express their objections without leaving behind their fingerprints. For instance, the Associated Press sought reactions from southern ballplayers—and not northern players—who were more likely to criticize the signing. By doing so, northern newspapers could identify racial discrimination with the South and deny that racism existed in their own region of the country.[26]

The *Sporting News* published several articles on the signing of Robinson, including its main story that included this revealing description of Robinson: "Robinson is definitely dark. His color is the hue of ebony. By no means can he ever be called a brown bomber or a chocolate soldier." The *Sporting News* also included reactions from a number of the nation's sportswriters, who responded with banal platitudes but failed to capture the story's significance.

In an editorial, J. G. Taylor Spink downplayed the story's importance and doubted whether Robinson was good enough to play in the major leagues. If Robinson were white and six years younger, he might be good enough for Brooklyn's AA team, Spink said. He did not say whether he had ever seen Robinson play or talked to anyone who had.[27]

In his *Sporting News* column, Dan Daniel, the president of the Baseball Writers' Association, agreed with his editor that the story "had received more attention than it was worth." *New York World-*

Telegram columnist Joe Williams wrote that Robinson must ignore "pressure groups, social frauds, and political demagogues," who would try to exploit him to advance their personal objectives. A number of sportswriters and baseball officials said they didn't object to Robinson in baseball as long as he was the "right type" of black and that he was "a credit to his race." Robinson, they said, would get a fair chance in baseball as long as he was a "good black," like Jesse Owens, and not a "bad" one, like former heavyweight champion Jack Johnson.[28]

Most baseball executives said they had no comment. But when Philadelphia sportswriters asked Connie Mack about Robinson, he said he no longer had respect for Rickey and the Athletics would not take the field if the Dodgers brought Robinson to his team's spring training site in West Palm Beach, Florida. The sportswriters who heard Mack's racist tirade agreed not to publish it.

"I decided I'd forgive old Connie for his ignorance," Red Smith later said.[29]

Shortly before the players, managers, coaches, and sportswriters left for Florida for spring training in February 1946, the New York Baseball Writers' Association had their annual banquet. Arthur Daley, the revered sports columnist of the *New York Times*, wrote that the sportswriters spoofed the sensitive subject of Jackie Robinson but did so in such a way that "no one's feelings really were hurt."

To make his point, he published the dialogue of the skit: A writer dressed as Commissioner Albert "Happy" Chandler summoned a butler in blackface who appeared in a Montreal uniform and responded, "Yassah, Massa. Here ah is."

"Ah! There you are, Jackie," the Chandler character responded. "Jackie, you old wooly-headed rascal, how long you been in the family?"

"Long time, Kun'l," the Robinson character said. "Evver since Mistah Rickey done bo't me."[30]

On to the Stage

(Curtain rises showing Southern mansion. Darky in satin knee breeches is dusting table with back to audience. He turns slowly, disclosing that upper part of uniform is a Montreal shirt. Waits for laugh, advances center, peers into wings.) .

Butler—Looks lak de massa will be late dis ebning. (Exits.)

(Off-stage singing of "For He's a Jolly Good Fellow." Four colonels enter, vigorously patting the back of Chandler. He detaches himself and walks center.)

Chandler—Ah loves baseball. (Pause). Baseball, that is. (Longer pause.) Mighty fine to be home. Ah loves the South, too. The South, that is. When Ah comes to New York, Ah only stays at the Hotel Dixie. Dixie, that is. And Ah insists on a room with southern exposure. Southern, that is. .

Spink—Mighty fine speech, Senator. Mighty fine.

Chandler—Thank yo' kindly, Colonel Spink, thank yo' kindly. Shall we all partake of some refreshments? (Colonels nod assent.) No reason why we all shouldn't enjoy a little Southern hospitality. Southern, that is. (Claps hands and calls) Robbie-eee. Robbie-eee. (Butler enters.)

Butler—Yassuh, Massa. Here Ah is.

Chandler—Ah, there you are, Jackie. Jackie,

A description of the 1946 skit in which a blackfaced white sportswriter depicted Robinson as a butler to the baseball commissioner. *New York Times.*

When Wendell Smith learned of the skit, he excoriated sportswriters for their bigotry. Rickey, too, who was recovering in the hospital from a bout with Meniere's disease, was privately incensed.[31]

Rickey, to his credit, did everything he could to give Robinson the best chance of succeeding in Florida. He signed a second black prospect, Johnny Wright, and hired Wendell Smith to serve as Robinson's chauffeur, bodyguard, and father confessor. He also went to Daytona Beach before spring training to work out accommodations for Robinson and Wright, who would not be allowed to stay in the same hotel with the rest of the organization.[32]

There wasn't enough room for all the players in the organization to train in Daytona Beach. The Montreal team began spring training forty miles away in rural Sanford.

Robinson spoke to sportswriters after his first day of practice on March 4. The next day's stories included biographical information about Robinson such as his athletic success at UCLA, his military background, his statistics in the Negro Leagues, and his recent marriage to Rachel. Sportswriters praised him for his poise, intelligence, athletic ability, and sense of humor. When Robinson told reporters he weighed about 195 but wanted to get down to the 180 pounds he weighed when he played for UCLA, a reporter remarked that the extra weight didn't show. "It's in my feet," he said.[33]

Robinson later criticized sportswriters for being combative during spring training. "They frequently stirred up trouble by baiting me or jumping into any situation I was involved in without completely checking the facts," he said.[34]

In fact, sportswriters rarely, if ever, treated Robinson with outright hostility. Rather, they ignored him. White sportswriters treated Robinson as if he were a curiosity or a novelty—like a one-armed player or a thirty-five-year-old rookie.

After the second day of practice, a Klansman told Smith there would be trouble if Robinson was not out of town by sundown. Smith, Robinson, and Wright left immediately, and the Montreal team went to Daytona Beach the next day.[35]

Robinson struggled at the plate and injured his throwing arm trying to impress the coaches. He couldn't hit and he couldn't throw. Rickey moved him to first base, where he didn't have to throw, and encouraged him to use his speed. Robinson began bunting his way on base and then stole second and third. His armed healed.[36]

The bigotry at Sanford surfaced in other cities. The city of Jacksonville locked the gates to its ballpark rather than allow Robinson to take the field in its segregated ballpark. Deland canceled a day game because the lights weren't working. He was escorted off the field by a police officer in another town. Only Daytona Beach let him play that spring.[37]

Robinson made the Montreal roster and became its most valuable player as the team won the International League championship. Rickey signed Robinson the following spring, and he played his first game for Brooklyn on April 15, 1947.

The story had become too big for the mainstream press to ignore.

Robinson and the integration of baseball became, according to William Simons, the most talked-about story involving race relations in the years immediately following World War II.[38]

But you wouldn't know that by reading the country's mainstream newspapers. White sportswriters kept Robinson at a distance—as did Brooklyn players.

Sportswriters perpetuated the fiction that Robinson and his teammates had become good friends, reporting that Dixie Walker, a hardcore segregationist, had taken Robinson under his wing and was giving him batting tips. One columnist referred to Walker as "Robinson's best friend and chief advisor." Jackie's wife, Rachel, clipped the article and wrote the following: "Some sportswriters fall for anything." Robinson later said he had no relationship—let alone a friendship—with Walker.[39]

White sportswriters failed to tell the story of the integration of baseball because they made little attempt to get close to it. According to Red Smith's biographer, the sportswriter was opposed to racial discrimination but did not feel comfortable challenging the issue in print. When Smith was later asked how he felt about the story of Robinson and the integration of baseball, he answered, "I don't remember feeling any way except for having a lively interest in a good story."[40]

If he indeed had such an interest in the story, why did he not write anything about it?

The same could be asked of most of the white sportswriters who failed to tell the story of Robinson and the integration of baseball and, in doing so, denied their readers the opportunity to understand what the story meant not just to baseball but to society. They thus denied their readers the context necessary to make sense of a changing America.

Too many white sportswriters simply believed that the signing of Robinson meant that baseball was now integrated and that it had solved what J. G. Taylor Spink had called baseball's "race issue."[41] That conclusion was incalculably wrong because it denied the long history of racism in baseball. These same sportswriters failed to help their readers appreciate that what Robinson did on April 15, 1947—and during his rookie season and subsequent baseball career—transcended baseball.

Jonathan Eig writes in *Opening Day* that Robinson, by demonstrating grace under unceasing pressure, provided an example for others who would confront racial inequality. "He proved that black Americans had been held back not by their inferiority but by systematic discrimination," Eig writes. "And he proved it not with printed words or arguments declaimed before a judge. He proved it with deeds. That was Jackie Robinson's true legacy."[42]

More than seventy years after Robinson integrated baseball, his stature as a baseball player remains secure. But he has not yet been fully recognized for his contributions to civil rights. If white America still doesn't appreciate Robinson's legacy in the civil rights movement, it's because white journalists, commentators, and historians have failed to put him in the context of the civil rights movement. If white America is ever to give Robinson the credit he deserves, the nation's sportswriters and the rest of us must quit seeing him as just a ballplayer who broke baseball's color barrier and recognize him as a civil rights icon who played baseball.

7

ON RETIRING 42

DAVID NAZE

In 1997, fifty years after Jackie Robinson radically transformed the landscape of baseball, and America, through racial integration, Major League Baseball retired his jersey number—42. There's a strong likelihood that anyone reading this chapter can conjure the iconic image of that beautiful Dodger blue filling in the 4 and 2 on the back of Robinson's jersey. We've seen it on baseball stadium walls, stadium banners, and commemorative jersey patches, among many other places. The retirement of Robinson's number has certainly given fans something significant to remember and revere. But it's important to keep in mind that this ceremonial gesture, no matter how significant, can never capture his legacy.

The retirement of a player's number is certainly nothing new to sports. In some organizations, like the Boston Celtics and the New York Yankees, it has become practically commonplace. Several reasons have fueled this increasingly popular practice: to commemorate an individual's impact on an organization; to highlight a player's athletic accomplishments and longevity; to thank the player for his or her commitment to and excellence within the organization; and to cement the number in organizational history to the point that no other player will wear it again.

In Robinson's case, 1997 marked a first: his was the first number retired across an entire sport. At the 1997 commemorative ceremony, acting Major League Baseball commissioner Bud Selig said, "In

MLB retired Robinson's number in 1997. Osvaldo Salas / National Baseball Hall of Fame.

honor of Jackie, Major League Baseball is taking the unprecedented step of retiring his uniform number in perpetuity. Number 42, from this day forward, will never again be issued by a major league club. Number 42 belongs to Jackie Robinson for the ages."[1] The players who were wearing number 42 at that time included Mo Vaughn of the Boston Red Sox, Butch Huskey of the New York Mets, Tom Goodwin of the Kansas City Royals, Buddy Groom of the Oakland Athletics, and Marc Sagmoen of the Texas Rangers. Each was allowed to wear the number for the remainder of his career.

Perhaps the most famous 42 that fell under this grandfather clause was the one worn by Hall of Fame New York Yankees pitcher Mariano Rivera. In January 2019, Rivera became the first player unanimously elected to the Hall of Fame. Reflecting on the moment, he said, "One thing I will always remember is wearing No. 42 and representing Mr. Jackie Robinson. He, I assume, was the first No.

42 elected, and me being the last player to wear No. 42 and being elected to the Hall of Fame unanimously is amazing." While Dayn Perry of CBS Sports did not see an exact equality between the two men, he appreciated the star pitcher's continuation of Robinson's legacy. "Rivera, though, will be just behind Robinson when it comes to those most associated with this canonized uniform number," Perry wrote. "Given Rivera's generous spirit and his sterling reputation on and off the field, he again makes a fitting capstone for the proud history of No. 42."[2]

What was the impetus behind the retirement of Robinson's number in 1997? Obviously, something significant was going to be planned for the fiftieth anniversary of Robinson's debut, but the decision to retire his number across all Major League Baseball teams was not as obvious. As Jayson Stark of ESPN recounts about those involved in the decision, "They were there to do something that had never been done before: retire a number, Jackie Robinson's 42, across an entire sport. And to do their part to ensure that the power of Robinson's major league debut, 50 years earlier to the day, would keep resonating through history."[3]

In 2017 Stark recorded an oral history of the minds behind the retirement proposal, including Len Coleman, then the National League president, later the chairman of the Jackie Robinson Foundation for eighteen years; Bud Selig, then the acting commissioner of Major League Baseball; Sharon Robinson, Jackie's daughter, now MLB's educational consultant; and Claire Smith, who covered the ceremony for the *New York Times*.

In his comments, Coleman recalled the origin of the decision:

> I actually got put in charge of orchestrating the festivities for the 15th, and I was struggling in thinking about what we were going to do to capture the moment . . . that would be totally distinctive, that would separate Jackie from every other ballplayer and capture the significance of his accomplishment. I was driving on the Gar-

den State Parkway, and it was like a lightning bolt hit: "Retire his number from the whole game." I thought about it as I was driving, and I said, "That's it. I'm going to go to Bud and say: 'Let's retire the number.'"

According to Selig, he found Coleman's idea compelling:

You know, there's always pressure on [retiring] numbers. And you've got to be so careful, and I really mean that. But this one, to me, there was just no question about it. This Jackie Robinson thing was really special, and so it just appealed to me greatly. . . . In the [college] course I teach—which is "Baseball in American History, 1945 to the Present"—I start with Jackie Robinson. He's my first lecture every September. I really believe [his first game] was the most powerful and important moment in baseball history.

Sharon Robinson remembered that she and Rachel had initial questions and slight reservations about the proposal:

Len called us first and gave us the heads-up that this was going to happen, just a few days in advance. And my mom and I were like, "Is that a good thing? Is that a bad thing?" What about Mo Vaughn? What about all the players that we knew at the time were wearing No. 42? Some of them were wearing it to honor my dad. . . . So when they walked out on that field, I remember sort of holding my breath, because we had anxiety over how the retirement of the No. 42 would be received. We weren't sure how the fans were going to take it. But when Bud announced it, they jumped out of their seats. We just couldn't believe it. The fans jumped out of their seats and stood up and cheered. So we knew it was the right decision.[4]

The historic decision to retire Robinson's jersey followed a number of earlier commemorations. The first occurred on June 4, 1972, when Robinson was invited to Dodger Stadium to celebrate the quarter century that had passed since his rookie year in 1947. This particular ceremony was designed to provide Robinson with the ultimate organizational legacy: the retirement of his number across the entire Dodger organization. The Jackie Robinson spectators saw that day was a physically altered version of the one they were used to. He was suffering from a number of ailments, including diabetes, blindness, a limp, and high blood pressure. Former teammates Sandy Koufax and Roy Campanella also had their numbers retired that same day.

On October 15, 1972, Major League Baseball commissioner Bowie Kuhn invited Robinson to make an appearance in a ceremony prior to game 2 of the World Series. At one point, Robinson had protested baseball's poor record on minority hiring, particularly for managerial and front-office positions. Despite this, he agreed to attend the televised event. But after he threw out the ceremonial first pitch, he stepped to the microphone and said, "I am extremely proud and pleased to be here this afternoon but must admit I'm going to be tremendously more pleased and more proud when I look at that third base coaching line one day and see a black face managing baseball."[5] Nine days later, Robinson passed away due to his poor health.

The 1997 ceremony at Shea Stadium garnered significantly more attention compared to the 1972 event. Robinson's pioneering spirit was marked with a big celebration that included musical entertainment by Tevin Campbell. During Campbell's performance, video screens in the outfield displayed images of Robinson on and off the field. President Clinton, Selig, and Rachel Robinson then delivered brief remarks. The elements of this ceremony proved to be more dynamic compared to the 1972 ceremony.

But there was a major voice of dissent: Hank Aaron. In his *New York Times* editorial, the former Negro League star and Major League Baseball Hall of Famer stated, "Now, 50 years later, people are saying that Jackie Robinson was an icon, a pioneer, a hero. But that's all they want to do: say it. . . . It is tragic to me that baseball has fallen so far behind . . . in terms of racial leadership. People question whether baseball is still the national pastime, and I have to wonder too." Aaron continued to lament the concerns that are invisible in the integration narrative: "Here's hoping that . . . baseball will honor [Robinson] in a way that really matters. It could start more youth programs, give tickets to kids who can't afford them, become a social presence in the cities it depends on. It could hire more black umpires, more black doctors, more black concessionaries, more black executives. It could hire a black commissioner."[6]

On April 15, 2004, thirty-four thousand fans attended the first "Jackie Robinson Day" at Shea Stadium, home of the New York Mets. In the run-up to the event, Major League Baseball announced that it would mark Robinson's shattering of the color barrier every April 15. The intention was to preserve the legacy of a man who made baseball, and American, history in 1947. With Rachel and Sharon Robinson present, Commissioner Bud Selig led a ceremony that included a video montage of Robinson from his days as a baseball player. Jackie Robinson's impact on the game, society, and history, along with his memory and legacy, were now "official."

The prominent theme surrounding the 2004 commemoration focused on Major League Baseball's inability, or unwillingness, to cultivate a culture that included more African American baseball players. Many members of the African American community, including present and former players, expressed concern that the game still suffered from racial inequality.

Dave Stewart, a four-time twenty-game winner in the late 1980s and early 1990s, put it this way: "In Bud's words, the game is better today than it has ever been, but I think it has taken a drastic step backward. When you look at the numbers of blacks playing the game and the numbers in decision-making positions off the field, they're way down from even three years ago." When asked about the celebrations that started in 1997 to honor Robinson, Stewart replied, "There was good progress and a feeling among black players I think that baseball was trying to do something positive. Now . . . it's as if there's been a quick turnaround. . . . Why that's happened only the people internally know, but it's not good." Veteran Major League Baseball scout John Young followed suit, arguing, "I think there [are] societal changes to which baseball was slow in responding."[7]

The *San Francisco Chronicle* weighed in, too: "What has changed since Robinson's arrival? Still no black owners. Only three black general managers, one currently. What appeared to be a progression in 1975 turned out to be a peak." The *Chronicle* also reported on another point ignored in the anniversary celebration: "The number of African-American big-leaguers is under 10 percent for the first time since full integration—that was 1959."[8]

Rachel Robinson also expressed disappointment with MLB's racial landscape. When asked how her husband would view the ongoing racial inequality, she said, "Jack would be disappointed, obviously, and he would be fighting back, as he always did in his lifetime, and saying, 'Let's not forget what it took to get us to this point.' . . . I think there is a perception that there is a level playing field now, and that things have progressed. That is not true."[9]

The version of "Jackie Robinson" that MLB presented during the 2004 commemoration highlighted his role as a great athlete and a racial pioneer. Robinson appeared apolitical. Rather than encompassing his entire legacy, this version functioned more as a convenient, uncomplicated representation of racial equality in MLB and America; it served the ideal patriotic narrative that MLB has typically portrayed through Robinson.

Mystery still surrounds the impetus behind the creation of Jackie Robinson Day. Selig has often insisted that he did it because he wanted to ensure that people, especially young people, know who Jackie Robinson was. But the year 2004 seemed an odd choice, even arbitrary; it was an off year, unlike the significant twenty-fifth and fiftieth anniversaries. But it was a year marked by issues that garnered more national notoriety for baseball—including rumors of a possible player lockout and of players utilizing performance-enhancing drugs at an unprecedented level. Perhaps the best remedy to cure these ills, as well as waning fan interest, was for Major League Baseball to divert attention away from them by focusing on the positivity of Jackie Robinson's legacy.

In 2007, Cal Fussman published *After Jackie: Pride, Prejudice, and Baseball's Forgotten Heroes: An Oral History*. In the introduction, Fussman frames the collection as a project designed to help us move forward by learning and unlearning our racial past: "Every step of progress made since the day Jackie Robinson integrated Major League Baseball has come from education, learning, knowledge." Fussman goes on to explain, "The more I spoke with the men who came after Jackie, the more certain I became of one thing: The only way to unlearn is to learn. The surest way for us to move forward is to know where the old have been."[10]

Later in Fussman's book, Hall of Famer Frank Robinson shares a compelling anecdote about the number of black players in Major League Baseball:

> When I came into professional baseball, we used to leave our gloves in the outfield after the third out. That was 1953. You left your glove right there on the field. If you ask people who played back then when gloves stopped being left on the field, they can't tell you. They just know the practice stopped. And that's what's so disturbing about this business of the dwindling number of African-Americans in the major leagues. It's happening right in front of us. We see it. If we don't address it pretty soon, there's not going to be any of us here to remember when there stopped being blacks in baseball. Just like the gloves in the outfield.[11]

Frank Robinson's anecdote makes a crucial point about the role history plays in our ability to cultivate the legacy that Jackie Robinson left us. And that is why it is so incredibly important to ensure we find creative ways to spotlight Robinson beyond an annual ceremony. We owe it to Robinson to provide an active and sustainable space for the remembrance of his social impact. While Jackie Robinson Day serves that role to a certain extent, we can, should, and need to do more. For instance, author Jeff Snider offers one such option that might serve baseball fans well:

Every April 15, Jackie Robinson Day, the league honors Robinson's memory by having every player wear his number 42. Originally, Ken Griffey Jr. received special permission to wear number 42 on April 15, 2007, the 60th anniversary of Robinson's MLB debut. The idea spread (much to the chagrin of many players), and more than 240 wore 42 that day. In 2008, the number jumped to more than 330, and in 2009, it became official that every player and coach would wear the number on that day.[12]

So the number of players participating has been maximized. But why limit a commemorative tribute to Robinson's legacy to just once a season? As Snider continues,

But let's go back to Griffey's original idea: one player wearing a number as tribute to a great player. What is a better way to honor a player: putting his number in mothballs, or letting a player who exemplifies his greatness wear that number as a tribute? You want to honor a player by slapping his number on an outfield wall? That's great, and there's no reason to stop that. But let's separate that honor from the idea of retiring a number, and let's accept the fact that the best way to honor a player is by letting another great player follow in his footsteps.[13]

I believe we could benefit from Snider's proposal. Let's consider the impact of taking an increasingly commonplace practice of jersey retirement and turn it on its head. As more and more jerseys are retired, the ultimate impact is diluted. Certainly, the idea of a jersey number hanging from the rafters or being posted on a stadium wall or upper deck façade is compelling and without question represents that player's impact on an organization or even an entire sport. But that number, sitting among so many other retired jersey numbers, lying static, isolated, and inactive, loses its power.

Robinson's 42 has been put on a shelf to be dusted off and rolled out for a celebration every April 15. While that's a meaningful commemorative gesture in its own right, it's only one day per year. What if we allowed players to wear 42 again? What if we reactivated 42, allowing it to breathe life into his legacy once again?

Imagine it. Instead of players wearing 42 just once a year, a good number of players would have the opportunity to wear it every single game for six months a year. Imagine the conversations that could be sparked on a daily basis for 162 games per year. Or imagine the World Series MVP wearing 42 and using that opportunity to create a space that identifies and commemorates Robinson's legacy at an even greater level.

Pulling Robinson's number out of retirement would encourage us to talk more about him; to keep him front and center in our discussions about baseball, race, and culture; and to create new and fresh ways to honor his legacy. Commemorating Robinson's legacy through Jackie Robinson Day and retiring his number is helpful but not sufficient. There is room for creativity. There is room for expansion. There is room for further distinction. In fact, creativity, expansion, and distinction might be the most fitting options for remembering a man who embodied each of these characteristics on and off the field.

PART III

CIVIL RIGHTS AND POLITICS

8

BEFORE THE WORLD FAILED HIM

SRIDHAR PAPPU

Once again, he is alone. Though one might argue that he might have always been here, in this spot, forced to deal with this feeling of estrangement and of emotional distance, of being out of place even when surrounded by others. It was with him as a young black man growing up in Pasadena and on the day he took his place at first base at Ebbets Field on Opening Day 1947, as the first and only Negro player in Major League Baseball. Some part of him must have felt this even in 1960 as he made a choice that would be with him forever—well past his own death. As other African Americans had decided to cast their lot and allegiance to John F. Kennedy for president, he continued to side with the man who he felt was more able, more genuine in bringing about a more equal nation: Richard M. Nixon.

And yet, this is different. On this April day in 1968 in Atlanta, staring out at his surroundings, at the fellow mourners, Jack Roosevelt Robinson has the look of a man unable to share in the comfort one sometimes feels in the collective grief of others. Physical ailments make him seem far older than his age, and one gets the sense he is looking past everyone, or within himself. Maybe it's both. At the funeral for Martin Luther King Jr., his friend and fellow traveler, Robinson is left to think not only about King, but about his own future and past.

That's because from the time Robinson walked away from the game that made him an idol to millions, he had fought, even as his health began to fail him, for the ideals he shared with King. They were kindred spirits when it came to the idea of using nonviolence in the service of social change, even as the ranks that believed in this method began to dwindle. Both sought out an integrated America when the disillusioned young turned to black separatism. Each in his own way had aligned themselves with white power brokers, when, in Robinson's case, he would suffer the ultimate indignity of being called an "Uncle Tom."[1]

Now, with King felled in Memphis, Robinson is left with that terrible question all of us face at some point: What did it mean? This fight, this struggle? The years that now seem wasted? He had bloodied himself in fights with all comers: from the establishment ranks of civil rights organizations to the keepers of Camelot to men like Malcolm X. He had begun his life after baseball as the champion of a defined movement with defined goals. Now, though, he had seen a trail of largely unfulfilled promises, with the future he believed he could help usher in one that would never truly come to pass.

In this he is not alone. But in the aftermath of King's assassination, Robinson himself must be assessing what had been *his* role, *his* impact, with his days as a public figure now waning. What did he really achieve? Once he boldly embodied the brave, ambitious belief that fundamental change was coming—and fast. But at some point everything had turned against him and he found that his views no longer had currency, that the great goals of a great cause could never fully be reached. As much as Robinson was part of the civil rights movement, in many ways he was the very embodiment of the civil rights movement—one that began with such bluster but that was unable to recover from stumbles, to reform in a real way so that it might retain the strength to truly last.

Make no mistake: This was Robinson's fight as much as anyone's. He didn't watch it on television or comment on it from afar. He was there, in the thick of it, almost from its beginning to its end. And for a man who had endured so much tragedy in his life, his role

At the funeral of Martin Luther King Jr.
in 1968. Magnum Photos.

in all of this might be the most tragic. Because his life after baseball is ultimately a story of great struggle and sacrifice, of staking
everything—his family, his professional aspirations, a quiet existence
in suburban Connecticut—for something greater than himself. As he
milled around the great dignitaries at the funeral, with Coretta Scott
King in mourning with her children, with Jackie Kennedy there to
lend her support, his solemn gaze is not merely that of a mourner,
but that of a person who knew he had given everything possible, as
he had once done as a ballplayer, only to come up far too short. He
had not reached home.

* * *

That moment must have seemed so far away from the world that
Robinson briskly entered upon exiting from his stage in baseball
following the 1956 season. Robinson's initial foray into the crusade
marked a new life for him, one that began almost as soon as he
walked away from his old one, and he approached it with the same
vigor that he had once done with the game. As with baseball, in

this fight he wanted to be more than good. He needed to strive for perfection. He was determined to make clear that his time as Jackie Robinson, the ballplayer, was over. It was time for him to move on, for the world to know him as Jackie Robinson, the man. And he was going to make damn sure his voice would be heard.

"When they say the NAACP is moving too fast, take your time, be patient," Robinson said in a radio interview not long after his retirement in 1957. "Be patient, the Negro has proven beyond a doubt that we have been more than patient. And the Civil War's been over for about ninety-three years. If that isn't patience, I don't know what is."[2]

This was in response to a question about what some saw was the overaggressiveness of the NAACP, the unfathomable belief held by people that the organization was moving "very, very fast to get the rights of the Negro." Before the Black Panthers and the Nation of Islam and Stokely Carmichael provided a new, angry blueprint for African Americans, Robinson's statement carried a militant undertone to it. But it needed to be said. And by him. With it, he had given voice to the frustration of so many who had heard the patronizing words of the white establishment, most notably President Dwight D. Eisenhower, who urged a measured resolution to the thing that had cast a shadow over the country since its inception.

In truth, he had been developing this new voice even before his retirement, beginning with June 1956, in a moment that biographer Arnold Rampersad has pointed to as the occasion when Robinson decided publicly that he had to become part of a greater cause. This came with the NAACP awarding him the Spingarn Medal, given each year to one individual who had furthered the cause of equality for African Americans. No athlete had ever won the award. Once again he would take on the responsibility of being first.

"I was so often advised not to press issues," he told those in attendance at the ceremony, "not to speak up every time I thought there was an injustice. I was often advised to look after the Robinson family and not worry about other people." He now looked back to ask if "my course had been the proper one."[3]

And that was it. Within months of his retirement, there he was, working with the NAACP's Fight for Freedom Fund, speaking before crowds across the country. Aided by his patient adviser, Franklin H. Williams, he held his own speaking about the nuanced issues facing the country. There was no going back from this. Not that he wanted to.

"There was a time when I erred in being complacent," he told one crowd. "I was tempted to take advantages I received for granted. Then I realized my responsibility to my race and my country."[4]

What Robinson didn't understand at that moment was what precisely he had taken on and the price he would have to pay—not from those on the outside but from men seeking power as the momentum toward desegregation and racial equality grew. He seemed unaware of the growing discord and resentment building among the leaders of organizations who should have been working in unison with one another, but increasingly were not. But for him it didn't matter who headed what, who belonged to what. In the end, why should the credit actually matter?

Enter then King, the young pastor whose Southern Christian Leadership Conference had gained traction in its fight against injustice and cruelty, the cause that the NAACP once wholly owned. The two had met before Robinson's retirement, and as with so many, in Robinson's story, King, according to one biographer, saw a blueprint: this is how someone could carry on, move forward with courage even as he carried the weight and danger that comes with such a role.

Robinson immediately took to the man. Who wouldn't? That King and SCLC posed any real threat to Roy Wilkins, first the executive secretary and later the NAACP's executive director, was not evident to Robinson then. Nor was it readily apparent that the organization that he had raised money and lobbied for itself was bickering within.

If anything, even after such frictions became aware to him, Robinson seemed intent on trying to act as someone who might bridge divides, ones that would dramatically dwarf in comparison with those that came later. He was there at the behest of King in 1961 in the much-maligned Albany Movement in Albany, Georgia. He continued to act in support of the NAACP, though he spoke frankly and openly about his growing disenchantment with Wilkins and others, even before his call for Wilkins to step aside and let the "Young Turks" rise to power.[5] This was not about personal feelings or slights or scores, at least not yet. If anyone could live between worlds as he had, in baseball, in life, Robinson could do so now. This was something he could fix so this shared cause might actually move forward.

It could be called hubris. Or naïveté. A more apt description is a well-earned belief in himself and in his own ability to make people listen. As the 1960s began, one could argue that there was perhaps no more powerful African American figure in America. He had a newspaper column. He could speak freely to political figures from both parties. He was part of the unofficial civil rights roundtable at the Manhattan home of Arthur and Marian Logan. He aided Medgar Evers in Mississippi. Once he had desperately wanted to be something more than a baseball player. And now he was.

At the very same time, Robinson was beginning to see his own limits. His efforts to raise the money needed to rebuild the churches he stood in anguish over in Georgia would ultimately fail. He would lose both his newspaper column in the *New York Post* and his political standing when he sided with Nixon. His public war with the Harlem congressman Adam Clayton Powell Jr. had not sat well with those who were beginning to see him as a traitor to his race. And the grand gesture meant, it seemed, to placate both King and Wilkins would only exacerbate his standing with the latter.

It was supposed to be a happy occasion, honoring his induction into the Baseball Hall of Fame in 1962. In this celebratory dinner at the Waldorf Astoria, Wilkins was plucked to serve as the evening's "honorary" chair. Yet it was beneath the banner of the SCLC, which would reap the proceeds. As Rampersad recounted, for some time Wilkins had seethed over the press adulation over King and his upstart organization. The NAACP, he believed, through its vast network, had done so much more. But now he would lend his name to an event that helped replenish the coffers of King's organization. And it was because of the man who had once been his group's great ambassador, Jackie Robinson.

In some ways that evening foreshadowed the problems Robinson now faced, with his relevancy coming into question. Who was *he*, some now openly asked, to speak out in an increasingly caustic tone. The growing cacophony was enough for King himself to address it in a speech written by him but read by Reverend Wyatt Tee Walker in his absence.

"There are those, black and white, who have challenged the right of Jackie Robinson to ask these questions," King through Walker said. "He has the right. He has the right because he is a citizen. He has the right—more rightly—because back in the days when integration wasn't fashionable, he underwent the trauma and the humiliation and the loneliness which comes with being a pilgrim walking the lonesome byways toward the high road of Freedom. He was a sit-inner before sit-ins, a freedom rider before freedom rides."[6]

Yet as the decade moved forward, those credentials would increasingly be forgotten, even mocked. With the rise of reactionary forces within the GOP, his idea, however noble, that blacks should not be considered a solitary voting bloc loyal to the Democrats alone seemed increasingly fanciful. Worse, the concept of an integrated society seemed not only antiquated but unwanted. Why, many began to ask, should they try to shoehorn into place with people who would never really want them? If they wanted a better world, they would have to build their own.

Increasingly, of course, they had leaders who were willing to take them there. These were the people they wanted to hear, not Robinson. They certainly had little use for his words that day in September 1963 when he had organized a rally on 125th Street in Harlem in his effort to rebuild Birmingham's Sixteenth Street Baptist Church.

In earlier years this would have been Robinson's moment. He had traveled to Birmingham himself, inspecting the site, his anger undeniable, as he looked at what had been a house of worship until a bomb leveled it, ending the lives of four young girls. Now back north, he sought to help in the best manner he could, to do what he had so many times before.

He had enlisted celebrities and other notables to speak directly to the people. But it had been the very first one, Malcolm X, whom Robinson was now in open war with, that captured the crowd. And as the rally ended and Robinson told them it was time to go, one could hear the increasing chants of "We want Malcolm!" They had little interest in listening to Robinson, much less following his direction. It would take Malcolm X to return to the rally, to tell them it was really over, for everyone to go home.

Everything, it appeared, was coming apart for Robinson and those like him. That November, as their headlong ideological battles invariably played out in the press, Malcolm X wrote to Robinson, claiming, "You have never shown appreciation for the support given you by the Negro masses, but you have a record of being very faithful to your White Benefactors."[7]

To this, Robinson had a solid defense, both to his own character and to the white men he worked for and with. The same can't be said when Malcolm X brought up the idea of Paul Robeson. For years, since that day in 1947 when Robinson testified before the House Un-American Activities Committee, the fall of Robeson and Robinson's part in it threatened to undo every good thing that happened since.

By now, most everyone knows the story of what happened to the man, whom Jackie's friend Harry Belafonte would later describe as "the tallest tree in our forest," who "stood that strong in our midst in the kind of voice not only for the issues affecting black people but for the issues affecting poor people."[8]

But now the government sought to silence that voice. Robeson, with the Cold War building to a fevered pitch, with the Red Scare beginning to ruin the lives of so many deemed to be traitors, had made clear his affection toward the Soviet Union. Worse, he had said that blacks would not fight for the United States should the two great powers come to war. As they would do with authors and academics, actors and directors, HUAC set its sights on questioning the loyalty of the singer, and they would do it with help from baseball's newest star.

Of course Robinson's visit to Washington had not been his idea. That notion rested with his father figure, Branch Rickey, the person who had given him the chance to do what no other black man had done in the modern era: play professional baseball. Now the same man who had guided him through Montreal and then on to Brooklyn would help direct Robinson to speak before HUAC in a move that would very quickly ruin Robeson's life.

The sight is a haunting one. The dashing, handsome black man who had already become a transformative figure now testifying against the words of someone who had made so much possible for those like him. Robinson believed the idea that blacks might not defend their home was, among other things, "silly."[9] Though he would later come to say he had grown appreciative of Robeson, and he would not accept such an invitation in retrospect, he stuck by the sentiment surrounding his testimony. Robeson could speak for himself, but he didn't have the right to speak for an entire race.

"There are whites who would love to see us refuse to defend our country," Robinson would write with his ghostwriter Alfred Duckett in his autobiography, *I Never Had It Made*, "because then we could relinquish our right to be Americans."[10]

Robinson would never let go of the idea that somehow civil rights was the bedrock of a patriotic platform, one meant to reach the ideals of a country set forth so long ago, not only here but across the world. As such, he could not understand that his vision of the civil rights movement needed to broaden its scope beyond the arbitrary boundaries, particularly when it came to the very thing that young people black and white now took to the streets against—the Vietnam War.

This was something that King, at great risk to his own standing with other socially progressive Democrats, reluctantly took on. Before his speech in April 1967 at Riverside Church in Manhattan, he had given only a brief glimpse into what he thought of the unjust and ultimately pointless war. Thousands of young men, so many of them black, were boarding planes uncertain of their goals, not knowing whom they were defending and why. It was time for King to make clear his definitive stance on the war and what it meant for the nation.

The speech today ranks perhaps as one of the strongest, most evocative of King's career. Four years earlier, he spoke of the dream he had for the future. But now he found that our present military conflict ran counter to everything the marches, the speeches, the sit-ins sought to bring about. We were, he said, a country who saw the protection of freedom in military defense as more important than allocating funds to programs that might fundamentally bridge the gap between not only rich and poor, but whites and blacks. Moreover, we had sent men into battle in an arbitrary way, using violence as a wholesale tool against people who didn't ask for this war and were now subject to its devastation.

"We have destroyed their two most cherished institutions: the family and the village," King said. "We have cooperated in the crushing of the nation's only noncommunist political force, the unified Buddhist Church. We have supported the enemies of the peasants of Saigon. We have corrupted their women and children and killed their men."[11]

Later on, by Robinson's own accounting, the two spoke at length about these words. Nothing had changed between them, not really. King, he declared in his column, now carried by the *New York Amsterdam News*, was "still my leader—a man to whose defense I would come at any time he might need me. That is a personal commitment and a public pledge."

But he had to question the logic of his leader. Robinson simply couldn't get around the idea of merging the movements. Was King really "advocating a marriage of the civil rights and peace movements—and, if so, would such a marriage be a disastrous alliance"?[12]

Great men can sometimes have great failings. His failure to see the need for the civil rights and peace movements to work in unison was one of Robinson's greatest. Like so many actions of the U.S. government that would help define the twentieth century, the war was meant as a blow against communism. And while King had correctly come to see this as propaganda, his friend could not. At the moment when people might have looked to Robinson for his moral leadership, he seemed unmoved to see that the peace movement was very much rooted in morality. If they needed a champion, they could turn elsewhere, to Muhammad Ali.

"I think he's hurting the morale of a lot of young Negro soldiers over in Vietnam," Robinson said of Ali. "And the tragedy to me is that Cassius has made millions of dollars off of the American public and now he's not willing to show his appreciation to a country that's giving him, in my view, a fantastic opportunity."[13]

Two weeks after the 1967 World Series, Robinson spoke with reporters at Boston University's George Sherman Union. Many things were addressed, including his own acrimonious history with the Red Sox, the last team to integrate in Major League Baseball. Down the hall, within the school's newspaper quarters, hung a photo of Ali. By now the boxer had famously refused induction into the military, with great cost to his own career. Robinson hadn't minded Ali calling himself "The Greatest." But this was something he simply could not accept.

"I don't think in a country such as ours that you can reject your responsibilities," Robinson said of the stand that in principle, if not practice, he admired. "Everybody thought Cassius Clay would be a big martyr. It worked out just the opposite. I think he was tremendously misguided in this area."[14]

Speaking more broadly, Robinson addressed the violent acts driven by poverty and frustration that had become too prevalent in northern U.S. cities. He had seen it and felt its backlash earlier that summer when he'd been dispatched by Nelson Rockefeller to Buffalo, now dealing with the effects of its own race riot, with well-armed white police and black citizenry at odds with one another. Watching him then, one could see a man lost, his body gaunt, listening to the complaints, growing more and more exasperated as he tried to talk.

"Young people nowadays are learning to hate," Robinson told those gathered in Boston. "We've got to show them that moderate leaders can accomplish something. That's the problem with Negro leadership today. We're losing. Kids today are looking for success. They're looking for achievements. The kids aren't like we were. They're not fearful. They're not afraid of dying."

At the same time, Robinson's world was collapsing around him. Diabetes had slowed him, increasingly stripping him of his eyesight, of his freedom of movement, of his relative youth. Jackie Jr. had returned from Vietnam no longer a troubled young man but a dangerous one—to both himself and others. His wife Rachel had found a career of her own. Now, his rhetoric toward both young upstarts and older, established leaders showed the same militancy he had once reserved for those who urged patience.

"I don't think it was bitterness," Rachel later said. "I think what he was withdrawing about and maybe being more critical of things was his disappointment that *he* could no longer be a force in anything. It was enough for him to make it around the house and make it to manage his own life and so it wasn't bitterness so much as it was disappointment that he hadn't seen major change.

"He'd seen some change in the society," she continued, "but not major. There was a lot of work left to do and he couldn't participate in it. I feel that what he was feeling was that kind of disappointment, both in the country, that we didn't move faster towards change, and secondly, that he couldn't participate any longer."[15]

That didn't mean he wouldn't try. He couldn't ever stop trying, no matter the cost. In 1968 he failed, despite his best efforts, in his quest to stop the ascendency of Nixon, now running on a campaign of "law and order," to the top of the Republican presidential ticket. He would do whatever he could to help drive black votes to his friend and Democrat Hubert H. Humphrey. In his own way, Robinson once again tried to demonstrate that no party should ever believe they could count on your vote. They had to earn your trust or risk being forsaken.

The last months of 1967 and 1968 would mark Robinson's last real days as a figure in public life and an active civil rights icon. And despite losing King in the midst of them, one saw Robinson reach out to young leaders (largely in athletics) as he never did before. Perhaps because he knew he was at the end of things. He could no longer endure the movement's physical toll. Now he had to size up the merits of who would come next.

This didn't start off well. But rarely in history did anything good come from an early-morning call from Howard Cosell. Robinson had stayed away from the boycott now being discussed by some black athletes of the Olympic Games set to take place in October 1968. But with less than a year left before the games, in late 1967, Cosell pressed Robinson for his thoughts. He told the broadcaster he didn't support the idea. But over the next day, he reconsidered.

In some ways, he had been where these athletes were. He had endured the cruelty of crowds and that of opposing players. It took courage to stay in it. Now he understood it took perhaps greater courage to walk away. We needed African Americans in both professional and amateur sports. Unlike Jesse Owens, the onetime teammate of his brother Mack in the 1936 games, he felt kinship with Tommie Smith, the San Diego State sprinter with a chance to win gold. Robinson saw the true conviction in a man who would sacrifice this chance if it might help the stalled state of racial progress.

"Maybe we, as Negro athletes, have 'been around' too long, accepting inequities and indignities and going along with the worn-out promises about how things are going to get better," Robinson wrote in his column. "If this is the way the youngsters feel, believe me, I can sympathize with their point of view."[16]

He then turned to the words of Malcolm X, of all people. Following his death, Robinson remained silent, unwilling to express his final assessment of his onetime antagonist who had questioned his bravery and independence and beliefs in integration. Now, Robinson declared him as a brilliant man, a leader, who once told him, "Jackie, in days to come, your son and my son will not be willing to settle for things we are willing to settle for."

"I am certain this is correct," Robinson wrote, "and this is the way it should be."

This marked a new moment for Robinson. This wasn't a man in retreat. He still stood firm against those who called for violence. But he understood the impatience. And he was beginning a period of self-reflection of what he had and hadn't done before his retirement when he was still an All-Star for the Brooklyn Dodgers. What if he had begun to speak out on civil rights while he was playing, knowing that putting out such statements might endanger his livelihood? He was forcing himself, perhaps unfairly, to judge himself and his convictions when that kind of introspection was unnecessary. But it was a much-needed look inward as the man began to assess his legacy.

One certainly saw that in Robinson after the games. No boycott had taken place. But something as powerful, perhaps as emboldening had. In the 200-meter final, Smith did win that gold medal, with his teammate John Carlos winning bronze. The two would be known forever not by the race but by what followed on the victory stand—the two men with their heads down, their black-gloved fists raised in a symbol of Black Power.

One might have expected Robinson, of all people, to castigate the two men and what they had done. Jesse Owens, his brother's teammate on the 1936 Olympics, certainly had. Robinson had spent years attacking the very concept of Black Power. After the fact, on a television panel, he called Carlos and Smith's demonstration "the greatest demonstration of personal conviction and pride I've ever seen."[17]

"I take pride in their proudness in being black," he said. "What they did had nothing to do with shaming this country.

"Sometimes I wish we had done the very same thing when we were playing ball," he continued. "If we had stood up, I doubt very seriously that the youngsters would be having the kind of troubles they're having today."

He was reaching out. To the youth who had turned away from him. To the new heroes who were desperately needed. In the coming years he would find at least one in Reverend Jesse Jackson, whom he called "a tall, young, brave, Black Moses who can take us some giant steps along the way to that Promised Land of which Dr. King spoke."[18] In Jackson, the man who would later eulogize Robison in 1972, he saw someone who might recharge whatever remained from the 1960s. Jackson, he believed, could do more than lead marches. He offered a "salvation for national decency." He was someone best suited to rise out of "this deepening pit of polarization between us as a people."[19]

This darkened view of America would come toward the end of his life when he wanted to continue to act, but simply couldn't. He had reached a point, in looking back, disillusioned with what he had done. He had reached a point where many of the people he once rallied had, to a sunken, hardened place where they saw the end goals they believed were coming slip away from them, farther away from where they had been at the start.

"If you've been an activist and you label yourself that way," Rachel said, "you think of yourself that way and then along comes something that you can't control and it takes away that strength to do it, the ability to do it, to be an activist, you feel hopeless.

"Sometimes there's a retrenchment that factors into that change and so it was more like that than just being bitter. One of the things he put in his *I Never Had It Made* was that it was difficult for him to salute the flag. I hated for him to put that in there because I felt it would be misunderstood that he hated the country or whatever. He loved the country but it wasn't functioning the way he hoped it would."[20]

We are forever guilty of seeking simple summary of a movement, of a man. Though Robinson believed that no man's voice should stand for an entire population, he is maybe the civil rights struggle's truest avatar. His battles and fights, his moments of reconciliation remind us that the movement can never be defined by a statue or a paragraph or even in a single historical volume. He had been at the center of the movement, and he suffered when it did. He represented the best of intentions and could not be there to help write the next chapter.

Because of this, as with the rest of his contemporaries who passed too soon, we are left with unresolved questions. What would have happened had he not grown sick, or fully understood the toll of the war? Had he lived, he most certainly would have tried his best to stop Ronald Reagan, whom he already viewed as a bigot in the same vein as Barry Goldwater, only smarter. Robinson might have helped Jackson make good on his ambitions, to move forward and advance more complex civil rights initiatives. He might have shed that unfair label of the bitter solider and could have been the steady hand, the older adviser, as young black men and women were elected to office.

Or perhaps it would have been too late. Too late to make up for the missed opportunities, for the infighting, to make the United

States understand that it had not made good on the promise just with the passage of Civil Rights Bills in 1964 and 1965. We only know he would have been there, to tell us what had gone wrong or right, speaking his mind as he forged new alliances and called out old allies for their transgressions.

And if we must think of his legacy as one of unmet goals, we must then remember him for the goals themselves. It means not remembering the sullen, darkened Robinson, deep in his thoughts and anguish. It means remembering how he was before the world began to fail him.

Now, there he is, with his young son David, holding him close. He is not a superstar or spokesman. He is a father, one of thousands who've come to the capital, a city built by slaves. He is simply a man who at that moment has seen, if only for a moment, the world open in ways that he could have never imagined. Today he sees a way for a better future. He hopes he might help lead us to it. Perhaps he still can.

9

THE DILEMMA OF THE BLACK REPUBLICAN

GERALD EARLY

Jackie Robinson was a Republican. Had he lived his adult life at the turn of the twentieth century, this fact would hardly have been surprising or even noteworthy. For African Americans, the Republican Party was the party of Lincoln, Thaddeus Stevens, Charles Sumner, the Emancipation Proclamation, the radicals who gave us the Thirteenth, Fourteenth, and Fifteenth Amendments, Reconstruction, the Civil Rights Act of 1866, the Reconstruction Act, the Second Reconstruction Act, the Ku Klux Klan Act of 1871, and the Civil Rights Act of 1875. It was the only political choice for black people.

As the Republicans dominated national politics and the presidency during the rest of the nineteenth century, the party became more "establishment," less radical, a victim, it might be said, of its own success. (Grover Cleveland and Woodrow Wilson were the only Democratic Party presidents between Abraham Lincoln, 1861, and Franklin D. Roosevelt, 1933. Both served two terms.) The GOP, the Grand Old Party, became the party of high tariffs, big business, crony capitalism, and the status quo. It was increasingly embarrassed and encumbered by its reputation among white Democrats and the white electorate generally as the party of the Negro, and became less and less concerned with racial matters or protecting African Americans in the South from a vengeful white backlash, waffling on the most pressing issue for African Americans of the latter part of the nineteenth century, a federal law against lynching. Indeed, one of the major acts of white reconciliation after the war was the Republican willingness to end federal occupation of the South in a deal to win the presidency for Rutherford B. Hayes. In this acquiescence, the Republicans also agreed to leave the "Negro Problem," as it was called, entirely in the hands of white southerners, as it was understood that the white southerner knew and understood Negroes and knew how to handle them. In effect, the Republicans made a deal with white southerners to make race a *regional* rather than a *national* issue. And by being a regional problem, the rest of the nation was taken off the hook, so to speak. So blacks were left on the doorstep of the white South as if they were an unwanted baby. But in doing so, abandoning the rights of black citizenship in the South, the Republicans became as much a sectional or regional party as the Democrats did. This was the cost of white reconciliation.

But even as the Republican Party grew more conservative, African Americans remained remarkably loyal to it. After all, it was still the party through which they won their freedom and gained constitutional guarantees, the party that legislatively safeguarded their presence in a segregated U.S. Army, the party that employed them in considerable numbers in the nation's capital without segregating them. In fact, Theodore Roosevelt secretly consulted with African American educator and national leader Booker T. Washington about making black (and even some white) federal appointments. Roosevelt even invited Washington to the White House to dine in 1901, a move of such controversy that Republicans for decades that followed tried to downplay it by making it a working lunch in Roosevelt's office, as this seemed a bit less suggestive of social equality than a dinner. But it was a dinner, make no mistake. Many, especially blacks, believed that Roosevelt's precipitous action in the 1906 Brownsville affair, where an entire 167-member black regiment was dishonorably discharged without trial for allegedly shooting up the Texas town resulting in one death, was his attempt to make up for the Washington dinner. Washington, in fact, pleaded with Roosevelt to reconsider his decision, but to no avail. (The discharged men were pardoned in 1972 as the result of a new investigation that was opened during the Nixon administration, another controversial Republican administration on racial matters.)

To be sure, the Republicans had their Progressive, liberal wing, of which Wisconsin's Bob La Follette was one of the leaders; Roosevelt another. But early twentieth-century Progressivism had little interest in blacks, as the movement mostly concentrated on breaking up urban political machines and challenging the hegemony of unchecked capitalism. In the North, Progressivism was largely indifferent to African Americans; in the South, it was worse. As Dewey Grantham described it, "The strongest group of Southern Progressives—those who sponsored the major reforms—were insurgent politicians who came to power not only because they denounced corporations and sponsored a program of neo-Populism, but also because many of them made the race issue their chief stock-in-trade and led such anti-Negro movements as that of disfranchisement. The strongest of these political leaders were the most rabid Negrophobes."[1]

Progressivism offered blacks little; but in addition, the GOP also produced the lily-white movement of the late nineteenth and early twentieth centuries, an attempt by conservative whites to rid the party of its black support and black influence in an effort to counter the power of the segregationist Democratic Party, which came to control the entire South. This struggle between conservative whites and liberal and moderate blacks would adumbrate the party's post–World War II division and ultimate alienation of blacks from the party.

Black dissatisfaction with the Republicans resulted in an attempt by black activists like the NAACP's W. E. B. Du Bois and newspaper editor William Monroe Trotter, both northerners, Harvard grads, and harsh critics of southerner Booker T. Washington, whom they considered to be a conservative accommodationist, to switch the race's vote in the 1912 presidential election to Democratic New Jersey governor and Progressive Woodrow Wilson, who uttered some pre-election blandishments when he met with them. The switch was not successful, although Wilson received more black support than any Democratic candidate had since the Civil War. Wilson, who identified as a southerner and whose scholarship supported the "lost cause" interpretation of white southern history, was true to himself, segregating black federal workers in the nation's capital and dismissing a considerable number of them. Not to put too fine a point on it, Wilson intensely disliked Negroes. Chastened black leaders would not try to switch the vote again for another two decades.

The GOP faced its biggest identity crisis with the rise of Franklin Roosevelt and the coming of the New Deal in 1932. Republican president Herbert Hoover received most of the black electoral support in 1932, as the thought of voting for the Democratic Party, with its implacable southern segregationist wing, was still unconscionable for black voters. Franklin Roosevelt was not seen at this time as a "friend of the Negro," and his selection of Texan and Speaker of the House John Nance Garner, whose hometown allegedly did not even permit blacks to enter, as his running mate was a cause not merely of concern but of alarm. Garner, black Hoover supporters pointed out, "had fired thirty-three black employees, voted against appropriations for Howard University three times, and against antilynching legislation seven times."[2] Roosevelt's polio and seemingly less than robust health convinced many blacks that he would die in office if he were elected and that Garner would be president, a horrifying thought to them.

But black support for the Republicans was weakening. Prominent blacks like Du Bois (again), Walter White, Marian Anderson, Robert R. Church Jr., and Reverend Reverdy Ransom were strenuously opposed to Hoover, linking him, somewhat unfairly, to the lily-white movement in the GOP, and encouraged blacks to vote for the Democrats. Newspaper publisher Robert L. Vann (of the *Pitts-*

burgh Courier) was vehemently calling for blacks to switch party allegiance. The northward and westward urban migration of blacks that had begun around 1915, liberating them from the harsh, unconstitutional sanctions against their voting in the South, made the group an increasingly important political bloc in major cities. Black voting power in some cities was enough to tilt a state one way or another in a close election. Also, black voting power increased with women gaining the right to vote in 1920.

To be sure, blacks were disproportionately affected by the onset of the Great Depression and were upset that the War Department's downsizing of the Army was having a disparate impact on the all-black Tenth Cavalry. Hoover supposedly refused to be photographed with black leaders, although on October 1, 1932, he was photographed at the White House with two hundred invited black politicians. He was, shall we say, cautious about it. He was also accused of reducing the participation of black delegates at the 1932 Republican National Convention to the smallest ever in the history of the party. Hoover did nothing about lynching, never publicly supporting any sort of anti-lynching legislation. Nonetheless, Hoover won the majority of the black vote; little good it did him as he lost the election in a landslide. This was the last time a Republican presidential candidate would win the national black vote. Up to this point, it would have been understandable, even predictable, that Jack Roosevelt Robinson would have been a Republican. After this, it becomes a bit more of an enigma, a mystery. After 1932, what was the Republican Party to black Americans?

Roosevelt was no great advocate for African Americans, but his wife Eleanor was. She may have been more responsible for the great party realignment than anyone else in Roosevelt's administration. Many New Deal programs offered blacks very little help as the federal government permitted the states to run them, with predictable discrimination, especially in the South. But programs like the Public Works Administration, Works Progress Administration,

Civilian Conservation Corps, National Youth Administration, and Federal Theatre and Federal Music Projects did help blacks greatly. And overall there was something of a bracing effect from the New Deal; blacks, more importantly, were affected by the idea of an activist federal government and by the idea of massive aid programs. The idea of the welfare state appealed to blacks as ultimately the method and philosophy that would improve their plight. All they had to do now was to get the federal government to condition its massive aid with the requirement that no state could practice racial discrimination in administering it. That lever would break the back of Jim Crow, and it was more likely to happen with a party that was wholeheartedly behind the idea of an assertive federal power in domestic affairs. This is why the shift happened. As one scholar put it, "African Americans saw the federal government as a positive force."[3] This would always put most black voters at odds with a Republican Party that began to preach "smaller" government and to look upon federal power with suspicion, if not outright disdain.

The tide had turned. In the 1936 election, although only 44 percent of black Americans identified as Democrats, 71 percent voted for Roosevelt, while only 28 percent voted for the Republican Alf Landon. Even with a popular black hero like heavyweight champion Joe Louis supporting him and making strong appeals to the black community, Republican Wendell Willkie, who had been a Democrat only six months before he was nominated, got only 32 percent of the black vote in 1940, only slightly better than Landon, who made no special outreach effort. And neither Landon nor Willkie ran as a conservative.

Here began the Republican Party's long wandering in the wilderness. What could the party stand for? If the GOP endorsed the welfare state but argued that they could manage it, they were simply another version of Democrats, Democrats-Lite. We will give you the welfare state, only more slowly and efficiently. But if you are the opposite of welfare state advocates, what precisely are you? Are you like the Protestants of the Reformation who argued for a return to the primitive church? Do you now argue for a return to primitive, minimal government and the freedom of the individual not to be coerced by the ever-expanding welfare state and its promises of security? What does it really mean to be, as conservative Phyllis Schlafly so famously put it, a choice and not an echo? This exile in the political desert of national politics was inextricably bound to the GOP's connection to black voters, and how to get them back, if they did want them. Or whether black voters, in the end, were really worth having? Was the party better off without them?

The divide between blacks and the Republican Party was clear: in 1945, when Senator Robert Taft, son of former president William Howard Taft and known as Mr. Republican, proposed legislation for a permanent Fair Employment Practice Committee (FEPC), extending the life of the temporary FEPC that was created in 1941 by Franklin Roosevelt's Executive Order 8802, most blacks found this unacceptable. Taft's agency would have no enforcement powers; it could not compel those practicing discrimination in hiring to cease with legal or economic sanctions, hurting the business so that it would find practicing discrimination not in its interests. Blacks and their white liberal allies wanted a compulsory FEPC: moral suasion no longer cut it. Taft, though sympathetic, replied that he could not do so as such an agency would be federal overreach, giving it immense power to make businesses do whatever it wanted them to do in hiring workers. A compulsory FEPC would cause an endless stream of lawsuits and perhaps even violence on the part of those opposed to it. In the end, it would produce a racial spoils system (which conservatives argue is exactly what affirmative action is). Those who wanted a compulsory FEPC argued that it would prevent violence, not start it, that discrimination was easy to discern, and the practice could be easily discontinued if businesses were disincentivized by the power of the federal government. When a bill for a compulsory FEPC was put before Congress, many Republicans joined

A portrait of Abraham Lincoln hung on the wall of Rickey's office. National Baseball Hall of Fame Library.

with white southern Democrats to defeat the measure. Here was the shape of American politics to come.

In 1960, Jackie Robinson supported Republican candidate and then–vice president Richard Nixon for the presidency. In 1956, Dwight Eisenhower, World War II hero and one of the most popular Republican politicians of the twentieth century, received 39 percent of the black vote, not bad, but one would have expected more, especially as Democratic candidate Adlai Stevenson had, the first time he ran in 1952, chosen a southern segregationist, John J. Sparkman, as his running mate and was lukewarm on civil rights, believing in gradualism. He disagreed with the 1956 southern manifesto against the 1954 *Brown v. Board* decision that mandated the desegregation of public schools, but he did not oppose it. He also was not inclined to use federal force to counter segregationists' slow-walking school integration or terrorizing blacks who wanted quicker compliance.

Although he criticized Eisenhower's plea for patience on the part of blacks, Robinson was favorably disposed to Eisenhower after the federal government protected black children newly integrating a public high school in Little Rock by sending in federal troops and after the passage of the 1957 Civil Rights Act, which did not have much government muscle behind it but did establish the Civil Rights Division of the Justice Department and the U.S. Civil Rights Commission. (To this point, all federal civil rights legislation had been launched by Republicans. Eisenhower would sign another civil rights bill in 1960 that tried to strengthen some of the voting safeguards of the earlier act. This was the first civil rights legislation since Reconstruction.) Eisenhower brought a large number of blacks into the federal government during his presidency and actively enforced Truman's desegregation executive order for the military. In 1955, he hired E. Frederic Morrow as his assistant on special projects, giving a black man a visible, if minor, position in his inner circle. On the basis of this, plus the fact that Eisenhower made a special effort to win back the black vote in 1956, he should have done better with blacks and the party should have been poised for even greater gains in 1960.

But on the whole, in retrospect, it might seem odd to people that Robinson endorsed Nixon, someone who became so identified with the 1960s Republican "southern strategy" of attracting disaffected whites to the GOP, which enabled him to win the presidency in 1968. But Nixon's record on civil rights, despite his record as a Commie-hunting, take-no-prisoners Cold War conservative, was far stronger than that of John Kennedy, his Democratic opponent; indeed, his only political opponent whose record on civil rights would be better was Hubert Humphrey. Nixon had genuflected to the eastern, liberal wing of the party by meeting with Nelson Rockefeller, Robinson's political friend, much to the chagrin of conservatives, so backing Nixon was certainly reasonable for Robinson, especially as Kennedy's running mate was Texas senator Lyndon Johnson, who was, at this point in his career, no supporter of civil rights, and was the person the white recalcitrant South wanted on the ticket.

In fact, Robinson was registered as an independent, which meant that he wanted to keep his political or at least voting options open. "But Robinson was a Republican at heart," writes biographer Arnold Rampersad, "albeit a liberal Republican on the key matter of civil rights. . . . He liked [the GOP's] toughness on communism, its image of moral austerity that was unsullied, unlike the Democratic Party's, by Southern bigotry or by the seedy corruption of some urban Democratic machines; he liked the Republicans' association with capitalism and business, an area Robinson was determined to learn and even conquer."[4]

Robinson had been a high-performance amateur and professional athlete. This meant that, as an overachiever, he had considerable respect for both merit and competition, the two cornerstones of sports and, in some respect, the two values that black people greatly admired and felt to be defining aspects of their cause for freedom or renewed emancipation from the thralldom of white supremacy. African Americans wanted their merit recognized by whites and to not be penalized by needing to have an excess of merit (twice as good as white) to succeed. They wanted fair competition with whites, objective, color-blind (for lack of a better term) measures to ensure that the best person got the prize. Baseball, once it integrated, was professing to be such a sphere of recognized merit and fair competition. Robinson was an example of the new American Negro—fearless in the face of performing with whites as an equal—in a new American Age, the Age of Integration. (Think of the two Sidney Poitier films that bracket the Age of Robinson, Joseph Mankiewicz's *No Way Out*, released in 1950, where Poitier plays a doctor in a white hospital whose competence is challenged by racist whites, and Hall Bartlett's war drama *All the Young Men*, released in 1960, where Poitier, a tough Marine sergeant, must lead a company of white soldiers who doubt his ability. Both films are Robinsonesque portrayals of fearless black men under fire in a world of whites, trying to establish their merit through a kind of merciless but ultimately justified competitive fire.)

One has to consider only Robinson's article in the June 1948 issue of *Ebony*, "What's Wrong with Negro League Baseball?," where he emphatically criticized the slipshod, unprofessional operation of the Negro Leagues, to see an essential sort of conservatism in his makeup that made him, in some ideological ways, more suited to the Republican Party. What Robinson was arguing was that racial oppression and structural disadvantages were no excuses for lack of standards in the management of the sport for blacks. (It was similar to the argument that trumpeter Wynton Marsalis and critic Stanley Crouch made about black music in the 1980s and 1990s: black music is a professional endeavor that must and indeed does have standards, and anyone who asserts that this view is elitist or that blacks labor under conditions that make the application of canonical standards unjust or oppressive is ipso facto racist and patronizing. What Marsalis and Crouch were trying to do was to free black music from the romance of hipsterism, from being, in the white gaze, merely some sort of atavistic anti-bourgeois challenge to white conformity and mores.) Interestingly, black people who would take Robinson's view of Negro League Baseball as their view of black cultural and institutional life today would likely be conservative and Republican.

Robinson was never enamored of radical race thinking or leftism. His disagreements with black nationalist Malcolm X and Harlem congressman Adam Clayton Powell Jr. amply demonstrate this. He strongly asserted on many occasions that he was an American.

He was not seeking some non-Western identity, nor did he seek to be anti-American. He vehemently rejected communism and Third World ideology. He did not reject American values and did not see himself or black people as having some separate destiny or fate apart from the nation. Whatever else can be said about Robinson, he was certainly not a hipster type and was not seeking nonconformity.

In addition to these views, his belief in a two-party system and in black people having a role in both parties led him to be Republican. There was a strategic as well as ideological component to his affiliation. And he strongly believed that black people should start businesses and own and manage financial institutions. He himself was an executive with Chock full o'Nuts and was accused of being anti-union; in short, he was something of a businessman. Robinson believed in something that was characterized during the Nixon administration as "black capitalism" or "black capital ownership," an attempt to move blacks away from government assistance or dependence on federally generated wealth transfers and into private equity markets, which would be the only real way that they could finally achieve any sort of substantial wealth. For this reason, in 1969 Nixon established by executive order the Office of Minority Business Enterprise (OMBE), which, despite its problems and relatively modest funding, had considerable impact. According to Joan Hoff, "Independent surveys conducted by *Nuestro Business Review* and *Black Enterprise* in 1981 'showed that 45 of the top 100 Latino businesses had been formed between 1969 and 1976' and that 56 of the top 100 black firms had been established 'between 1969 and 1976, 30 of them in the years of 1969 through 1971 when the federal minority enterprise program was being launched.'"[5] Robinson, like many black people, believed in black business, in black people "buying black," and in the future of the black community being built on the idea of black economic self-sufficiency, on the idea of blacks becoming producers rather than merely consumers. This harkens back, of course, to Booker T. Washington and his National Negro Business

League, which preached the same set of ideas and aspirations. Blacks like Robinson might have opposed Republican hostility to the welfare state and wealth transfers to blacks, but they almost certainly would have agreed that without fully participating and taking their chances as players in the market economy, they would always remain supplicants and laborers and never obtain real wealth. The difference here would have been the insistence on the part of African Americans that racism rather than cultural orientation, as many white conservatives would have averred, prevented them from having success in the market economy. Particularly through Nixon, who put the concept into action with the OMBE, the Republican Party, chary of wealth redistribution in any case as a party that looked after the interests of the rich, became the party of black business enterprise rather than the Democrat Party. For this reason, too, it made a bit more sense for Robinson to be a Republican than a Democrat.

Robinson's time as a Republican was mostly spent at war with the conservatives who took over in 1964 with the presidential nomination of Arizona senator Barry Goldwater and who have remained a force with the party ever since and a considerable political and social movement in their own right. Robinson voted for Lyndon Johnson in 1964 (voting for Goldwater, who voted against the 1964 Civil Rights Act, was unthinkable) and for Hubert Humphrey in 1968. He was not a loyal Republican (most black Republicans during the 1960s found it hard to be loyal to a party that they did not consider to be loyal to them) but rather an embattled warrior, fighting, at times, as most black Republicans did, to make the party their own in much the same way various factions fight over the direction of a church. In this respect, Robinson is something of the prototype, the emblem, and the icon of the black people who struggle to be Republican today, to be in a party that does not know how to want them or how to use them in a way that would free them of this dilemma of fighting against themselves to be themselves.

10

"I'VE GOT TO BE ME"

Robinson and the Long Black Freedom Struggle

YOHURU WILLIAMS

From the moment Jack Roosevelt Robinson put on a Dodgers uniform and strolled confidently onto the turf at St. Louis Sportsman's Park, there were questions about his legacy. On that April afternoon, they were limited to the experiment itself. Would Robinson perform, or would he succumb to the pressure? Would there be trouble from angry fans opposed to a black man playing Major League Baseball, or would the day pass peacefully? Would proud black fans stay away from the park concerned by the potential for violence, or would they storm the artificial segregation barrier imposed by the right field bleachers—St. Louis–style apartheid—in their excitement to see Robinson make history?

Of course, the story of how that day turned out is now well known. Yet in other areas Jack's legacy remains contested. Celebrated for his role in integrating Major League Baseball, Jack personifies the very symbol of black empowerment. At the same time, due in large part to a number of well-publicized feuds and disagreements with other, more radical voices within the civil rights and Black Power movements, he has been seen by some as a tool of the establishment, hand-picked because of his willingness to kowtow and be used to satisfy the demands of his powerful white benefactors. Caught between the two extremes, the historical Jackie Robinson remains for most elusive, lost in the cartoonish poles often painted of black leaders from Booker

T. Washington and W. E. B. Du Bois to Martin Luther King Jr. and Malcolm X.

But the question remains, how do we situate Jackie Robinson in the struggle for black equality in the latter half of the twentieth century, in which the integration of Major League Baseball figures so prominently?

Although he is best remembered for breaking the color line, Jack Roosevelt Robinson's involvement in the struggle for black equality began long before 1947 and reverberates well beyond the world of professional sports. His life in many ways reflects twentieth-century African American history. Had he not become a professional athlete, his story, like that of so many other African Americans, may have been lost. Born in Georgia in 1919, he barely remembered the harsh conditions of life on a planation for a family bound through tenancy. His mother defiantly escaped from that life as part of the great migration to the sun-kissed city of Pasadena, California. Like hundreds of thousands of other southern migrants to California, Robinson came to appreciate the opportunity but nagging limitations of northern-style apartheid. Distinguishing himself as the first four-letter athlete at UCLA, he left school to enlist in the military during World War II; he promptly became reacquainted with the ugly face of southern-style apartheid aboard a civilian bus in Texas in 1944. Facing a court-martial for his defiant stand in that case, he demonstrated the courage, wisdom, and tenacity that, along with his athletic prowess, would make him the ideal partner for Dodgers manager Branch Rickey in their pioneering joint effort to desegregate baseball in 1947. Their endeavor bore immediate fruit with Jack recognized as Rookie of the Year and, two years later, National League MVP. The crowning achievement, of course, came with a title for Brooklyn in the 1955 World Series.

Jackie Robinson's political activism did not end when he retired from professional sports the following year. In fact, he became deeply involved in black freedom struggles. He lent his celebrity to the NAACP, supported the Reverend Dr. Martin Luther King Jr. and the Southern Christian Leadership Conference, and, much later, offered a spirited if limited defense of the tactics of the Black Panther Party. A lifelong independent and later prominent supporter of New York Republican governor Nelson Rockefeller, Robinson was nothing if not complicated. His racial politics brought him at various times into harmony and conflict with all of the major civil rights organizations and leaders of his day, including King, Muslim minister Malcolm X, New York politician Adam Clayton Powell Jr., and NAACP head Roy Wilkins. Jackie embraced a blueprint for black empowerment that he saw through the lens of black capitalism. As he explained in his autobiography, "During the post-baseball years, I became increasingly persuaded that there were two keys to the advancement of blacks in America—the ballot and the buck. If we organized our political and economic strength, we would have a much easier fight on our hands."[1] (Du Bois pursued a similar position in the 1930s.) By examining the life of Jackie Robinson, we glean insight into not only the politics of this enigmatic sports icon but also his contributions and legacy to the black freedom movement.

By his own admission, Jackie Robinson claimed that baseball was his fourth-best sport, and yet over the course of his nine seasons with the Brooklyn Dodgers, he helped to redefine the game. In civil rights, Robinson likewise claimed to be nothing more than a follower, but he proved instrumental to civil rights leaders and organizations that tapped into his celebrity to advance the quest for black equality. Unlike some other entertainers and celebrities, with Jack the civil rights movement got more than a face. His powerful embrace guaranteed publicity but also his opinion, which he voiced without reservation, at times to the chagrin of adversaries and allies from King and Wilkins to Powell and Malcolm X.

Jack was never afraid to admit when he was wrong before the public and behind the scenes, and his views morphed, hardened, and matured based on a myriad of factors. Those who knew him appreciated not only the complexity of his positions but also his thoughtfulness in sharing them. To others, he remained and remains a symbol whose words and actions are often awkwardly adjusted to fit a simple American progress scenario. That narrative serves neither the man nor, in most cases, the nuances of the situations in which it is deployed. This is especially true when we consider Jack's participation in the civil rights movement and his ardent, though over time less than dogmatic, critique of the Black Power movement.

Through a critique of Adam Clayton Powell Jr. in March 1963, Jack unintentionally waded into a fight with Malcolm X. In the course of criticizing Powell for misleading the African American community, Robinson invoked Powell's alleged support of Malcolm X and the Nation of Islam as proof of his being out of touch with the needs of the black community. As he wrote in a widely published open letter to Powell, "You know . . . in spite of the fact that you and I share a deep respect for minister Malcolm X as an individual, the way pointed by the Black Muslims is not the true way to the solution for the Negro problem."[2]

As expected, Malcolm X took umbrage at these remarks, unleashing a blistering critique of his own that became one of the bases for the depiction of Jackie Robinson as a tool of the "white power structure" and a sold-out "Uncle Tom."

In his response, Malcolm referred to his own initial fandom of Robinson and by extension integration. "In those days," he observed, "I was one of your ardent fans: your speed and shifty base running used to hold me spellbound . . . and according to the attack you leveled against me and Congressman Powell in your recent column, I must confess that even today you still display the same old 'speed,' the same 'cunning' and 'shiftiness,' and you are still trying to win 'The Big Game' for your White Boss."[3]

In reality there was little validity to Malcolm X's critique. Jack Roosevelt Robinson was his own person and at the core a "race man" for whom race consciousness was essential. In their 1945 tome *Black Metropolis*, St. Clair Drake and Horace Cayton sought to explain the advent of the idea of the race man as a by-product of racial segregation. "Race consciousness," they wrote, "is not the work of 'agitators,' or 'subversive influences'—it is forced upon Negroes by the very fact of their separate-subordinate status in American life."[4]

While Jack clearly displayed such consciousness, he refused to let it define him. In this sense, he seemed to embody the very essence of the concept of "double consciousness" defined by W. E. B. Du Bois in his 1903 book *The Souls of Black Folk*. Du Bois described double consciousness as "a peculiar sensation" and "this sense of always looking at one's self through the eyes of others, of measuring one's soul by the tape of a world that looks on in amused contempt and pity. One ever feels his twoness, an American, a Negro; two souls, two thoughts, two unreconciled strivings; two warring ideals in one dark body, whose dogged strength alone keeps it from being torn asunder."[5]

As Jack later observed betraying his own struggle with his twoness, "I admit freely that I think, live and breathe black first and foremost." Nevertheless, he maintained, "I am opposed to enforced separatism and I am opposed to enforced segregation. The first freedom for all people is freedom of choice."[6]

His war of words with Malcom X began in the spring of 1963, just as the nation was getting its first sustained glimpse of the movement ultimately known as the Black Power movement. Positioned later as the counterpoint to King and the national nonviolent civil rights movement, Black Power has generally been situated as oppositional to civil rights rather than working in tandem. The disagreements among famous leaders often reinforced this notion.

In fact, Black Power was its own vibrant movement that had grown up alongside the civil rights movement—but with a very different orientation. Decentering integration as the goal of black liberation, it focused instead on black self-determination and community building, consciously linking the black freedom struggle in America with the struggles of other oppressed and colonized peoples across the globe. Both movements were instrumental in toppling segregation in America. As Peniel Joseph observed, "The black power movement, in its challenge of postwar racial liberalism, fundamentally transformed struggles for racial justice through an uncompromising quest for social, political, cultural, and economic transformation."[7]

In this sense, Jack stood at the nexus of both the civil rights and Black Power movements—unquestionably moored in the camp of civil rights but with a deep connection to some of the core tenets of Black Power. He seemed more akin to a loner like the equally enigmatic James Meredith than to a leader like Malcolm X or Martin Luther King Jr. With no organization or constituency to be beholden to, Jack could speak with a freedom of conscience that often landed him in hot water with adherents to both movements.

Jack's independence of thought made him difficult to categorize except in the one-dimensional way that dismissed him in the same way Malcolm had done. At the same time, his friends and supporters also chose to see him through their own lens as the famous first who could be enlisted to speak for and bolster their causes—mostly as defined by them, not Jack.

Despite his many published columns and speeches, his name and legacy were constantly invoked to tell a singular story of integration and diminish other black athletes—especially those who did not fit the "Jackie" mold. That story suggested that Robinson happily accepted inclusion at the expense of being able to speak his mind. He served as a convenient target. For critics, his relationship with Branch Rickey provided ample evidence of his purported submissiveness to white authority. This became increasingly common in the 1960s as a new generation of black athletes, unbound by the circumstances that helped to define Robinson's entry into the major leagues, increasingly used their platforms to call attention to racial prejudice in America.

In 1964, for instance, sports columnist Murray Olderman took aim at Cleveland Browns fullback Jim Brown for saying that "the Black Muslim's basic attitude toward whites is shared by almost 99 percent of the Negro population." As part of his rebuke, Olderman harkened to the year 1958 when Brown won the Jim Thorpe Trophy: "At the time the crusade for the Negro athlete was led by Jackie Robinson, late of the Brooklyn Dodgers and a vociferous claimant for human dignity." He continued, "Jackie attracted some criticism because he was pugnacious in an era before Malcolm X and Muhammad Ali and when it was still clever to say Joe Louis was a true champion to his race—the human race."[8]

This deployment of the "Good Negro" trope plagued Robinson throughout much of his post-baseball life. It obscured the depth and complexity of thinking he brought to many issues impacting the black community.

In *The Audacity of Hope*, another famous first, Barack Obama, wrote, "I serve as a blank screen on which people of vastly different political stripes project their own views. As such, I am bound to disappoint some, if not all, of them."[9] It is the burden Jack Roosevelt Robinson shared—except that Robinson never embraced or projected himself as a blank screen or bemoaned those he disappointed. Jack's first year in the league, or the oft-told story about it, in some sense transformed him into that blank screen, reinforcing the myth of Jackie. Despite being celebrated for not fighting back in both his pre- and post-baseball lives, he actually pursued a militant civil rights agenda at odds with the passive notion of integration promoted by apostles of black nationalism like Malcolm X. Both his supporters and detractors nevertheless crafted this identity for him. They invariably attempted to deploy their version of Jack to satisfy elements of their agenda. To go in search of Jack's legacy in relation to the larger civil rights and Black Power movements is to sift through the haze and smoke of what others said or projected and interrogate Robinson in his own words and actions. The historical

Robinson is a far more interesting and complicated character who illustrates both the tension and the symbiotic relationship of the civil rights and Black Power movements.

No one understood this better than his widow Rachel Robinson, who refused to allow the myth to overshadow the man. "One of the popular songs he always loved," she recalled in 1975, "was Sammy Davis's 'I've Got to Be Me.'" She explained, "It reflected his insistence that he be allowed to be himself." At the same time, Rachel quickly acknowledged that Jack "didn't always encourage that in other people." As she conceptualized the problem, "He was an organizer and he often felt that people should bend their will to his and follow him in order to get things done. It was kind of a contradiction. He was often disappointed that other ballplayers wouldn't join the battles he waged."[10]

As daughter Sharon Robinson likewise recalled, "Well, he did reach a point where he was sort of at a crossroads himself, as was the movement. He did not feel that the NAACP, which he'd supported in the '50s and early '60s, was an organization he could any longer support. He had a falling out with Dr. King—they'd been marching buddies—over the war, over the peace movement. My father had a son who fought in Vietnam, and my father was sort of, 'We've got to support these boys.' And Dr. King was adamant that we stop the war."[11]

Jack's break with King over the war paled in comparison with his strong views on Black Power. By the close of the 1960s, Black Power—as articulated by black leaders such as Stokely Carmichael and H. Rap Brown—had become synonymous with revolutionary violence. The Black Panther Party for Self Defense in many ways became the living embodiment of that strain. The black leather jackets and berets were accents to the guns that became the most visible sign of the Panthers' expansive program for change. Jack's opposition to some of the elements of the Black Power movement was strategic. As Sharon Robinson later recalled, "I couldn't have this

Huey Newton poster in his house. He told me to take it down. What he said to me was, 'Sharon, black people cannot take up arms and win. They're not going to do it, it won't work; it's not going to happen.' So, he was at odds with everyone, and believe me, it was really tough at home."[12]

Rachel Robinson was more generous in her assessment in 1975: "But someone said to me the other day, 'Why was he so bitter?' I don't think he was. I think he has a healthy aggressiveness that he found outlets for. He was outspoken and ready to go to battle. But that's different from being bitter or sitting on a lot of unexpressed anger that incapacitates a lot of people."[13]

This same independence of thought and blank-screen phenomenon colored and continues to color Jack's controversial 1949 testimony before the House Un-American Activities Committee. His seeming condemnation of Paul Robeson solidified, in the public imagination at least, the dichotomy between the two men. In reality, Jack's stand in favor of a more militant pursuit of civil rights was largely distorted by the press and by his unfortunate choice of words in characterizing Robeson's position as a "siren song sung in bass."

Lost in the hullabaloo over his word choice was his clear warning about black opposition to Jim Crow. "White people," Robinson boldly proclaimed, "must realize that the more a Negro hates Communism because it opposes democracy, the more he is going to hate any other influence that kills off democracy in this country—and that goes for racial discrimination in the Army, and segregation on trains and buses, and job discrimination because of religious beliefs or color or place of birth." Robinson did not stop there:

And one other thing the American public ought to understand, if we are to make progress in this matter: The fact that it is a Communist who denounces injustice in the courts, police brutality, and lynching when it happens doesn't change the truth of his charges.

Just because communists kick up a big fuss over racial discrimination when it suits their purposes, a lot of people try to pretend that
the whole issue is a creation of Communist imagination. But they
are not fooling anyone with this kind of pretense, and talk about
"Communists stirring up Negroes to protest" only makes present
misunderstanding worse than ever. Negroes were stirred up long
before there was a Communist Party, and they'll stay stirred up long
after the party has disappeared—unless Jim Crow has disappeared
by then as well.

Ignoring in part the powerful message forecasting continued black
agitation to challenge Jim Crow, newspapers of the day chose to
interpret Robinson's words according to their own agenda. Thus,
while the *St. Louis Post-Dispatch* praised his statement as "distinguished by its good sense and moderation," the official news outlet
of the Communist Party USA, the *Daily Worker*, denounced him for
"playing ball with the Ku Kluxers of the Un-American Committee."

After the Connecticut Bar Association selected Jack as its 1964
man of the year, the *Hartford Courant* revived Jack's testimony to
make its own statement about his legacy. "In many ways the successful life of Jackie Robinson is a striking contrast to that of another
Negro, Paul Robeson," the newspaper observed. "Robeson was a superior man of education and outstanding talent. But Robeson chose
the course of rebellion against the society in which he lived. It was
an understandable reaction. But of the two, Robinson's life has been
productive of much more good for his race, because he stayed inside
the national structure, and worked for betterment. The betterment
is coming, slowly but surely. Jackie Robinson can be credited with
part of the progress that has been made."[14]

Such outside pronouncements of legacy aside, it is important to
note how those within the movement judged Jack's participation
and contribution. Asked to comment on Jack's legacy as he was
being honored by Montreal in 1966, comedian Dick Gregory ini-

tially quipped, situating him between both movements: "What has he done for the civil rights movement? Man, he ran up a lifetime batting average of over 300. That's Black Power, boy."

Jokes aside, Gregory offered a more thoughtful reflection identifying the three main areas of impact Jack had on sports, business, and the civil rights movement. "But, as you know," he began, "Jackie is an extremely intelligent man. He could have chosen any profession and mastered it. Yet he chose to make his name in baseball; to become the first Negro to play in the major leagues." Gregory ultimately chose to situate Jack's legacy, however, in terms of the example he set as a hero and as a role model for black America. "For the Negro in America, it's vital that there be great and respected members of our race like Jackie," he observed. "It was his attitude that inspired us. The attitude that no matter what you can be great."[15]

NAACP executive director Roy Wilkins echoed Gregory's assessment in speaking of Jack's legacy on the black freedom struggle beyond words and symbols. As he observed, "Jackie's contributions have been threefold. First, his conduct and performance as the pioneer Negro in major league baseball broke down barriers across the board for other Negroes. Secondly, his direct involvement in his work for the NAACP, his speeches, his writings have given our cause incalculably greater momentum. Thirdly, his present activities in the business field are helping to bridge the wide gap that separates the Negro from positions in business and industry."[16]

What Wilkins left out and what the Montreal award recognized as an important fourth area of influence was Jackie Robinson's unmistakable impact on youth. Over the course of his career in professional baseball and beyond, Jack was a role model for youth, a role he wholly embraced and one that was not limited to the baseball diamond. In January 1957, for instance, Jack paid a visit to Baltimore, where he met with the members of the NAACP Youth Council. His remarks about the urgency of the struggle so inspired the young people in attendance that the members of the group decided to rename their chapter after him. The move did not sit well with NAACP national director of branches Gloster Current, who advised national youth secretary Herbert Wright to "take the necessary steps to have the name changed in accordance with accepted procedure." Wright elected to forego Current's advice and continued to refer to the Baltimore youth division as the Jackie Robinson Youth Council.

The Jackie Robinson Youth Council evolved into one of the most active and well known in the country. They participated in voter registration drives and engaged in demonstrations often at odds with the staider image of the NAACP, yet firmly within the framework of the civil rights movement. Jack continued to engage with the Youth Council, returning to Baltimore in April of 1959 at the group's request to speak at the Sharp Street Memorial Church. Billy Maxwell, then serving as council president, announced that the event would be free and open to the public to expose as many people as possible to the man whom the Youth Council idolized as a strong patron, spokesperson, and activist for civil rights.

These same labels might have confounded those familiar only with Jack's foray into politics. His controversial support of Richard Nixon in 1960, which he later regretted, further fueled the image of the sellout conjured by Malcolm X. His political opponents also seized on this as well. After it became clear that Jack would not be endorsing his brother's campaign, Robert Kennedy not only called out his support of Nixon but accused him of executing the anti-labor agenda of Chock full o'Nuts owner William Black for his efforts to block unionization of the company's employees. Robinson's position on unionizing within the company also raised the ire of black nationalists and labor organizers.

And yet one of the principal tenets of Black Power along with self-determination was economic empowerment. While Robinson's efforts clearly barred unionizing, they also helped to ensure a pathway to black economic opportunity for black workers who were often excluded from union membership. In the fall of 1963, while the newspapers were reporting on the conflict between Jack and Malcolm X, the city of New York launched an inquiry into Chock full o'Nuts. The complaint alleged what amounted to reverse discrimination against the company, citing the low number of whites employed by the chain. In July of that year, nine white students even staged a picket at one of the restaurants to dramatize their concerns over the alleged discrimination. Although the New York City Commission on Human Rights ultimately found no probable cause for a charge of reverse discrimination, Jack informed them the company would take immediate steps to rectify the situation by utilizing both city and private employment agencies to solicit qualified white candidates.

These nuances in understanding Jack should ultimately impact the way we see his legacy with regard to the long black freedom struggle and the double consciousness described by Du Bois that informed it. In response to one of the most identifiable moments associated with Black Power, Jack demonstrated the independence of thought and action that defies the mischaracterizations of his detractors. Months before John Carlos and Tommie Smith raised their hands in protest at the 1968 Olympics, Robinson offered his view over a proposed boycott of the games. During an early-morning phone call with Howard Cosell, Jack had expressed strong reservations. Later that day, as he observed in a subsequent edition of his *Pittsburgh Courier* column,

I began to give the matter some careful thought and I got hold of the clips from the media which told of the boycott movement. After doing this, I was not so certain the proposed boycott was a bad idea. I decided it is something the American public ought to at least look at.

Maybe that is our problem. Maybe we, as Negro athletes have "been around" too long, accepting inequities and indignities and going along with the worn-out promises about how things are going to get better.

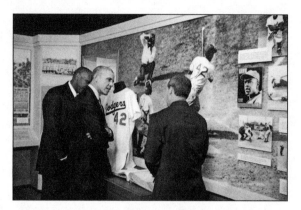

Barack Obama saw a direct line between his election to the presidency and Robinson's pioneering role in baseball. Pete Souza / White House.

If this is the way the youngsters feel, believe me, I can sympathize with their point of view. Malcolm X, the late and brilliant leader, once pointed out to me, during the course of a debate, that: "Jackie, in days to come, your son and my son will not be willing to settle for things we are willing to settle for." I am certain that this is correct and that this is the way it should be.

Also, I can't help thinking that one of the reasons the boycott idea sprung up originally was because of the snatching of the Cassius Clay crown. I can't help remembering that, if it hadn't been for the Olympics, Clay might have remained an unknown. I just hope that this beautiful cause doesn't end up a lost cause. That's why, although I honor the brave young men who have begun it, I have mixed emotions.[17]

His conclusion betrayed his ever-growing understanding of the need for multiple pathways to full equality. Such mixed emotions perhaps best explain the complicated historical figure over the symbol and trope. They highlight at least part of his legacy that remains true. In 1997, when MLB commissioner Bud Selig directed the retirement of Jack's number 42 throughout the major leagues, President Bill

Clinton sought to encapsulate Jack's legacy by noting that Robinson scored "the go-ahead run that day, and we've all been trying to catch up ever since." Robinson's legacy, Clinton continued, "did not end with baseball, for afterward, he spent the rest of his life trying to open the doors and keep them open for all kinds of people." Rachel Robinson was much more expansive in her view: "I believe the greatest tribute we can pay to Jackie Robinson is to gain new support for a more equitable society"—a goal that both the civil rights and Black Power movements also shared.[18]

PART IV

THE WIDE WORLD OF SPORTS

11

THE FIRST FAMOUS JOCK FOR JUSTICE

PETER DREIER

Part of Jackie Robinson's legacy is as a role model for athletes who want to express their political and social views. But Robinson was not simply a sports figure who lent his celebrity status to the civil rights movement. He viewed himself as much an activist as an athlete. He recognized that his opportunity to break baseball's color line was the result of a protest movement, and he repaid that debt many times over through his own participation in the struggle for civil rights.

Robinson was the first well-known professional athlete in post–World War II America to use his celebrity to speak out against social injustice. He laid the groundwork for Muhammad Ali, Roberto Clemente, John Carlos, Tommie Smith, Jim Brown, Bill Russell, Dave Meggyesy, Jim Bouton, Curt Flood, Kareem Abdul-Jabbar, Bill Walton, Arthur Ashe, Billie Jean King, Carlos Delgado, Adonal Foyle, Steve Nash, Sean Doolittle, Colin Kaepernick, LeBron James, Megan Rapinoe, and others.

In 2019, members of the U.S. women's soccer team announced that they wouldn't accept an invitation from President Donald Trump to visit the White House after they won the World Cup. Trump, some sportswriters, and some fans criticized them for injecting politics into the sport. Alex Morgan, the team's co-captain and women's soccer Player of the Year in 2018, told *Time* magazine, "We don't have to be put in this little box. There's the narrative that's been said hundreds of times about any sort of athlete who's spoken out politically. 'Stick to sports.' We're much more than that, O.K.?"[1] Robinson heard the same criticisms during and after his playing career (1947–56) with the Brooklyn Dodgers, and he gave a similar answer. He believed that as an American citizen, and as a black man in a racist society, he had an obligation to use his fame to challenge the social and political status quo.

All social movements try to recruit high-profile celebrities—entertainers, writers, artists, and athletes—to help promote their causes. This is true across the political spectrum. On the right, celebrities like singers Anita Bryant and Ted Nugent, actors Tom Selleck, Chuck Norris, and Charlton Heston, and athletes like Pete Sampras, Jack Kemp, Jim Bunning, Mike Ditka, Charles Barkley, Tom Brady, and Curt Schilling have embraced conservative causes and candidates. On the left, entertainers like Pete Seeger, Woody Guthrie, Harry Belafonte, Bruce Springsteen, Marvin Gaye, Phil Ochs, Aretha Franklin, Joan Baez, Holly Near, Mark Ruffalo, and Jane Fonda have been identified with civil rights, antiwar, gay rights, and feminist movements, as have writers like John Steinbeck, James Baldwin, Langston Hughes, Adrienne Rich, Arthur Miller, Gloria Steinem, and Tony Kushner.

Celebrities can perform a variety of roles on behalf of social movements. They can lend their names; raise money; appear at rallies and other events; write books, articles, poems, and songs; start or join movement organizations; and engage in marches, protests, and even civil disobedience to draw public attention to the issues and groups they want to promote.

When it comes to political dissent, few athletes have spoken out on big issues like war, workers' rights, environmental concerns, racism, sexism, or voter suppression. Nor do many of them endorse political candidates.

In 1990 basketball star Michael Jordan, who had a multimillion-dollar contract with Nike, refused to endorse his fellow black North

Carolinian Harvey Gantt, then running for the U.S. Senate against right-winger Jesse Helms. "Republicans buy sneakers, too," Jordan explained at the time.[2]

Early in his professional career, golfer Tiger Woods stirred some political controversy with one of his first commercials for Nike after signing a $40 million endorsement contract. It displayed images of Woods golfing as these words scrolled down the screen: "There are still courses in the United States I am not allowed to play because of the color of my skin. I've heard I'm not ready for you. Are you ready for me?" At the time Woods told *Sports Illustrated* that it was "important . . . for this country to talk about this subject [racism]. . . . You can't say something like that in a polite way. Golf has shied away from this for too long. Some clubs have brought in tokens, but nothing has really changed. I hope what I'm doing can change that."[3]

According to Richard Lapchick, executive director of the National Consortium for Academics and Sports at the University of Central Florida, Woods was "crucified" by some sportswriters for the commercial and his comments. Nike quickly realized that confrontational politics wasn't the best way to sell shoes. "Tiger seemed to learn a lesson," Lapchick explained in a 2004 interview. "It is one that I wish he and other athletes had not learned: no more political issues. He has been silent since then because of what happened early in his career."[4] For example, Woods remained on the sidelines during the 2002 controversy over the intransigence of the Augusta National Golf Club, host of the annual Masters Tournament, on permitting women to join.

Fear of losing commercial endorsements is only one reason that few professional athletes speak out about controversial social and political issues. Many are simply not interested in politics or believe that they don't know enough about issues to express their opinions in public. Athletes are expected to perform, not pontificate.

On those occasions when they do express themselves, they are often met with derision and contempt. In 2018, Laura Ingraham, a host for right-wing Fox News, scolded the Cleveland Cavaliers' LeBron James for "talking politics," including criticizing President Donald Trump. Ingraham said she wasn't interested in the political views of "someone who gets paid $100 million a year to bounce a ball." She said that James should just "shut up and dribble."[5] Most notably, NFL quarterback Colin Kaepernick faced censure from Trump and blacklisting by NFL teams when he protested American racism by kneeling on the field during the national anthem, starting in 2016, a gesture that sparked considerable controversy.

There is, of course, an obvious double standard when it comes to sports and politics. Most professional sports team owners regard political involvement as essential to doing business. They make large campaign contributions to both Republicans and Democrats. They invite elected officials to sit next to them at games. They lobby city, state, and federal officeholders on legislation and tax breaks for new stadiums. After President Trump attacked Kaepernick, every NFL owner—Democrat and Republican alike—fell in line with the NFL's quickly revised policy to require players to stand.[6]

The public is used to seeing athletes participating in a wide variety of charity and community service activities. For example, Boston Red Sox star Ted Williams often visited children with cancer in the hospital and lent his name to the Jimmy Fund, which has raised millions of dollars for cancer research. Today, many professional athletes start foundations that fix inner-city playgrounds, create scholarship funds to help poor students attend college, make commercials urging kids to stay in school and say no to drugs, play in golf tournaments to raise money for charitable causes, give talks at schools, and participate in workshops to teach kids the fundamentals of their sport. Professional teams encourage players to engage in such community service activities, which they view as good for public relations.

Only a handful of professional athletes, however, move beyond charity and social service to challenge the larger system through both words and deeds, including activism in social and political movements. In that way, Robinson was a pathbreaker.

* * *

Robinson engaged in both kinds of work for social reform—charity and social justice activism. As a youngster in Pasadena, he frequently got in trouble, engaging in activities that at the time were described as "juvenile delinquency," including his membership in a street gang. During his rookie year with the Dodgers, and throughout the rest of his life, Robinson participated in many acts of charity and social service, particularly, but not exclusively, in the black community, including Harlem. He mentored young people at the YMCA and the Police Athletic League. He visited sick children in hospitals and brought toys and baseballs autographed by himself and his teammates. He gave speeches at schools and universities. But during and after his playing days, he also spoke out about American racism, specifically identifying the institutions that perpetuated racial injustice, including banks and other businesses, politicians, the media, and Major League Baseball, and he participated in civil rights rallies and protests, and endorsed candidates for office. He not only talked the talk. He walked the walk.

Robinson wrote regular columns for the *Pittsburgh Courier*, *New York Post*, and *New York Amsterdam News*.[7] He hosted radio and TV talk shows. He was frequently interviewed and quoted by mainstream media outlets on civil rights issues. He raised money for a wide variety of civil rights causes and organizations, including the NAACP, Southern Christian Leadership Conference (SCLC), Congress of Racial Equality, and Student Nonviolent Coordinating Committee (SNCC). He sat on the boards of several civil rights and social reform organizations. He was a well-traveled speaker at meetings, conferences, and rallies around the country on behalf of civil rights and social justice causes. He was an active participant at demonstrations, pickets, and marches for civil rights. He testified before

Congress about racial injustice. He endorsed and campaigned for political candidates whom he believed to be allies of the civil rights movement. He began his engagement with the civil rights movement during the ten years he played for the Dodgers and expanded his commitment after he retired from baseball in 1956 until his death in 1972.

Robinson set the stage for other athletes to speak out, but no other professional athlete, before or since, has been so deeply involved in social change movements. The scale, depth, and variety of Robinson's activism are so remarkable that it would be almost impossible to replicate. Robinson's engagement with the civil rights movement was not something he did on the side. During his playing days, it was a central part of his life, despite the demands of being a full-time athlete under enormous physical and psychological pressure for his pathbreaking role. When his playing days ended, Robinson's involvement deepened, as he took on an incredible diversity of responsibilities, often at the expense of his health and his livelihood.

Moreover, Robinson did so during a period when social justice activism in general, and especially by celebrities, was risky. Robinson joined the Brooklyn Dodgers in 1947, just as the Cold War was emerging. People who spoke out for liberal and progressive causes—civil rights, opposition to nuclear testing, equality for women, workers' rights—could be branded radicals or communists and face economic sanctions (including loss of their job) and social ostracism. It is important to recall that the modern civil rights movement had not yet emerged. The Supreme Court's *Brown v. Board of Education* ruling, outlawing school segregation, did not occur until 1954. The Montgomery bus boycott, which brought both Rosa Parks and Martin Luther King into the national spotlight, began the following year. Students in North Carolina launched the first lunch counter sit-ins in 1960.

Some writers and activists, looking back at Robinson's life and career, claim that he was insulated from right-wing attacks because he was a pro-business, anticommunist Republican and was opposed to black separatism. But none of these beliefs shielded Robinson from severe criticism for being outspoken and militant on behalf of racial equality. In fact, the FBI kept a file on Robinson because it was concerned about his activism and influence.

A similar dynamic can be seen in the reputation of Reverend Martin Luther King. Today King is viewed as something of an American saint. A recent Gallup poll discovered that 94 percent of Americans viewed him in a positive light. His birthday is a national holiday. His name adorns schools and street signs. Americans from across the political spectrum invoke King's name to justify their beliefs and actions. But during his lifetime, in his own country, King was considered a dangerous radical. He was harassed by the FBI and vilified in the media. In August 1966—two years after he was awarded the Nobel Peace Prize at age thirty-five—a Gallup poll found that 63 percent of Americans had an unfavorable opinion of King, compared with 33 percent who viewed him favorably.

To many Americans, Jackie Robinson's success on the baseball diamond was a symbol of the promise of a racially integrated society. It is difficult today to summon the excitement and fervor that greeted Robinson's achievement. He did more than change the way baseball was played and who played it. The dignity with which Robinson handled his encounters with racism drew public attention to the issue, stirred the consciences of many white Americans, and gave black Americans a tremendous boost of pride and self-confidence.

Robinson Was a "Race Man"

Due to his upbringing and his early experiences, Robinson had little tolerance for bigotry. The grandson of a slave and the son of a sharecropper, Robinson was fourteen months old in 1920 when his mother moved her five children from Cairo, Georgia, to Pasadena, a wealthy, conservative Los Angeles suburb. During Robinson's youth, black residents, who represented a small portion of the city's population, were treated as second-class citizens. Blacks were allowed to swim in the municipal pool only on Wednesdays (the day the water was changed) and could use the YMCA only one day a week. Robinson learned at an early age that athletic success did not guarantee social or political acceptance. When his older brother Mack returned from the 1936 Olympics in Berlin with a silver medal in track, he got no hero's welcome. The only job the college-educated Mack would find was as a street sweeper and ditch digger.

Robinson was a star athlete at Pasadena Junior College before enrolling at UCLA, where he became its first four-sport athlete (football, basketball, track, and baseball), twice led basketball's Pacific Coast League in scoring, won the NCAA broad jump championship, and became an All-American football player. But, like his brother's, his success on the athletic field did not change the way he was treated as a black man in a racist society.

Robinson was particularly incensed by his mistreatment in the Army during World War II. Many of the Negro League's finest ballplayers saw military service during the war, but like other African Americans they faced discrimination and humiliation as soldiers. Most black soldiers with baseball talent were confined to playing on all-black teams. When Robinson went out for the baseball team at Fort Riley, Kansas, a white player told him that the officer in charge said, "I'll break up the team before I'll have a nigger on it."[8] When he was reassigned to Fort Hood in Texas, his anger boiled over. On July 6, 1944, Robinson—a twenty-five-year-old Army lieutenant—boarded a military bus at Fort Hood with the light-skinned black wife of another black officer and sat down next to her in the middle of the vehicle. "Hey you, sittin' beside that woman," the driver yelled. "Get to the back of the bus." Robinson refused, knowing that buses had been officially desegregated on military bases. When the driver threatened to have him arrested, Robinson shook his finger in the driver's face and told him, "Quit fucking with me." Two military policemen soon arrived and escorted Robinson away.

He faced trumped-up charges of insubordination, disturbing the peace, drunkenness, conduct unbecoming an officer, insulting a civilian woman, and refusing to obey the lawful orders of a superior officer. Unlike the routine mistreatment of many black soldiers in the Jim Crow military, Robinson's court-martial trial, on August 2, 1944, triggered news stories in the black press and protests by the NAACP because he was already something of a public figure. Voting by secret ballot, the nine military judges found Robinson not guilty. By November, he was honorably discharged from the Army.

Describing the ordeal, Robinson later wrote, "It was a small victory, for I had learned that I was in two wars, one against the foreign enemy, the other against prejudice at home."[9] From that time on, and perhaps even earlier, Robinson viewed himself as a "race man"—a widely used term at the time that signified someone who was primarily committed to advancing the conditions of black Americans and viewed his own life and career as part of that effort.

While playing sports at UCLA, professional football in Hawaii, and Negro League baseball in Kansas City and while serving in the Army, Robinson was certainly aware that part of the wider movement to desegregate America included a specific campaign to dismantle baseball's Jim Crow system. Starting in the 1930s and accelerating during World War II, the black press, civil rights groups, the Communist Party, progressive white activists, left-wing unions, and radical politicians waged campaigns to eliminate discrimination in housing, jobs, and other sectors of society. The campaigns included protests against segregation within the military, mobilizing for a federal anti-lynching law, marches to open up defense jobs to blacks during World War II, and boycotts against stores that refused to hire African Americans under the banner "don't shop where you can't work." As soon as the United States entered the war in 1941, black newspapers enthusiastically supported the "Double V" campaign—victory over fascism overseas and over racism at home.

As Jules Tygiel, Arnold Rampersad, Chris Lamb, and others have documented, civil rights and progressive activists believed that if they could push the national pastime to integration, they could make inroads in other facets of American society.[10] The protest movement published open letters to baseball owners, polled white managers and players about their willingness to have black players on major league rosters, picketed at baseball stadiums in New York and Chicago, gathered signatures on petitions, and kept the issue before the public. They even pushed major league teams to give tryouts to black players. In 1945, Isadore Muchnick, a progressive member of the Boston City Council, threatened to deny the Red Sox a permit to play on Sundays unless the team considered hiring black players. Working with several black sportswriters, Muchnick persuaded the reluctant Red Sox general manager, Eddie Collins, to give three Negro League players—Robinson, Sam Jethroe, and Marvin Williams—a tryout at Fenway Park in April of that year. The Sox had no intention of signing any of the players, nor did the Pittsburgh Pirates and Chicago White Sox, who orchestrated similar bogus auditions. But the public pressure and media publicity helped raise awareness and furthered the cause.

In 1945, the New York State Legislature passed the Quinn-Ives Act, which banned discrimination in hiring, and soon formed a committee to investigate discriminatory hiring practices, including one that focused on baseball. In short order, New York mayor Fiorello La Guardia established a Committee on Baseball to push the Yankees, Giants, and Dodgers to sign black players. Left-wing congressman Vito Marcantonio, who represented Harlem, called for an investigation of baseball's racist practices. Branch Rickey, the Dodgers' general manager and part owner, was not enthusiastic about these efforts because he did not want people to think that his efforts to integrate the team were the result of public pressure.

Robinson Joins the Dodgers

Rickey's scouts identified Robinson, who was playing for the Kansas City Monarchs in the Negro Leagues, as a potential barrier breaker. Rickey could have chosen other Negro League players with more talent, experience, or name recognition, such as Satchel Paige or Josh Gibson, but he wanted someone who could be, in today's terms, a role model.[11] He knew that if the experiment failed, it would set back the cause of integration for years.

Robinson was young, articulate, and well educated. Although Pasadena was rigidly segregated, Robinson had formed friendships with his white neighbors and classmates in high school and college. Rickey knew Robinson had a hot temper and strong political views, but he believed that Robinson could handle the emotional pressure, help the Dodgers on the field, and attract more fans to Ebbets Field. Robinson promised Rickey that, for at least his rookie year, he would not respond to the verbal barbs and physical abuse he would face on a daily basis. In 1946, when Robinson played for the Dodgers' minor league franchise in Montreal, America remained a deeply segregated nation. That year, at least six African Americans were lynched in the South. Restrictive covenants, barring blacks (and Jews) from buying homes in many neighborhoods—not just in the South—were still legal. Only a handful of blacks were enrolled in the nation's predominantly white colleges and universities. There were only two blacks in Congress. No big city had a black mayor.

Robinson endured more verbal, psychological, and physical abuse than any professional athlete before or since. When he arrived at spring training in Florida in 1946, Robinson could not stay in the same hotel as his white teammates. A white man came to the home where he was staying and warned sportswriter Wendell Smith, Robinson's traveling companion, that a white mob was ready to run the black players out of town. Anyone living in or familiar with Florida at that time knew of the state's long history of lynchings. At a spring training game in Sanford, the police chief walked onto the field and ordered Robinson's manager Clay Hopper (for the Montreal Royals) to remove Robinson and black teammate John Wright from the stadium.

When Robinson played for the Royals, the team traveled to segregated cities like Louisville and Baltimore. When he played for the Dodgers, the team played in segregated cities like Cincinnati, St. Louis, and Philadelphia. In those cities, Robinson could not stay in the same hotels or eat in the same restaurants as his white teammates. He also had to endure segregated buses, trains, public parks, movie theaters, and other facilities. He received a torrent of hate mail and death threats. On the field, he heard constant racist taunts from fans and opposing players. A week after his first game in a Dodger uniform, while playing the Philadelphia Phillies, the Phillies' manager Ben Chapman called Robinson a "nigger" and shouted "Go back to the cotton field where you belong" and "They're waiting for you in the jungles, black boy," without rebuke from the umpire or National League officials. Throughout his rookie season, and even afterward, opposing pitchers threw fastballs at his head, brushed him back, and occasionally plunked him. Runners on opposing teams went out of their way to spike him when he was covering the bases.[12]

During spring training in 1947, some of Robinson's own teammates let it be known that they resented having a black man on the team. A handful of Dodgers, led by Georgia-born Dixie Walker, even circulated a petition asking Rickey to keep Robinson off the club. Rickey and manager Leo Durocher quickly squashed the revolt. Even so, Robinson often sat by himself in the clubhouse while his teammates played cards or just chatted. Describing Robinson's relationships with his teammates during his rookie year, columnist Jimmy Cannon called him "the loneliest man I have ever seen in sports."[13]

Robinson seethed with anger, but he kept his promise to Rickey, enduring the abuse without retaliating. But it took a toll. He developed stomach pains. His hair turned prematurely gray.

Robinson had an outstanding rookie season. He hit .297, led the National League with 29 stolen bases (including 3 steals of home), and led the Dodgers to the NL pennant. The *Sporting News* named him baseball's Rookie of the Year.[14] That year, the Dodgers set road attendance records in every National League park except Cincinnati's Crosley Field. His first appearance at the Chicago Cubs' Wrigley Field set an attendance record of 46,572. He appeared on the cover of *Time* magazine on September 22, 1947. At the end of the season, an Associated Press poll ranked Robinson second only to singer Bing Crosby as America's "most admired man." (Despite this, that year Robinson made the major league minimum of $5,000—$57,000 in today's dollars. In 1956, his final year in the majors, he earned $42,500—$400,000 in today's dollars, below MLB's current minimum salary of $550,000.)

The Robinson-Robeson Episode

In 1949—a year when he would be named the National League's Most Valuable Player and again led the Dodgers into the World Series—Robinson made his first major foray into the world of politics, although the circumstances were not of his own making.[15]

That summer, right-wing and segregationist members of Congress orchestrated a confrontation between Robinson and Paul Robeson—the two most well known and admired African Americans in the country. The media salivated at the opportunity to portray the clash of these larger-than-life figures as a surrogate for the Cold War between capitalism and communism.

In early July, Robinson received a telegram from Congressman John Wood (D-GA), an archsegregationist and former Ku Klux Klan member, who chaired the House Un-American Activities Committee (HUAC). He invited Robinson to address a hearing on "Communist infiltration of minority groups." Specifically, he wanted Robinson to attack Robeson for being a disloyal American and communist agitator who didn't speak for black people.

The pretext for the hearing was a statement that Robeson had made that April at a left-wing conference in Paris. The media ignored Robeson's main point—that most Americans, including blacks, did not want to go to war with the Soviet Union. Instead, most news outlets used the Associated Press report, which quoted Robeson saying that if a war broke out between the United States and Russia, "it is unthinkable that American Negroes would go to war on behalf of those who have oppressed us for generations against a country which in one generation has raised our people to the full dignity of mankind."

At the time, Robeson was at the height of his fame.[16] He was also a defiant activist. He gave free concerts for left-wing unions and progressive causes. He refused to perform in roles that demeaned African Americans. In 1945 he headed an organization that challenged President Harry Truman to support an anti-lynching law. That year the NAACP awarded Robeson the Spingarn Medal, its highest honor. He was an outspoken critic of European and American imperialism and a strong supporter of nations, in Africa and elsewhere, seeking to unleash themselves from the yoke of colonialism. He embraced the Soviet Union, which he believed had done more than his native country to battle racism and anti-Semitism.

Ironically, Robeson also played a key role in paving the way for Robinson's breakthrough. In 1943 he led a delegation of prominent African Americans, including the owners of major black newspapers, who met with baseball commissioner Kenesaw Mountain Landis and team owners to demand the sport's desegregation. "The time has come when you must change your attitude toward Negroes," Robeson told them. "Because baseball is a national game, it is up to baseball to see that discrimination does not become an American pattern."

Robinson was reluctant to testify against Robeson. He didn't agree with Robeson's communist views, but he admired his lifetime of activism. "I didn't want to fall prey to the white man's game and allow myself to be pitted against another black man," he later wrote. "I knew that Robeson was striking out against racial inequality in the way that seemed best to him."[17]

Branch Rickey was a fervent anticommunist and reminded Robinson that if he refused to testify, HUAC might subpoena him anyway. Robinson also felt a "sense of responsibility" to convey black Americans' loyalty. So on the morning of July 18, Robinson and his wife Rachel flew to Washington, DC, a city where first-class hotels were still racially segregated. On this occasion, HUAC waived its rule against media photographs.

As expected, Robinson criticized Robeson, but it was far from the harsh attack that Wood and his HUAC colleagues were hoping for. Instead, Robinson made an impassioned demand for racial integration and challenged America's hypocrisy around race relations.[18]

Regarding Robeson's Paris speech, Robinson said that Robeson "has a right to his personal views, and if he wants to sound silly when he expresses them in public, that is his business and not mine. He's still a famous ex-athlete and a great singer and actor."

In contrast to Robinson's testimony, at the time many Americans— and certainly most HUAC members—believed that communists and communist sympathizers did not have the right to express their views or hold jobs. Robinson insisted that blacks were loyal Americans who would "do their best to help their country stay out of war. If unsuccessful, they'd do their best to help their country win the war—against Russia or any other enemy that threatened us." Robinson also challenged HUAC's view that black Americans' anger and activism was the result of communist agitators. "The fact that it is a Communist who denounces injustice in the courts, police brutality, and lynching when it happens doesn't change the truth of his charges. Just because Communists kick up a big fuss over racial discrimination when it suits their purposes, a lot of people try to pretend that the whole issue is a creation of Communist imagination." In fact, Robinson insisted, "Negroes were stirred up long before there was a Communist Party, and they'll stay stirred up long after the party has disappeared—unless Jim Crow has disappeared by then as well."

Robinson's appearance was a major news story, but the white press focused on his criticism of Robeson and virtually ignored his condemnation of racism. It was part of a wider campaign to isolate Robeson, who was denounced by the media, politicians, and conservative and liberal groups alike as being a traitor and Soviet shill. Radio stations banned his recordings. Concert halls and colleges canceled his performances. In 1950, the State Department revoked Robeson's passport so he couldn't perform abroad, where he was still popular. His annual income plummeted from over $150,000 to less than $3,000. His voice was marginalized during the 1960s civil rights movement. His name and photo were even stricken from the college All-America football teams.

Robinson faced a similar dilemma with regard to the film *The Jackie Robinson Story*, which was released in 1950. Robinson played himself and Ruby Dee portrayed his wife Rachel. The film depicted some of the racism that Robinson faced growing up and during his first few years with the Dodgers, but its central theme reflected the celebration of America, at the height of the Cold War, as a land of opportunity where anyone could succeed if they had the talent and will. The movie opens with the narrator saying, "This is a story of a boy and his dream. But more than that, it's a story of an American boy and a dream that is truly American." At the time, Robinson was a fierce patriot, but he recognized that America's claim to equal opportunity flew in the face of the nation's racial caste system, a topic that the film skirted.

Robinson Unleashes His Outrage

By 1949, after his initial two years establishing himself as a Dodger, Robinson began to unleash his frustrations and his temper. He argued constantly with umpires and opposing players. He was less willing to stifle his anger at the second-class accommodations and mistreatment he, and the handful of other black major leaguers, had to endure. In 1950, for example, he wrote National League president Ford Frick complaining that umpires treated him differently than white players in terms of calling balls and strikes and ejecting him from games for arguing calls. Robinson saw a racist double standard when, in 1950, sportswriters chose the Giants' Eddie Stanky over Robinson as the second baseman for the All-Star team, even though Robinson was having a much better season in every category and even though Stanky, like Robinson, was known as an aggressive player, even a hothead. Appearing on a local TV talk show in 1953, Robinson publicly accused the New York Yankees—the only one of the three New York City teams without a black player—of racism. He started to speak out more forcefully on social issues, particularly the persistence of racism in America. He got more directly involved in organizations working for change.

Throughout his playing career, Robinson was constantly criticized for being so frank about race relations in baseball and in society. Many sportswriters and many other players—including some of his fellow black players, content simply to be playing in the majors—considered Robinson too angry, vocal, and ungrateful for the opportunity he was given. Syndicated sports columnist Dick Young of the *New York Daily News* complained that when he talked to the Dodgers' black catcher Roy Campanella, they always talked solely about baseball, but when he talked with Robinson, "sooner or later we get around to social issues."[19] The same forthright comments or assertive behavior by white players was out of bounds for Robinson. A 1953 article in *Sport* magazine, "Why They Boo Jackie Robinson," described him as "combative," "emotional" and "calculating," as well as a "pop-off," a "whiner," a "showboat," and a "troublemaker." A Cleveland paper called Robinson a "rabble rouser" who was on a "soap box." The *Sporting News* headlined one story

"Robinson Should Be a Player, Not a Crusader." Others called him a "loudmouth," a "sorehead," and worse.

During and after his playing career, Robinson utilized the media to express his views. In 1947, he wrote a column, "Jackie Robinson Says," in the *Pittsburgh Courier*—one of the most influential black newspapers—documenting his rookie season. In the off-season after his second year in the majors, he hosted a daily radio program. The following year, he hosted a TV show. After he retired from the Dodgers, he wrote a three-times-a-week column in the *New York Post*, a liberal daily, and then in the *New York Amsterdam News*, a black weekly. He used these venues to discuss racial injustice, politics, sports, and other topics.[20]

In 1949, he agreed to chair the New York state committee of the United Negro and Allied Veterans of America, which helped returning World War II veterans readjust to life in the United States, including help with education, jobs, and housing. He also joined the advisory board of Harlem's Solidarity Center, which provided health insurance and medical services. (It was sponsored by the International Workers Order, a left-wing group.) In 1954 and 1955, he chaired the Commission on Community Organizations, a civil rights campaign of the National Conference of Christians and Jews, and he toured the country during the off-season on its behalf. In 1955, he became co-chair of New York's Committee of the United Negro College Fund.

Robinson's Post-baseball Activism

After he retired from baseball in 1956, no team offered him a position as a coach, manager, or executive. He went to work as an executive with the Chock full o'Nuts restaurant chain. He wasn't simply a token figure but was given considerable management responsibilities. But the firm's liberal owner allowed Robinson to engage in his community service and civil rights activities, even though much of it was controversial. That gave Robinson the opportunity to spend a great deal of time traveling around the country giving speeches on behalf of civil rights groups, participating in rallies and protests, raising money for civil rights causes, and serving on boards of civil rights and social reform organizations. He served as the NAACP's fundraising chair, eventually raising a record amount for the nation's premier civil rights organization. His willingness to speak out and his involvement with civil rights and social reform groups led the NAACP to give Robinson its highest award, the Spingarn Medal, in December 1956; he was the first athlete to receive that honor. In his acceptance speech, he explained that although many people had warned him "not to speak up every time I thought there was an injustice," he would continue to do so.[21] In 1957, he publicly urged President Eisenhower to send troops to Little Rock, Arkansas, to protect black students seeking to desegregate the public schools.

Robinson went beyond making public statements, serving on committees, and lending his name to letterheads for good causes. He was often on the front lines of the civil rights movement. In 1960, he was impressed with the resilience and courage of the college students engaging in sit-ins at southern lunch counters. Several of the student activists traveled to New York City to meet with Robinson, who agreed to raise bail money for the students lingering in southern jail cells. Within a few days he'd raised $20,000, and then organized a fundraiser at his Connecticut home that featured jazz greats Ella Fitzgerald, Sarah Vaughan, and Duke Ellington. This became the first of Robinson's annual "Afternoons of Jazz" at his home to raise money for civil rights causes. He also joined civil rights activists in picketing the Woolworth lunch counters in New York in solidarity with the southern sit-inners.

In 1961, Robinson used his column to support the Freedom Riders, even writing a public letter to the chair of the federal Interstate Commerce Commission demanding that he immediately order the desegregation of interstate bus travel. Robinson drew on his own anticommunist credentials to criticize segregationist senator James

Eastland of Mississippi, who attacked the Freedom Riders as communists. The next year, at King's request, Robinson traveled to Albany, Georgia, to draw media attention to three black churches that had been burned to the ground by segregationists. He then led a fundraising campaign that collected $50,000 to rebuild the churches and returned to Georgia once they were rebuilt to demonstrate the civil rights movement's resilience and resistance to intimidation. In 1963, he devoted considerable time and travel to support King's voter registration efforts in the South. He also traveled to Birmingham as part of King's campaign to dismantle segregation in that city. Although he was personally close to King, he did not confine his fundraising efforts to SCLC. He continued to raise money for the NAACP, SNCC, and other civil rights groups. "His presence in the South was very important to us," recalled Wyatt Tee Walker, chief of staff of King's SCLC.[22]

Robinson's Forays into Politics and Business

Once he retired from baseball, Robinson took a more active interest in partisan politics, but he was never interested in running for office. Although he was frequently criticized by liberals for his support for Republicans, his embrace of candidates was based almost entirely on their views and track record on civil rights issues, not party affiliation. In fact, in the 1960 presidential election, he initially supported Hubert Humphrey, a Democratic senator from Minnesota and longtime civil rights stalwart. He traveled to different cities to speak on Humphrey's behalf during the Democratic primaries. By May, however, Senator John Kennedy's primary victories forced Humphrey to drop out.

Both Kennedy and Vice President Richard Nixon, the GOP candidate, actively sought Robinson's endorsement. Robinson met with both candidates. He was not impressed with Kennedy's commitment to civil rights (including his waffling on the 1957 Civil Rights Act) and worried that the Massachusetts senator would be beholden to the segregationist Democrats who controlled Congress. At the time, there were a significant number of liberal Republicans who supported civil rights, and many African Americans still viewed the GOP as the party of Abraham Lincoln. Robinson even used his *New York Post* column to criticize Kennedy "as long as he continues to play politics at the expense of 18,000,000 Negro Americans."[23]

Nixon had been cultivating Robinson as early as 1952, when they met by accident in Chicago.[24] They occasionally exchanged letters. When they met in 1960, Nixon persuaded him that he would be more forceful on civil rights issues than Eisenhower and that he would appoint black people to positions of responsibility in his administration. In September 1960, Robinson shocked his liberal fans by endorsing and campaigning for Nixon. He quickly regretted his choice, especially after Nixon refused to make an appearance in Harlem and refused to take action after Martin Luther King was arrested for participating in an Atlanta sit-in and sent to an isolated prison in rural Georgia, where his family and friends feared he would be killed. (In contrast, JFK's aides secured King's release from the jail, which turned many blacks into Kennedy voters.) Three weeks before Election Day, Robinson said that "Nixon doesn't deserve to win."

In 1962, Robinson endorsed the reelection campaign of New York's governor Nelson Rockefeller, the last of the high-ranking liberal Republicans who supported activist government and civil rights, even donating money to King's civil rights crusades. After the election, Robinson briefly worked as an aide to Rockefeller and in 1964 supported him for president, but when reactionary senator Barry Goldwater of Arizona won the nomination, Robinson left the GOP convention commenting that he now had "a better understanding of how it must have felt to be a Jew in Hitler's Germany," and left the Republican Party behind.[25] In 1968, he supported Humphrey over Nixon for president.

Robinson was not naïve about the realities of racial segregation and white racism. He and Rachel had to use a white intermediary in order to buy a home in white, affluent Stamford, Connecticut. His children faced racism in the local public schools. He was rejected for membership in a local country club. Even so, he was a firm believer in racial integration. In his newspaper column and in other public forums, he clashed with Malcolm X, who accused Robinson of being a puppet of "white bosses." Some young black nationalist militants called Robinson an "Uncle Tom" because of his support for racial integration.

Ironically, Robinson's ventures into the business world reflected some of the ideas of black nationalists, who believed in the creation of black-owned businesses as an alternative to black ghettos being colonized by white corporations. Robinson openly criticized American business for discriminating against blacks as executives, employees, and consumers. He was particularly angered by white-owned banks and by slumlords. He lent his name to several businesses, including a residential construction company and a black-owned bank in Harlem, to help address the affordable housing shortage and white banks' persistent redlining. Both businesses fell on hard times and dimmed Robinson's confidence in black capitalism as a strategy for racial advancement and integration.

As he grew older, Robinson became more impatient with the slow progress against racism in sports and society. In 1964, Robinson expressed his displeasure with Muhammad Ali when the boxer announced he had joined the Nation of Islam (under the tutelage of Malcolm X) and refused to submit to the draft during the war in Vietnam due to his religious convictions. "He's hurting, I think, the morale of a lot of young Negro soldiers over in Vietnam," said Robinson, whose son was serving (and would later be wounded) in Vietnam.[26] But by 1967, after Ali was convicted, Robinson talked about the "heroism and tragedy" of Ali's situation and said that Ali "has won a battle by standing up for his principle."[27] Even so, he was upset when King came out against the Vietnam War that year. In 1967, too, Robinson resigned from the NAACP board for its failure to include "young, more progressive voices." The following year, he publicly supported track stars John Carlos and Tommie Smith's fist-raising protest at the Olympic Games in Mexico City.

He was frustrated by the slow pace of racial progress in baseball. It was not until 1959 that the last holdout, the Boston Red Sox, brought an African American onto its roster. In 1970, Robinson was one of two former ballplayers (the other was Hank Greenberg) to testify in federal court in support of Curt Flood's challenge to baseball's reserve clause, which kept players in indentured servitude to their teams.

Robinson refused to participate in a 1969 Old Timers' Game because he did not yet see "genuine interest in breaking the barriers that deny access to managerial and front office positions."[28] Robinson's statement irked fellow Hall of Famer Bob Feller. He and Robinson happened to be at the same press conference in Washington, DC, to celebrate baseball's alleged hundredth anniversary. Feller, who in 1946 predicted that Robinson was not good enough to make it in the majors, took the opportunity to attack Robinson. "Robinson has always been bush," Feller said. "He's always been a professional agitator more than anything else. He's just ticked off because baseball never rolled out the red carpet when he quit playing and offered him a soft front office job." An angry Robinson responded, "My big thing is I don't believe that the black players are getting an equal opportunity with the whites after their playing days are through. I think the public is more ready for a black manager than the owners."[29] At his final public appearance, throwing the ceremonial first pitch before game 2 of the 1972 World Series, shortly before he died, Robinson accepted a plaque honoring the twenty-fifth anniversary of his major league debut; he then observed, "I'm going to be tremendously more pleased and more proud when I look at that third base coaching line one day and see a black face managing in baseball."[30] No major league team had a black manager until the Cleveland Indians hired Frank Robinson in 1975. The majors' first black general manager—the Atlanta Braves' Bill Lucas—wasn't hired until 1977.

"I cannot possibly believe," Robinson wrote in his autobiography *I Never Had It Made*, published shortly before he died of a heart attack and complications from diabetes at age fifty-three in October 1972, "that I have it made while so many black brothers and sisters are hungry, inadequately housed, insufficiently clothed, denied their dignity as they live in slums or barely exist on welfare."[31]

He also apologized to Robeson, writing that he would reject HUAC's invitation to testify "if offered now." He added, "I have grown wiser and closer to the painful truths about America's destructiveness and I do have an increased respect for Paul Robeson, who, over the span of that 20 years sacrificed himself, his career and the wealth and comfort he once enjoyed because, I believe, he was sincerely trying to help his people."[32]

Years before Colin Kaepernick was born, Robinson wrote, "I cannot stand and sing the anthem. I cannot salute the flag; I know that I am a black man in a white world."[33]

Athletes Climb on Robinson's Shoulders

During the 1960s and 1970s, other athletes began to follow Robinson's example, using their celebrity status to speak out on key issues, particularly civil rights and Vietnam. Bill Russell (born in 1934) was an All-Star center with the Boston Celtics from 1956 to 1969 and later became the team's first black coach. He was the first black superstar in the National Basketball Association. Reflecting his growing racial consciousness, in 1959 he traveled to Africa, including Libya, Ethiopia, and Liberia. In a Liberian classroom, a student asked him why he was there. "I came here because I am drawn here, like any man, drawn to seek the land of my ancestors," he responded.[34] Prior to the 1961–62 season, the Celtics were scheduled to play an exhibition game in Lexington, Kentucky. After Russell and his black teammates were refused service at a local restaurant, he persuaded them to refuse to play in the game and flew home. The boycott was a bold move at a time when black athletes were supposed to accept such indignities without complaining, and it drew a great deal of publicity and controversy. Russell subsequently was outspoken on civil rights issues. After NAACP leader Medgar Evers was assassinated in 1963 in front of his home in Jackson, Mississippi, Russell flew down to lead the city's first integrated basketball camps. He frequently spoke out about the widespread racism he and other blacks encountered in Boston.[35]

Jim Brown (born in 1936) was an outstanding running back with the Cleveland Browns from 1957 through 1965. During his playing days, he founded the Black Economic Union (BEU), through which professional athletes helped establish black-owned and black-run businesses, athletic clubs, and youth motivation programs. After the BEU folded, Brown persuaded some companies to adopt the program. In 1986, he founded Vital Issues to teach life management skills to inner-city gang members and prison inmates. By 1989, Vital Issues had evolved into Amer-I-Can, which sponsored programs in several cities. His efforts to create black-owned enterprises were based in part on his own experiences confronting racism as one of the NFL's few black superstars. "I was a highly paid, over-glamorized gladiator," he told the *Washington Post*. "The decision-makers are the men who own, not the ones who play. I was never under an illusion as to who was the boss."[36]

Even as the civil rights movement was gaining momentum, black baseball players still had to put up with segregated housing, hotels, and restaurants in the southern towns that hosted minor league teams. They faced constant insults on and off the field. In addition, most teams still held spring training in Florida, where public facilities, restaurants, hotels, and ballparks remained segregated through the mid-1960s. Black fans were consigned to the stadium's "colored" sections, and black players had to stay in second-rate black hotels or at the homes of local black families rather than in the same hotels as their white teammates.

In 1961, Bill White, the St. Louis Cardinals slugger, complained to an Associated Press reporter about the team's segregated accommodations in St. Petersburg, where they held spring training. The *St. Louis Argus*, a black newspaper, picked up the story, adding an editorial comment suggesting that black Cardinals fans consider boycotting beer made by Anheuser-Busch (the Cardinals' owner). That same year, under pressure from the Dodgers' black players, owner Walter O'Malley told local officials in Vero Beach that he would no longer comply with laws requiring segregated entrances, bathrooms, water fountains, and seating at Holman Stadium, where his team played its spring games.[37]

In 1963, Arthur Ashe (born in 1943) became the first black player ever selected for the U.S. Davis Cup team and was soon recognized as one of the greatest tennis players of all time as both an amateur and a professional (at a time when pro tennis players were not well paid). In 1969, Ashe was denied a visa by the apartheid government in South Africa to travel to that country to play in the South African Open. In subsequent years, he continued to apply for visas, but each time the racist government turned him down. Angered by such blatant discrimination, Ashe became an early leader in the American and global movement to dismantle South Africa's apartheid regime. He campaigned for U.S. sanctions against South Africa and the expulsion of the nation from the International Lawn Tennis Federation (ILTF). In March 1970, the country was expelled from the Davis Cup competition.

Ashe also led a campaign to improve tennis professionals' pay, which he believed was not commensurate with the sport's growing popularity and revenues. He was an early supporter of the Association of Tennis Professionals and become its elected president in 1974. In 1973, with the South African government hoping to end their Olympic ban and rejoin the Olympic movement, it finally granted

SYA166 BB893

B STA319 NL PD=STAMFORD CONN 10=

LIEUTENANT ARTHUR ASHE=

CARE WESTPOINT MILITARY ACADEMY WESTPOINT NY=

PROUD OF YOUR GREATNESS AS A TENNIS PLAYER PROUDER OF
YOUR GREATNESS AS A MAN YOUR STAND SHOULD BRIDGE THE GAP
BETWEEN RACES AND INSPIRE BLACK PEOPLE THE WORLD OVER AND
ALSO AFFECT THE DECENCY OF ALL AMERICANS.=

JACKIE ROBINSON.

Like Robinson, Arthur Ashe took a vigorous stand against apartheid in South Africa. International Tennis Hall of Fame.

Ashe a visa to enter the country for the first time to play in the South African Open. By 1977, he believed that it had been a mistake to play in South Africa and called for South Africa to be expelled from the professional tennis circuit and Davis Cup competition. Ashe's activism helped draw attention to the global divestment movement and the eventual dismantling of apartheid in 1994.[38]

Muhammad Ali (born in 1942) is probably the most well-known example of an outspoken athlete. The heavyweight boxing champion publicly opposed the war in Vietnam and refused induction into the Army in 1967 on the grounds of his religious beliefs as a conscientious objector. However, Ali also explained his antiwar feelings on straightforward political grounds, including America's mistreatment of black people as second-class citizens. "I ain't got no quarrel with them Vietcong," he told reporters. He also observed that "no Vietcong ever called me nigger." Ali was stripped of his heavyweight title and sentenced to five years in prison. (He eventually won a Supreme Court appeal and didn't serve any time.) During and after his involuntary hiatus from boxing, he was a frequent antiwar speaker on college campuses and elsewhere. At the time, sportswriters and politicians relentlessly attacked him and he lost millions of dollars in potential paydays and endorsements. By the 1980s, however, he was among the world's most admired people for his convictions and his efforts to promote human rights around the world.[39]

After Martin Luther King was assassinated on April 4, 1968, many baseball players refused to play the last few spring training games out of respect for his memory and in defiance of their teams' owners. The following week, Commissioner William Eckert announced that each team could decide whether to play or cancel Opening Day games. Players took the matter into their own hands. Led by star outfielder Roberto Clemente, Pittsburgh Pirates players held a closed-door meeting and voted to sit out the opener. They also asked the general manager to postpone the next game, which would take place on the day of King's funeral. Their statement explained, "We are doing this because we white and black players respect what Dr. King has done for mankind."[40] Players on other teams followed the Pirates' lead. In response, Eckert announced that Opening Day would be postponed until the day after King's funeral.

The civil rights movement was the impetus for Curt Flood's challenge to baseball's reserve clause, which had enormous ripple effects across the sports world.[41] Flood was only thirty-one and in his prime—an outstanding hitter, runner, and center fielder with Hall of Fame statistics—when he stood up to baseball's establishment. Flood played for the Cardinals for twelve seasons. After the 1969 season, the Cardinals tried to trade him to the Philadelphia Phillies. Under the reserve clause, part of the standard player's contract, players could be traded without having any say in the matter. But Flood didn't want to move to Philadelphia, which he called "the nation's northernmost southern city." More importantly, he objected to being treated like a piece of property and to the reserve clause's restriction on his freedom. Flood considered himself a "well-paid slave." In a letter to Commissioner Bowie Kuhn, Flood wrote, "After 12 years in the major leagues, I do not feel I am a piece of property to be bought and sold irrespective of my wishes. I believe that any system which produces that result violates my basic rights as a citizen and is inconsistent with the laws of the United States and of the sovereign States."

With the backing of the Major League Baseball Players Association and its executive director Marvin Miller (who recruited former U.S. Supreme Court justice Arthur Goldberg to be Flood's lawyer), Flood became the plaintiff in the case known as *Flood v. Kuhn*, which began in January 1970. In June 1972, the case reached the U.S. Supreme Court, which ruled against Flood by a five to three vote and upheld baseball's absurd exemption from federal antitrust statutes. Although the Supreme Court ruled against Flood, he had paved the way. In 1975, in a case involving pitchers Dave McNally and Andy Messersmith, arbitrator Peter Seitz invalidated the reserve clause and gave them the right to free agency. This allowed ballplayers the ability to veto proposed trades, bargain for the best contract, and decide where they wanted to work.

Flood paid a huge financial and emotional price for his course. His 1970 salary would have been $100,000, but he was no longer employable—and blacklisted by the owners—despite his talent. Instead, he spent years traveling to Europe, devoting himself to painting and writing, including his autobiography, *The Way It Is*. Looking back, Flood explained,

I guess you really have to understand who that person, who that Curt Flood was. I'm a child of the sixties, I'm a man of the sixties. During that period of time this country was coming apart at the seams. We were in Southeast Asia. Good men were dying for America and for the Constitution. In the southern part of the United States we were marching for civil rights and Dr. King had been assassinated, and we lost the Kennedys. And to think that merely because I was a professional baseball player, I could ignore what was going on outside the walls of Busch Stadium was truly hypocrisy and now I found that all of those rights that these great Americans were dying for, I didn't have in my own profession.

In 1999, *Time* magazine named Flood (who died in 1997 at age fifty-nine) one of the ten most influential people in sports in the twentieth century.

In November 1967 San Jose State University professor Harry Edwards organized a workshop about the Olympic Project for Human Rights (OPHR), urging athletes to boycott the upcoming Summer Olympic Games in Mexico City as a protest against racism in the United States and overseas. Some athletes boycotted the games, while others decided to participate but use the event as an opportunity to protest. Track medalists John Carlos and Tommie Smith generated international media attention and controversy with their Black Power salute during the medal ceremony. Smith explained his protest this way: "If I win, I am American, not a black American. But if I did something bad, then they would say I am a Negro." Their protest hurt their subsequent professional careers.[42]

Kareem Abdul-Jabbar (born in 1947)—who played in the NBA for twenty seasons and was a record six-time NBA Most Valuable Player and a record nineteen-time NBA All-Star—had attended Edwards's workshop and was one of the athletes who boycotted the games. Born Lew Alcindor, he was politically conscious as early as high school, influenced by the civil rights movement. In the summer of 1964, an incident of police abuse triggered riots in Harlem, where he lived. He wrote an article for the Harlem Youth Action Project newspaper based on interviews with black residents frustrated by the persistence of police violence against blacks, segregated schools, slum housing, and job discrimination.

In June 1967, while a student at UCLA, Abdul-Jabbar joined Jim Brown, Bill Russell, and six other black professional athletes at a meeting in Cleveland to lend support to Ali, who had just been stripped of his heavyweight title for refusing induction into the U.S. military and his opposition to the Vietnam War. He was the only college athlete at the gathering, and it had a significant influence on his thinking. Years later, in his autobiography *Becoming Kareem*, he wrote, "Being at the summit and hearing Ali's articulate defense of his moral beliefs and his willingness to suffer for them reinvigorated my own commitment to become even more politically involved."[43] Alcindor addressed the two hundred people at the church: "Everybody knows me. I'm the big basketball star, the weekend hero, everybody's All-American." But on the streets of Harlem, he explained, he was just another black man who could be a victim of police brutality.

The following year, he (along with his UCLA teammates Mike Warren and Lucius Allen) boycotted the 1968 Summer Olympics by not trying out for the U.S. basketball team. As the most famous college basketball player in the country, he was a target of much criticism, including those who called him ungrateful and unpatriotic. On the *Today Show*, host Joe Garagiola, a former Major League Baseball player, suggested that "maybe you should move" out of the United States. But he stood his ground. Instead of participating in the Olympics, he spent that summer working for Operation Sports Rescue, leading basketball clinics and mentoring black and Puerto Rican young people, encouraging them to get an education.

In 2011, Abdul-Jabbar was awarded the Double Helix Medal for his work raising awareness for cancer research. In 2014, he wrote an article in the left-wing magazine *Jacobin* urging fair compensation for college athletes: "In the name of fairness, we must bring an end to the indentured servitude of college athletes and start paying them what they are worth."

As a convert to Islam, he has often challenged prevailing stereotypes about the religion. Appearing on the TV talk show *Meet the Press* in 2015, he said that Islam should not be blamed for the actions of violent extremists, just as Christianity should not be blamed for the actions of violent extremists who profess Christianity. In 2017, he condemned Donald Trump's travel ban, explaining, "The absence of reason and compassion is the very definition of pure evil because it is a rejection of our sacred values, distilled from millennia of struggle." He has written several books on black and sports history and wrote a regular column for *Time* magazine.

Bill Walton, who entered UCLA in 1970, followed Abdul-Jabbar as the school's star basketball player. He led the team to eighty-eight consecutive wins and two national championships. He also led campus protests against the Vietnam War, including getting arrested for participating in a civil disobedience action in 1972 that stopped traffic on busy Wilshire Boulevard, despite the fact that his mentor, coach John Wooden, objected to his stance and activism. He recorded a message on his answering machine in favor of Richard Nixon's impeachment.[44]

Dave Meggyesy, an All-Pro linebacker for the St. Louis Cardinals in the late 1960s, was a vocal opponent of the Vietnam War. He allowed a local antiwar group to hold meetings at his house. In 1968, he refused to put his hand over his heart or stand at attention during the playing of the national anthem. Instead, he "dropped his head, scuffed the dirt with his cleats and spit on the ground."[45] Local sports writers and fans criticized him, and team executives told him to keep his political views to himself, but as he recounted in his memoir *Out of Their League*, Meggyesy refused to back down, was consequently benched, and retired in 1969 at age twenty-eight while still in his athletic prime. He taught courses at Stanford University on sports consciousness and social change and on the athlete and society.[46]

The 1969 World Series between the Mets and Orioles coincided with the nationwide Vietnam Moratorium Day, which included protests outside the Mets' Shea Stadium. An offshoot of the antiwar group, calling themselves Mets Fans for Peace, circulated a leaflet with a photo of the Mets' twenty-four-year-old pitching ace Tom Seaver and a reprint of a *New York Times* article from the previous week headlined "Tom Seaver Says U.S. Should Leave Vietnam." The story quoted Seaver promising to pay for an ad in the *New York Times*: "If the Mets can win the World Series, then we can get out of Vietnam."[47] Seaver, who had served in the Marines and attended the conservative University of Southern California, was upset by the leaflets and refused to wear a black armband that day, as the antiwar demonstrators were doing. But the Mets won the World Series and Seaver kept his promise. On December 31 that year, he and his wife Nancy put an ad in the newspaper that was more tepid than his original statement. It read, "On the eve of 1970, please join us in a prayer for peace."[48]

In his iconoclastic 1970 book *Ball Four*, former Yankees pitcher Jim Bouton expressed his opposition to the Vietnam War with reference to a member of his Yankee fan club: "It just doesn't seem right that a member of my fan club should be fighting in Vietnam," Bouton wrote. "Or that anybody should be."[49] In 1972, Washington Redskins lineman Ray Schoenke organized four hundred athletes to support Senator George McGovern's antiwar presidential campaign, despite the fact that his coach, George Allen, was a close friend of McGovern's opponent, Richard Nixon.[50] Pittsburgh Pirate pitcher Dock Ellis, who often spoke out against racism, stayed quiet on the war. When reporters asked him about the goodwill tour to Vietnam that he and other players participated in, he initially said, "I don't want to answer questions about Vietnam. I don't want to get political."[51] However, when the Nixon administration tried to get him to endorse the war, he angrily shot back, threatening to publicly describe all the drug-addicted American soldiers he saw there.

Billie Jean King's commitment to feminism, and later to LGBTQ equality, paralleled Robinson's full-scale involvement with the civil rights movement.[52] Like Robinson, she overcame barriers in sports and then used her celebrity to break barriers in society. King is one of the greatest tennis players of all time. She was ranked number one in the world five times between 1966 and 1972 and was ranked in the top ten for seventeen years, beginning in 1960. In total, she won 67 singles titles, 101 doubles titles, and 11 mixed doubles titles, amassing almost $2 million in prize money after turning professional in 1968 and before retiring in 1983. She coached the U.S. Olympic women's tennis team in 1996 and 2000.

King's advocacy for women's sports in the 1960s and 1970s revolutionized school, amateur, and professional athletics. There had been many great women athletes before King, but she helped make it more acceptable for girls and women to be athletes. In the late 1960s professional women's tennis was widely dismissed as a frilly sideshow. Male "amateur" tennis stars would get paid under the table, but women athletes were not taken as seriously. For winning her first two Wimbledon tournaments, she received nothing except the $14 daily allowance. In 1970, when King and eight other female players defied the tennis establishment to form their own professional circuit, many experts doubted that they could attract big enough crowds to generate prize money. Women's tennis is now as popular as men's.

In addition to her dominance on the courts, King made significant contributions to women's sports and feminism in general. King campaigned tirelessly for Title IX, which prohibits sex discrimination in all federally funded school programs, including sports. Her efforts, which included testifying before Congress, helped persuade lawyers to adopt the law in 1972, which President Nixon signed in June of that year. The year before Title IX passed, only 1 percent of college athletic budgets went to women's sports programs. At the high school level, male athletes outnumbered female athletes 12.5 to 1. Since Title IX's enactment, female participation in sports has grown by 1,057 percent at the high school level and by 614 percent at the college level, reaching close to parity.

In 1972, almost a year before the Supreme Court's landmark *Roe v. Wade* ruling, King was one of fifty-three women to sign an ad in the first issue of *Ms.* magazine boldly proclaiming "We Have Had Abortions," putting her on the front lines of the battle for reproductive rights. Also in 1972, she became the first woman to be named *Sports Illustrated*'s "Sportsperson of the Year." King pushed for higher fees for women athletes, which led firms like Philip Morris and Virginia Slims to sponsor women's tournaments. When she won the U.S. Open in 1972, she received $15,000 less than did the men's winner, Ilie Nastase. She threatened to boycott the 1973 U.S. Open if it did not equalize prize money between women and men athletes. The tournament agreed to do so, setting a precedent. In 1974 she was one of the founders and the first president of the Women's Tennis Association. That year, with support from Gloria Steinem and *Ms.*, King also founded *womenSports* magazine and the Women's Sports Foundation. With King's backing, the magazine and foundation became powerful voices for women in sports. In 1975 *Seventeen* magazine polled its readers and found that King was the most admired woman in the world. In 1981 King was forced out of the closet by a former girlfriend who sued her, unsuccessfully, for palimony, while she was still married. She soon embraced her new role as the first openly lesbian major sports star. She serves on the Elton John AIDS Foundation and has received numerous honors for her work with the LGBTQ community. King's foundation developed and promotes It Takes a Team!, an educational program to end homophobia in school sports.

In the 1970s, as the number of Latino ballplayers increased, some players began speaking out against human rights abuses and other international issues. Pirates outfielder (and future Hall of Famer) Roberto Clemente condemned American support for the Somoza dictatorship in Nicaragua. Pitcher Albert Williams, a native of that country, fought with the rebels to defend the Sandinista Revolution in 1977 and 1978. White Sox and Tigers outfielder Magglio

Ordóñez and White Sox shortstop Ozzie Guillén, both Venezuelans, supported socialist Hugo Chávez. In 2013, Ordóñez was elected the socialist mayor of Juan Antonio Sotillo Municipality. The most notable dissenter from American policy and its war on terrorism was first baseman Carlos Delgado, the two-time All Star who played with the Blue Jays, Florida Marlins, and New York Mets during his seventeen-year career. Delgado, a Puerto Rico native, was no stranger to political protest. He had campaigned for years against the American naval presence in Vieques, a Puerto Rican island used for sixty years as a weapons-testing ground. Remembering older residents' horror stories about the explosions, Delgado believed the military was waging a form of war on the tiny island.

After the U.S. Navy left, Delgado and others called for the American government to clean up the economic, psychological, environmental mess it left behind, which included high cancer rates. Rallying others, he contributed hundreds of thousands of dollars to the campaign. As sportswriter Dave Zirin has noted, Delgado "viewed the people of Vieques as casualties—collateral damage—from the war on Iraq because they served as guinea pigs."[53] Delgado created the Extra Bases Foundation in Puerto Rico as a platform to express his commitment to social justice. The foundation has assisted ill and disadvantaged children, promoted local hospitals, and publicized the island's education crisis.

After the September 11, 2001, attacks on the World Trade Center, Commissioner Bud Selig required teams to play "God Bless America" at each game's seventh-inning stretch. "After all," he claimed, "we do have troops in Iraq and Afghanistan." For three years, Delgado joined players and fans and stood while the song played, but in 2004 he decided to sit in the dugout instead, concerned that the song was being used to justify ongoing military intervention. Delgado claimed, "I don't stand because I don't believe it's right. . . . It's a very terrible thing that happened on September 11. It's also a terrible thing that happened in Afghanistan and Iraq. I feel so sad for the families that lost relatives and loved ones in the war. But I think it's the stupidest war ever."[54]

While Blue Jays president Paul Godfrey and catcher Gregg Zaun strongly supported the Iraq War, both honored Delgado's right to dissent. But when the team played at Yankee Stadium, boos and derision showered down on Delgado. After each of his outs, chants of "USA! USA!" went up in the crowd. Some right-wing fans and commentators labeled him "un-American," unfit to collect his paycheck, and even "a terrorist [who] should be jailed."

In response, Delgado reiterated his antiwar message: "I say God bless America, God bless Miami, God bless Puerto Rico and all countries until there is peace in the world." Delgado claimed that some fellow athletes supported him, but others attacked him, saying, "Go back to Puerto Rico." He wasn't surprised that some fans would object to his views. "I felt people booing me [but] when you do [something like this], you do it because it is the right thing to do. . . . The most important thing is to stay true to your values and principles." According to Delgado, "Athletes, who have this platform where they can reach millions of people, should use it."[55]

In 2003, just before the United States invaded Iraq, Dallas Mavericks guard Steve Nash wore a T-shirt to media day during the NBA's All-Star weekend that said "No War. Shoot for Peace." Numerous sports columnists criticized Nash for speaking his mind. (One wrote that he should "just shut up and play.") David Robinson, a U.S. Naval Academy graduate and former naval officer and then center for the San Antonio Spurs, said that Nash's attire was inappropriate. Flip Saunders, coach of the NBA's Minnesota Timberwolves, told the *Minneapolis Star-Tribune*, "What opinions you have, it's important to keep them to yourselves."[56]

During and after his thirteen years (1997–2010) as a center with three NBA teams—the Golden State Warriors, Orlando Magic, and Memphis Grizzlies—Adonal Foyle was an outspoken critic of America's political system. "This mother of all democracies," Foyle said, "is one of the most corrupt systems, where a small minority make the decisions for everybody else." In 2001, Foyle started Democracy Matters, a nonprofit group dedicated to educating young people about politics, mobilizing them to vote, and bringing pressure on elected officials to reform the nation's campaign finance laws. The group has chapters on fifty college campuses, staffed with paid interns.[57]

When he was not playing basketball, Foyle was frequently speaking at high schools, colleges, and conferences about the corrupting role of big money in politics. Foyle refused to be intimidated by those sportswriters and fans who objected to his beliefs and activism. "How can we say we are creating a society in Iraq based on democracy and freedom and tell people here who have the audacity to speak out to keep quiet?" he said in a 2004 interview. "If people shut down because they are afraid the media is going to spank them or fans are going to boo them, then the terrorists have won." He also observed, "When you talk about campaign finance reform, you are talking about all of the issues—war, civil rights, environment, gender, globalization—because they are all connected." He echoed similar views in 2018, telling the *San Francisco Chronicle*, "With the political climate we are in, there is a much bigger sense that this (money influencing politics) is the central issue of our time. If you look at what's happening with almost any policy now in Washington, there is still a force that is causing politicians to not really recognize the will of the American people."

A magna cum laude history major at Colgate University, Foyle explained, "If people want us [athletes] to be role models, it's not just saying what people want you to say. It's pushing the boundaries a bit, saying things that you may not want to think about. That's good for a society. Morality is much bigger than athletics." In 2005, Foyle founded the Kerosene Lamp Foundation, which serves children in Saint Vincent and the Grenadines, where he grew up. In 2008, he was elected to the board of Common Cause, an influential nonprofit organization committed to strengthening democracy. He also became a member of the executive committee of the NBA Players Association. In 2014, the Warriors appointed Foyle as the team's community ambassador.

Activist Athletes in the Trump Era

Presidents have sought to align themselves with athletes. They appear at professional sports events, where the American flag is ubiquitous, patriotic songs are played, and sometimes Air Force jets fly overhead. But on occasion, players have turned the tables. In 1991, for example, when President George H. W. Bush invited the Chicago Bulls to the White House to celebrate their NBA championship, Bulls guard Craig Hodges handed Bush a letter expressing outrage about the condition of urban America. On the other side of the political spectrum, in 2012 Boston Bruins goaltender Tim Thomas declined to visit the White House over disagreements with President Barack Obama's policies.

Pitcher Sean Doolittle had become the most outspoken contemporary professional athlete against social injustice. He explained to the *New York Times*, "When I was a kid, I remember my parents would say, 'Baseball is what you do, but that's not who you are'— like that might be my job, but that's not the end-all, be-all. I feel like I might even be able to use it to help other people or open some doors or explore more opportunities."[58] In 2015, when he was with the Oakland Athletics and ticket sales for the team's LGBT Pride Night were not going well, Doolittle and his girlfriend (now wife) Eireann Dolan hatched a plan to buy tickets from season ticket holders and donate them to LGBT youth who otherwise might not attend an A's game. They wound up purchasing nine hundred tickets.[59] In 2016, after Trump dismissed his vulgar "grab their pussy" comment as just "locker room talk," Doolittle denounced Trump on Twitter: "As an athlete, I've been in locker rooms my entire adult life and uh, that's not locker room talk." A week after his inauguration, Trump signed the first iteration of his travel ban, sparking nationwide protests. "These refugees are fleeing civil wars, terrorism, religious persecution, and are thoroughly vetted for 2 yrs," tweeted Doolittle. "A refugee ban is a bad idea. . . . It feels un-American. And also immoral."[60] He and Dolan also organized a Thanksgiving meal for seventeen Syrian refugees and got Chicago mayor Rahm Emanuel and several aldermen to serve as greeters and waiters to get publicity for the refugee cause. He and Dolan worked with Human Rights Watch and wrote an op-ed in *Sports Illustrated* urging the Veterans Affairs Department to provide adequate mental health services to military vets with less than honorable discharges, called "bad paper." They've supported Operation Finally Home, which builds houses for wounded veterans and their families. They started a registry to help furnish two such houses in Northern California and offered signed Oakland A's gear to those who donated. Within weeks, fans had filled every cabinet and drawer with the necessities for the recipients. He's also supported Swords to Ploughshares, a Bay Area organization devoted to helping veterans with housing and employment. After Nazis and white supremacists descended on Charlottesville, Virginia, triggering violent protests that resulted in the death of one anti-Nazi protester, Doolittle, who went to the University of Virginia, tweeted, "The C'Ville I knew from my time at @UVA is a diverse and accepting community. It's no place for Nazis." And "People say 'if we don't give them attention they'll go away.' Maybe. But if we don't condemn this evil, it might continue to spread." And "This kind of hatred was never gone, but now it's been normalized. They didn't even wear hoods. It's on us to condemn it and drive it out."[61]

Doolittle wasn't alone. President Trump inspired a new wave of protest by athletes. During the 2016 presidential election, Dodgers first baseman Adrián González refused to stay at a hotel owned by Trump. Asked to explain his action, González simply told reporters, "You can draw your own conclusions. They're probably right."[62] On election night, Dodgers pitcher Brandon McCarthy tweeted, "Tonight's result affects me none because I'm rich, white and male. Yet, it'll be a long time until I'm able to sleep peacefully."[63] Two months after Trump's inauguration, McCarthy was back on Twitter poking fun at Trump's campaign pledge to "drain the swamp" of corporate and Wall Street influence peddlers. "Was the 'swamp' Goldman Sachs itself?" McCarthy tweeted, referring to the powerful investment bank that has provided top officials in Trump's administration.[64] St. Louis Cardinals outfielder Dexter Fowler, whose wife immigrated from Iran, told ESPN that he opposed Trump's anti-Muslim executive order. In response to angry comments from fans, Fowler tweeted, "For the record. I know this is going to sound absolutely crazy, but athletes are humans, and not properties of the team they work for."[65] In 2016, to protest police brutality toward black Americans, San Francisco 49ers quarterback Colin Kaepernick decided to kneel, rather than stand, during the national anthem before his team's preseason games.[66] Throughout that season, other NFL players followed Kaepernick's example of silent protest. Their crusade widened after Trump launched an attack on the players' protest during a political rally in Alabama in September 2017. "Wouldn't you love to see one of these NFL owners, when somebody disrespects our flag, say, 'Get that son of a bitch off the field right now? Out! He's fired. He's fired!'" Trump bellowed.[67] The next weekend, more than two hundred players sat or kneeled in defiance of Trump. After his protest, Kaepernick was blacklisted by NFL teams, who refused to hire him, despite the fact that he was more talented than many NFL quarterbacks.

Kaepernick's act inspired many other professional and amateur athletes to follow his example. In May 2018, NFL owners capitulated to Trump by voting to require players to stand on the field for the national anthem or be subject to a fine. The next day, Trump applauded the owners for doing "the right thing." "Players who refuse to stand for the anthem," Trump declared, "shouldn't be in this country." Many NFL players reacted with anger over the league's policy and Trump's comments. "It's disgusting because of our First Amendment rights," said Denver Broncos linebacker Brandon Marshall.[68]

"[Trump is] an idiot, plain and simple," said Seattle Seahawks wide receiver Doug Baldwin.[69] Bruce Maxwell, the Oakland Athletics African American rookie catcher, son of an Army veteran, bashed Trump on Instagram: "Our president speaks of inequality of man because players are protesting the anthem! F- this man!"[70] Later that day, he became the first major league player to kneel for the national anthem before a game against the visiting Texas Rangers. Outfielder Mark Canha, who is white, stood behind Maxwell and placed his right hand on his teammate's shoulder. "My decision had been coming for a long time," Maxwell told the media, citing his own experiences with racism growing up in Huntsville, where Trump made his derogatory remarks about NFL players.

In 2017, Trump withdrew his White House invitation to the NBA champion Golden State Warriors after players criticized him. The next year, after the Warriors' Steph Curry and the Cavaliers' LeBron James said they wouldn't go to the White House if they won the championship, Trump didn't even bother extending an invitation to the victorious Warriors. (In January 2019, the Warriors met with former president Barack Obama at his Washington office when they were in town to play the Wizards.)

After most of the 2018 NFL Super Bowl champion Philadelphia Eagles announced that they were skipping the White House victory celebration in protest, Trump proclaimed that they were no longer invited. In May of that year, Houston Astro players Carlos Beltrán and Carlos Correa, both natives of Puerto Rico, skipped the team's visit to the White House to celebrate their 2017 World Series victory as a way of expressing their dismay with Trump's recovery efforts after Hurricane Maria devastated the island. In 2019, nine African American and Latino members of the 2018 World Series winners Boston Red Sox—Mookie Betts, Jackie Bradley Jr., Rafael

Devers, Hector Velázquez, Xander Bogaerts, Sandy León, Christian Vázquez, Eduardo Núñez, and David Price—refused to join Trump at a White House celebration. Manager Alex Cora, a native of Puerto Rico, also refused to attend because of Trump's failure to provide adequate aid to the island after it was devastated by the hurricane.[71] The University of Virginia men's basketball team—which won the 2019 NCAA championship—turned down an invitation to Trump's White House in part over their outrage over Trump's response to the white supremacist rally in Charlottesville two years earlier.[72]

The celebrity status of Megan Rapinoe reflects the growing popularity of soccer—and women's soccer in particular—in the United States over the past two decades. It is similar to the booming interest in women's tennis in the 1970s, except that more young girls participate in soccer than in tennis. Like Robinson and like Billie Jean King, Rapinoe has used her fame as a platform for social justice. In 2018 Rapinoe and WNBA star Sue Bird were the first openly gay couple to appear on the cover of *ESPN the Magazine*'s body issue. In 2019, twenty-eight members of the women's national soccer team filed a class-action gender discrimination lawsuit against the U.S. Soccer Federation demanding equal pay for female players.

A month after Kaepernick's take-a-knee protest in 2016, Rapinoe knelt during the national anthem in solidarity with the NFL star. After the U.S. Soccer Federation revised its rules to require all players to "stand respectfully" when the anthem is played, Rapinoe refused to sing the anthem and stood with her hand at her side instead of over her heart. In 2019, as co-captain of the U.S. women's national soccer team, she announced that she would refuse an invitation to visit Trump at the White House if her team won the World Cup. After Trump scolded Rapinoe on Twitter, her teammates voiced their support for her. Teammate Ali Krieger tweeted, "In regards to the 'President's' tweet today, I know women who you cannot control or grope anger you, but I stand by @mPinoe & will sit this one out as well. I don't support this administration nor their fight against LGBTQ+ citizens, immigrants & our most vulnerable."[73]

Until the 1960s and 1970s, many professional athletes earned little more than ordinary workers. Many lived in the same neighborhoods as their fans and had to work in the off-season to supplement their salaries. In both team sports like baseball, football, soccer, hockey, and basketball and individual sports like tennis and golf, professional athletes are better organized and better paid than were their counterparts a generation or two ago. The emergence of players' unions and associations has dramatically improved athletes' pay, working conditions, pensions, and bargaining clout. A growing number of pro athletes come from suburban upbringings and attended college, and they increasingly also come from Asia and Latin America. Regardless of their backgrounds, however, all pro athletes have much greater earning power than their predecessors. Since the 1970s, television contracts have brought new revenues that have dramatically increased salaries.

The Major League Baseball Players Association (MLBPA) was the first major professional players' union. When Marvin Miller, a former Steelworkers Union staffer, became the MLBPA's first executive director in 1966, he sought to raise players' political awareness. "We didn't just explain the labor laws," he recalled. "We had to get players to understand that they were a union. We did a lot of internal education to talk to players about broader issues." According to Ed Garvey, who ran the NFL players union from 1971 until 1983, the civil rights movement was critical to the union's early development. The union "was driven by the African-American players, who knew there was an unwritten quota on most teams where there would not be more than a third blacks on any one team," explained Garvey. "And they knew they wouldn't have a job with the team when their playing days were over." The players also understood that team owners were "the most powerful monopoly in the country," he says. Garvey brought the association into the AFL-CIO—the only professional sports union to do so—to give the players a sense that they were part of the broader labor movement. In the early 1970s several NFL players walked the picket lines with striking Farah clothing workers, joined bank employees in Seattle to boost their organizing drive, and took other public stands.[74]

Although today's professional athletes are better organized and better paid, they also face enormous job insecurity. There is massive competition for the few slots in the ranks of professional sports. The average career of a Major League Baseball player, for example, is only four years. Except for the superstars, athletes who speak out, or who are considered controversial or "troublemakers," can put their careers at risk, as Colin Kaepernick quickly discovered. Team executives and players' agents warn them not to risk their high salaries and commercial endorsements by taking contentious public stands. With some exceptions, the players' unions no longer view their mission as educating players about the broader labor movement or engaging them in social and political matters. Thus you had the spectacle, during the 2018 playoffs and World Series, of the New York Yankees and Los Angeles Dodgers crossing the hotel workers' union's picket lines at Boston hotels where workers were on strike. It would have been a significant gesture for a few Yankees, Dodgers, and Red Sox players to show up and join the hotel workers' picket lines.[75]

In early 2019, the MLBPA tried but could not stop the New Era Cap Company, which makes caps for all major league teams, from closing its union factory near Buffalo and moving production to nonunion facilities in Florida and overseas. In an op-ed in the *Washington Post*, Doolittle, then pitching for the Washington Nationals, expressed his concern that he and other players "will be wearing caps made by people who don't enjoy the same labor protections and safeguards that we do."[76] The MLBPA could insist that teams purchase players' uniforms, bats, and other equipment from union companies—or at least from those that provide decent pay, working conditions, and benefits. After the Washington Nationals won the World Series in October 2019, Doolittle announced that he would not join his teammates at the White House celebration with President Trump. "I don't want to hang out with somebody who talks like that,'" he told the *Washington Post*.[77] All-Star third baseman Anthony Rendon, outfielders Víctor Robles and Michael A. Taylor, and pitchers Javy Guerra, Joe Ross, and Wander Suero also boycotted the event.[78] Taking a knee or locking arms during the national anthem and tweeting and making public statements opposing Trump's racism and ignorance of the First Amendment give athletes a platform to speak out on controversial issues. But there is much more athletes can do to challenge the political status quo, as Jackie Robinson, Billie Jean King, Sean Doolittle, and others have shown.

When was the last time you saw a celebrity athlete standing in front of a post office or grocery store, holding voter registration forms, or walking precincts and going door-to-door in low-income and minority neighborhoods, urging people to vote? If athletes ventured onto the streets to participate in rallies, protests, and pickets about police abuses, voter suppression, workers' rights, or deportation of immigrants, their gestures would generate considerable media attention for these causes. Billboards and TV commercials saying "LeBron James wants you to vote" and "Megan Rapinoe wants you to call your Congressperson to raise the minimum wage and adopt paid family leave" could serve as a powerful rallying force to improve our democracy and society.

Jackie Robinson's legacy is to remind us of the unfinished agenda of the civil rights revolution, the importance of protest movements in moving the country closer to its ideals, and the role that athletes can play in challenging social injustice.

12

SUPPORTING BLACK WOMEN ATHLETES

AMIRA ROSE DAVIS

In 1955, fifteen-year-old Wilma Rudolph stood anxiously on the track at the historic Franklin Field in Philadelphia. She was not nervous about her races—she had won those handily. Indeed, her entire team had enjoyed a banner day. Led by Rudolph's nine victories, the small team of five high school girls from Tennessee State University's summer development program had swept the entire competition and walked away with the Junior National Amateur Athletic Union title. No, Rudolph was nervous for another reason. Her coach, the infamous Ed Temple, had just asked the girls to go take a picture with two black celebrities who had attended the meet. As she approached Don Newcombe and Jack Robinson, she worried about the thickness of her southern accent and was glad she wouldn't really have to talk. This was just a photo op, after all. What could these famous baseball players from the Brooklyn Dodgers possibly have to say to her?

Jack Robinson, as it turns out, had plenty to say. He pulled Rudolph aside and congratulated her on her victories. The two chatted for a few minutes, with Robinson complimenting her style of running and asking her about her family and life in Tennessee. Robinson was shocked to learn that Rudolph was still in high school and declared that she had a lot of potential. After pictures were taken, Robinson turned to Rudolph and gave her advice she would never forget. "You are a fascinating runner," he told the future Olympic gold medalist and track legend. "Don't let anything or anybody

Jackie Robinson with Don Newcombe and Wilma Rudolph in 1955. John W. Mosley / Temple University Libraries, Charles L. Blockson Afro-American Collection.

keep you from running. Keep running."[1] Those words stuck with Rudolph, and she turned them over and over in her head on the way back down to Tennessee. "I thought about Jackie Robinson and what he said, and for the first time in my life I had a black person I could look up to as a real hero," she recalled. "Jackie Robinson after that day was my first black hero."[2]

* * *

This brief encounter between Jack Robinson and Wilma Rudolph is more than a cool photo or compelling historical footnote. Their meeting and conversation cast light on a seldom explored side of the legendary Jackie Robinson—his support and amplification of black women athletes.

Robinson's respect for black women is well documented. He was fiercely devoted to his wife Rachel and constantly acknowledged her support and work. "She was my critic, my companion, my comforter and my inspiration," he wrote about Rachel. "She was my driving force to make good in this world."[3] Robinson often extolled his love for his wife and cited her support as a way to remind young girls and women how important they were and how vital they were to the success and future of the race. Many of Robinson's writings and speeches emphasized black women's value in heteronormative domestic life, yet he also acknowledged their political and social contributions, declaring, for instance, that "Negro women have been the backbone of our freedom movement."[4]

Robinson was not a vocal champion of gender equality in the way that he was a public voice on civil rights and electoral politics. Over the years, Robinson displayed a tension between a belief in traditional gender roles and a more progressive stance on women's autonomy and employment. Much of this tension was within his own home and in reaction to Rachel's ambition and tenacity. Rachel noted that being a "man, the main man, in a family of his own" carried a "profound appeal" for Jack.[5] Yet Robinson's vision of family life was at odds with Rachel's own professional opportunities. He admitted that if he had his way, Rachel would not work outside of the home and struggled with her desire for a professional career for many years. However, it is very clear that Rachel influenced his evolution on gender roles. Writing at the end of his life, Robinson acknowledged his personal growth and said that he was very proud of his wife's successful career.

Despite his personal struggle with Rachel's career aspirations, Robinson respected, and at times even celebrated, other black women who were breaking into traditionally male professional spaces. Legendary author Toni Morrison attested to this when she reflected on meeting Robinson in the late 1960s to discuss his potential autobiography:

> I already knew a great deal about the way many black men in that position often talked to black women who had a little power, which was to show the women that they really had none. Robinson was totally unlike that. He made no gestures to say "I'm more important than you; you have to accommodate me because I am a man." . . . He played none of the usual gender games. He respected me, felt comfortable with me. In hindsight, he was one of the few black men I had business dealings with in those days with whom I did not have to watch myself.[6]

Robinson's refusal to play the "usual gender games" was particularly apparent when it came to black women who were in sports.

Black Women in *Our Sports*

By the mid-twentieth century, black women and girls boasted a robust history of athletic participation. Black Americans understood sports to be a key space from which to refute their supposed inferiority, demonstrate the capabilities of the race, instill racial pride, and push for social and political equality. Competitive athletics for girls and women blossomed within black institutions. Still, black women, like their white counterparts, contended with prevailing notions that sports would make them less feminine and sexually deviant. Therefore, their participation was highly regulated by physical educators, coaches, and sports journalists, who constantly policed their appearances and behaviors.

The black press routinely covered women's athletics and often featured articles and updates on prominent women athletes. Many of these features attempted to emphasize their athletic achievements alongside their femininity and heteronormativity. It was common to see an article on a black woman athlete in black periodicals such as *Jet* or *Ebony* that featured the athlete in a dress or powdering her face or engaging in domestic work. The coverage juxtaposed their "inherently masculine" athletic exploits with not-so-subtle assurances that they were still feminine.

As editor in chief of the short-lived *Our Sports* magazine, Robinson offered a different portrayal of black women athletes. Heralded by Robinson as the "first and only publication of its kind," *Our Sports* offered readers a magazine that followed black athletes, from up-and-coming youth to the professional level. Robinson's magazine always featured black women athletes in a wide array of sports. One issue highlighted the growth of black women wrestlers, while another featured a profile on a top fencer. Additionally, the coverage featured images of the athletes playing sports as opposed to dainty model-like poses. Pictures of black women golfing or bowling were accompanied by in-depth articles that discussed their athletic achievements and goals. As one column asserted, "No readers of *Our Sports* would raise an eyebrow or cause excitement by coming up with the right answers to such questions as 'Who is Althea Gibson?' 'For what is Mae Faggs noted?' 'Can you identify Fanny Blankers-Koen, Maureen Connolly, The Bauer Sisters, Alice Coachman?'"[7]

Our Sports also went beyond showcasing athletes. The magazine amplified women in sports in a variety of ways and in doing so subtly created a space that welcomed and celebrated black women in many roles in the sports industry. *Our Sports* employed black women sportswriters and columnists and featured letters from black women readers. In one issue they even featured a spread titled "The Other Half of the Baseball Story" that featured the wives of well-known black major leaguers in order to give them due credit for the influence they had on their husbands' careers. While the article certainly reinforced traditional gender norms on one hand ("behind every successful man is a good woman"), it also helped to highlight the range of black women's involvement in sports and cast black women as an integral part of black major leaguers' success.[8] The amplification and support of black women—athletes or otherwise—in the pages of *Our Sports* reflected Robinson's sustained respect for them and provided a model for more substantial coverage of black girls and women in the sporting world.

A Picture's Worth a Thousand Words

In the years following Robinson's integration of the majors, Negro League Baseball struggled to stay afloat. Major league teams were plucking up Negro League stars left and right, often with very little compensation sent to the former teams. With their stars in the majors and their fans following close behind, the audience and viability of the league waned. After the departure of Hank Aaron in 1952, Syd Pollock, owner of the Indianapolis Clowns, went in search of the next star—or at least someone who would attract fans back to the Negro Leagues. Pollock found his gate attraction in a semiprofessional baseball league where a black woman by the name of Toni Stone was turning heads.

In 1953 Toni Stone signed a contract with the Clowns, replacing Aaron at second base and officially gender integrating the Negro Leagues. Pollock played up the spectacle of his "gal guardian of second base" from his first press release, where he boasted that "the latest masculine enterprise to fall before the advance of wearers of skirts and panties is the baseball diamond."[9] Pollock's bet paid off as thousands of fans packed into stadiums to see Stone play. The next year two more women, Connie Morgan and Mamie "Peanut" Johnson, would also enter the league.[10]

The presence of women in Negro League Baseball did not go over very well with many male sportswriters, despite their enthusiastic coverage of women's sports in their press pages. The baseball women were a cause for concern. For a number of black sports-writers, many of whom had been fighting to integrate the majors for years, the sight of Stone, Morgan, and Johnson was irrefutable proof that the Negro Leagues had run its course. They argued that women in baseball emasculated black men and devalued the rugged masculinity of the sport. "It is indeed unfortunate that Negro base-ball has collapsed to the extent that it has to tie itself to a woman's apron strings to survive," wrote one journalist. Another journalist agreed, arguing that "girls need to be run out of men's baseball with a softly-padded rail for their own good and the good of the game."[11]

Although Robinson was quite vocal about the poor state of the Negro Leagues, he never publicly admonished the women ball play-ers. In fact, he did quite the opposite. When barnstorming with his All-Star team, they stopped in Baltimore to face off against the Clowns. Pollock used this opportunity to stage a mini photo shoot with Robinson and Connie Morgan. Robinson obliged and took it upon himself to give Morgan batting tips as well. The image of Mor-gan "learning tips from the pros" was widely circulated as a way to legitimize the women athletes. Pollock plastered the image on pro-motional posters, scorecards, and postcards. Robinson's willingness to lend his image—and thus his tacit approval—to the promotion of the women athletes, as well as the Negro Leagues, was likely more supportive than any verbal statement or written column would ever be.

It also exemplifies the ways in which Robinson interacted with black women athletes. He respected them, amplified them, and of-fered support. However, this support was largely through photo opportunities and magazine spreads. Despite Robinson's public platform and vocal engagements with civil rights, electoral politics, and more, he never discussed women athletes at length. This was partially because his respect for black women as athletes was a given and did not require any grand statement. But it was also because the plight of black women athletes seemed largely tangential to Robinson's social concerns and political goals.

The Female Jackie Robinson

Even before he hung up his baseball cleats, Robinson enjoyed playing golf. After his retirement from professional baseball in 1956, golf became a more frequent pastime. Robinson was not the only legendary black athlete to enjoy a day on the links. Often he would golf alongside the great boxer Joe Louis and the tennis champion Althea Gibson. All three of them would advocate for access to golf clubs for black golfers and the dismantling of the color line in professional golf. Indeed, Gibson herself would go on to become the first black woman in the Ladies Professional Golf Association (LPGA). Robinson seemingly held black women golfers in particularly high esteem. They received considerable coverage in *Our Sports* under Robinson's editorial eye, and he frequently mentioned various black women golfers in his columns. Perhaps this fondness is best seen in his frequent pairing with Gibson in golf tournaments in the 1950s and 1960s.

The Choi-Settes, a black women's golf club in Chicago, hosted an annual golf tournament. Usually held at the Pipes-o-Peace golf course in Chicago, their tournaments were corporate-sponsored popular affairs that featured men's and women's competitions and the infamous celebrity showdown. For years the celebrity exhibition pitted Joe Louis and local golf superstar Ann Gregory against Robinson and Gibson. In subsequent years, the latter pair would take on a variety of challengers, including teen golf champions in 1963.[12] Their games were fun to watch and drew lots of onlookers and supporters. In many ways the Robinson-Gibson pairing was fitting—after all, she spent much of her career being labeled the "female Jackie Robinson."

As Gibson rose to prominence in the upper-class, lily-white, country club sport of tennis, it did not take long for the black press to hail her as Robinson's feminine counterpart. When Gibson won Wimbledon in 1957, many headlines instantly invoked Robinson while applauding her feat. The *Philadelphia Tribune* proclaimed that "Althea Gibson Makes History; Joins Jackie as Trailblazer."[13] While Gibson sometimes bristled at this comparison and the expectations it placed on her, it is helpful to consider the ways in which the label of "female Jackie Robinson" has been used to further his legacy.

The use of Robinson's name to describe barrier breakers is certainly not novel. Indeed, the first public mention of a "female Jackie Robinson" was almost immediately after his debut in 1947. A group of women from the American Girls Softball League penned a letter highlighting the achievements of their black teammate, Yvonne Coker. After extolling her phenomenal play in their league for the last three years, they mention that she is known in ballparks in the Northeast as "Jackie Robinson." The women add that "this is all well and good, but we prefer her own name—after all didn't she make the league first!"[14] The Robinson moniker was conferred on Coker, as it was on Gibson, as a black woman breaking the color line in white sports. For decades this was the most common application of the phrase "the female Jackie Robinson." It positioned athletes, such as Coker and Gibson, as contemporaries of Robinson, as barrier breakers replicating his achievements on parallel paths, not necessarily carrying on his legacy. Yet in the years following Robinson's death, the phrase would widen, extending beyond black women and directly situating athletes as the continuation of his legacy.

Trailblazers

In the months before Robinson's death, the Educational Amendment of 1972 was passed. The amendment included Title IX, a thirty-seven-word statement that would have wide-reaching effects and transform sports for girls and women in the United States. Title IX prohibits discrimination on the basis of sex for any federally funded educational program or activity. While athletics wasn't the central concern of the legislators who drafted this act, it would quickly become clear that the act would radically alter competitive sporting opportunities in youth sports, high schools, and colleges. Title IX ushered in a sporting revolution of sorts. Robinson would not live to see it.

In the week before his death, Robinson spoke candidly about the work that Major League Baseball still had to do to diversify. He spoke of his desire to see black managers and third base coaches. Not surprisingly he mentioned nothing about getting women involved in the game. However, a few years later, Hank Aaron would invoke his legacy as he advocated for women in baseball. "Why shouldn't women play professional major league baseball on the same team as men?," Aaron asked. "Women are capable of playing. And it's going to happen soon."[15] Aaron went on to explain that he was empathetic because of the discrimination he faced as a black man in the sport. "Everyone should be given a chance," he added. Aaron cited Robinson as the person who opened his eyes to the possibilities of playing in the majors as a way to point out that it takes only one person to break down the barrier and usher in new talent to the game. In many ways, Aaron was issuing a call for the next "female Jackie Robinson."

Unlike other calls or pronouncements of Robinson's female counterparts, Aaron's had rhetorically positioned a woman breaking into a men's professional league as an heir to Robinson's legacy as well. In the following decades, this implicit positioning would become an explicit and expressed view of Major League Baseball itself.

"Robinson's Legacy Reaches the Front Office," proclaimed a *New York Times* article from 1990. The article profiled a young black woman named Elaine Weddington, who was a scholarship recipient of the Jackie Robinson Foundation, which Rachel had founded in the year after Jack's death. Weddington had used the foundation's support to launch herself into a sports management career. She had just accepted a job as an assistant general manager with the Boston Red Sox. In many ways, Weddington embodied the vision of a diverse league from top to bottom that Robinson had articulated before his death.

In 1997, MLB hired Sharon Robinson, Jack and Rachel's daughter, to be the director of educational programming. She was to focus on "urban and women's issues" and pursue ideals championed by her father decades before.[16] Under Sharon's leadership, among other things, MLB has developed programs to market and grow the game of baseball and provide opportunities for unrepresented groups to get in the game as athletes, managers, and executives. This commitment to diversity and inclusion has expanded over the years to include a specific aim at supporting girls and women in baseball. Similar to Hank Aaron's call for the next "female Jackie Robinson," the educational programming from MLB seeks to incorporate girls and women athletes into the ideals and legacy of Jack Robinson. These programmatic initiatives expanded under Commissioner Bud Selig and continue today, including the Trailblazer Girls Baseball tournament held on Jackie Robinson Day each spring.

But the Trailblazer tournament remains overwhelmingly white. Mo'ne Davis aside, black girls are not participating in baseball at the same rates as their white peers. Moreover, the programming efforts that target black boys and (unintentionally) white girls to grow the game overlook and fail to reach black girls. Despite Robinson's documented respect for black women athletes and the long history of black women's baseball participation, the current demographics of the game—from the field to the front office—have yet to truly reflect the legacy of Jack Robinson's commitment to and amplification of black girls and women in the sport.

Robinson was outspoken about many things, but he certainly was not a leading voice on women's liberation. He had his own personal journey, fueled by his marriage to Rachel Robinson, with women's equality and evolving gender norms. Yet it's clear that throughout his life Robinson held space for black women in sports. It is important to note that his support was specifically for black girls and women. It was due to an immense respect for black women and their capabilities. Robinson respected, valued, celebrated, and amplified black women athletes when many did not. His legacy on women in sports could appropriately be considered Rachel's legacy. For it was Rachel Robinson who influenced and pushed her husband to evolve his gender ideals. It was Rachel Robinson who sustained his legacy and institutionalized it through the foundation. It was Rachel and Sharon who pushed MLB for the expansion of inclusion and outreach programs to marginalized populations, insisting they live up to the legacy of Jackie Robinson they were so eager to champion. The encouragement and advice Jack Robinson gave to young Wilma Rudolph in 1955 rings true to other black women in sports today. Don't give up, don't let others discourage you, and keep going.

13

THE CHALLENGES OF A GAY JACKIE ROBINSON

ADAM AMEL ROGERS

The gay Jackie Robinson.

This short phrase has populated headlines, media soundbites, and Hollywood scripts for decades. Jackie's legendary name is synonymous with "barrier breaker," so "the gay Jackie Robinson" has been used to describe any trailblazer in the lesbian, gay, bisexual, transgender, queer (LGBTQ) community.

Ellen DeGeneres was compared to Robinson when she came out as lesbian on her TV sitcom in 1997.[1] As was Harvey Milk, when he was elected as the first openly gay San Francisco supervisor in 1977. Milk mused that "every Black youth in the country was looking up to [Robinson], he was a symbol to all of them. In the same way, I'm a symbol of hope to gays and all minorities."[2]

Mostly though, "the gay Jackie Robinson" has been used in the sports world to describe LGBTQ athletes, both real and hypothetical. Its use is typically well intentioned, but ultimately it is problematic, flawed, and unhelpful. I have two major issues with "the gay Jackie Robinson" framework.

First, Jackie Robinson faced unimaginable hatred and bigotry every day of his journey. From not being able to stay in the same hotels as his teammates to facing death threats on the field, Jackie was forced to overcome monumental obstacles during Jim Crow. It is imperative that we do nothing to minimize that, which is why "the gay Jackie Robinson" isn't appropriate. There are certainly obstacles for queer and trans folks in 2019, and each out athlete described in the pages that follow has encountered bigotry and prejudice, but there is also a social and political capital that the LGBTQ community enjoys in 2019 that will stand behind and support openly queer and trans athletes.

My other issue with "the gay Jackie Robinson" framework is that Jackie's journey to the majors was handled with such mastery that it has inspired a standard and expectation that is unattainable in most other parts of society. This comparison has created completely unreasonable expectations for queer and trans athletes. We are obsessed with the idea of a singular hero—having one person or one symbol to serve as the shining star on the hill for others to follow. This was the path that worked for Jackie Robinson, Branch Rickey, and the Dodgers organization. They accomplished a huge feat, built the perfect Hollywood narrative, and established a larger-than-life legacy for Robinson that will be difficult for anyone else to achieve.

For the LGBTQ equal rights movement, there have been many successes in recent years—from nationwide marriage equality to the end of Don't Ask, Don't Tell, there are some real victories to celebrate. But the lack of a singular queer barrier breaker in sports has been a glaring gap in the story. It seems out of place that in 2019 I can take my husband and kids to an LGBTQ Pride event for every Major League Baseball team, where a queer artist will sing the national anthem, a gay TV star will throw out the first pitch, top out executive Billy Bean will give a speech, and any number of top corporations will proudly sponsor the rainbow-clad team giveaways, but we still won't see any openly gay players on any team. This is why there is such a hunger for "the gay Jackie Robinson." Media, corporate sponsors, and fans alike are desperate for the perfect Jackie Robinson–type figure to come along and break another barrier in sports.

The Jackie Robinson blueprint is an unproductive framework to follow—it isn't going to happen in the same way that it did in 1947.

The path to LGBTQ equality in sports does not include a singular hero; instead it involves several players chipping away at the rainbow ceiling. Women's professional sports are light years ahead in terms of out athletes. Some of the best WNBA players, including Elena Delle Donne and Brittney Griner, are out; and perhaps the biggest power couple in sports is U.S. soccer legend Megan Rapinoe and WNBA All-Star Sue Bird. On the men's side, we have had many success stories. A handful of athletes have come out publicly after retirement from the NFL, NBA, and Major League Baseball, and many openly LGBTQ athletes have thrived in individual sports. But we keep moving the measuring stick in pursuit of the singular hero—the Jackie Robinson figure who is going to serve as the modern symbol for equality in sports. We need to stop and look to the coming-out victories that have already happened, many of which took bits and pieces from the Robinson playbook. Here are some of their stories.

Glenn Burke

By many measurements, Major League Baseball has already had its "gay Jackie Robinson." It happened on the same team, thirty years later. Glenn Burke was called up to the Dodgers in 1977 and immediately made an impact on the field and in the locker room. He was a big-energy teammate who is credited with inventing the high five. He was also gay. There was no big press conference or media reveal, but it didn't take long for Burke's teammates to realize that he wasn't going to hide who he was. The Dodgers organization took notice as well. While Dodgers president Branch Rickey was instrumental in Jackie Robinson's successful career, Glenn Burke had a much different relationship with Rickey's replacement, Walter O'Malley. O'Malley and Dodgers general manager Al Campanis were concerned that word would get out that they had a gay player on the team, so they offered Burke $75,000 to get married. In turning down the money, Burke famously replied, "I guess you mean to a woman."[3]

His relationship with the Dodgers continued to sour when Burke started dating the son of legendary Dodgers manager Tommy Lasorda. To this day, Lasorda denies that his son dated Burke or that he was even gay. Two months into the 1978 season, Lasorda and Campanis traded Burke to the Oakland A's, which left the Dodgers players incredulous. When Dodgers outfielder Dusty Baker asked the team's trainer why they traded Burke, "He said, 'They don't want any gays on the team.' I said, 'The organization knows?' He said, 'Everybody knows.'"[4]

Burke's time in Oakland was tumultuous. A's manager Billy Martin made player introductions in spring training by saying, "This is Glenn Burke and he's a faggot."[5] Burke was also called anti-gay epithets by fans in the stands and felt isolated by his teammates.

Burke's teammates were reportedly afraid to shower with him—a story paralleled by Jackie Robinson's experience thirty years prior. When Dodgers outfielder Dixie Walker asked Branch Rickey to be traded, he said that when he went home to his hardware store in Alabama, he had to answer incredulous questions from his customers about whether he showered with Jackie Robinson. The shower wasn't just an issue for Walker: Jackie Robinson and fellow black teammates Roy Campanella and Don Newcombe all showered separately from the rest of the Dodgers players because white players were uncomfortable.

In 2014, ESPN faced a backlash from NFL players and coaches for inserting shower isolation into coverage of Michael Sam's first days with the St. Louis Rams as an openly gay man. ESPN's Josina Anderson reported, "Another Rams defensive player told me that 'Sam is respecting our space' and that, from his perspective, he seems to think that Michael Sam is waiting to kind of take a shower, as not to make his teammates feel uncomfortable."[6] Rams coach Jeff Fisher slammed the report as unethical and unprofessional.

Despite being a good player on one of the worst teams in baseball, Burke was sent down to the minors in Ogden, Utah, and he decided to retire from baseball. A few years later, he came out publicly and said, "People say I should still be playing, but I didn't want to make other people uncomfortable, so I faded away."[7] Burke found fanfare and adoration in the LGBTQ community when he publicly came out and embraced his role as a barrier breaker. He said, "If I can make friends honestly, it may be a step toward gays and straight people understanding each other. Maybe they'll say, 'He's alright, there's got to be a few more alright.' Maybe it will begin to make it easier for other young gays to go into sports."[8]

Burke's post-baseball life was riddled with tragedy. He ran out of money, turned to drugs, was hit by a car, and eventually died from AIDS-related illness in 1995. It took another two decades for Major League Baseball to officially acknowledge and honor Burke's role as a pioneer in the league.

Jason Collins

In 2013, NBA journeyman Jason Collins was featured on the cover of *Sports Illustrated* next to the words "The Gay Athlete." This. Was. It. The moment we had been waiting for was upon us—an active NBA player had come out publicly in a beautifully written piece. Collins was the perfect Jackie Robinson–esque candidate to be "the first." Branch Rickey said that first and foremost he "wanted a man of exceptional intelligence" to integrate the league, which is a big part of why Jackie was selected.[9] Years later, Collins fit this bill as well—he was Stanford educated, highly connected, and extremely intelligent. He had privately come out to his friends, Hillary and Bill Clinton, before the *Sports Illustrated* piece ran, and after the article came out he received a personal phone call from President Barack Obama. The only missing piece was that, as opposed to Jackie Robinson being the best player on the field when he broke the color barrier, Collins was at the end of his journeyman career, and it was unclear if he would be on an NBA roster the following season.

The beginning of the NBA season came and went with no Jason Collins. It seemed like this might have been another missed opportunity, but in February 2014 the Brooklyn Nets signed Collins to a midseason ten-day contract. His first game in uniform was in Los Angeles against the Lakers, so my husband and I rushed down to Staples Center to witness history. I thought it was going to be the modern version of Jackie running out onto Ebbets Field for the first time.

When my husband and I picked up our tickets at the game, I said, "Big game, huh?" The ticket office guy looked confused as to how the tragic Kobe-less Lakers could be in any kind of a big game right now. He clearly didn't know that a barrier was about to be broken. We took our seats, and I wondered why no one was talking about the fact that history was going to occur just a few feet in front of us. Finally, the sushi-eating couple behind us started talking about it. The man said, "Oh, Jason Collins is going to play tonight." His wife asked, "Which one is he again?" The man replied, "He's the local guy from Harvard-Westlake High School."

No one seemed to understand the gravity of the situation.

When Jason was announced into the game, we screamed our support and looked around to find polite applause and a smattering of people standing, but it wasn't the Jackie Robinson–type moment that it was in my head. Collins played the rest of the season without incident and then retired.

Dave Kopay

In 1975, Minnesota Twins public relations director Tom Mee responded to a question about gay athletes from *The Advocate*, an LGBTQ advocacy magazine, by saying, "The cop-out, immoral lifestyle of the tragic misfits espoused by your publication has no place in organized athletics at any level. Your colossal gall in attempting to extend your perversion to an area of total manhood is just simply unthinkable."[10] This response was seen by *Washington Star* editor

Dave Burgin, who decided it was time for his paper to explore the idea of gay players in professional sport. He assigned Lynn Rosellini to report on the topic, and her initial story, which was filled with conjecture from anonymous sources, in essence launched what Jim Buzinski at *Outsports* called "the start of the modern era of gays in sports."[11]

David Kopay, a running back who retired from professional football in 1972, read the article, and after seeing that no athletes were willing to use their names, he said, "Well, at least I could do that. At least I can be myself."[12] Kopay then came out as gay in the *Washington Star*, and in 1977 he wrote a best-selling autobiography about his experiences. He wrote candidly about trying to fall in love with a woman and undergoing hypnosis in an attempt to change his sexual orientation. He also detailed his family's negative reaction. When Kopay spoke with his father over the phone, his father told him, "If I were there he would kill me. He said he never wanted to see me again."[13] Negativity outside his family manifested in Kopay being "blacklisted" from football and not being able to get a job in coaching or scouting.

While many of the athletes who came out later were treated to significant media coverage, this surprisingly wasn't the case immediately after Kopay's announcement. In an article titled "The Cover-Up," reporter Hugh Harrison detailed his efforts to contact media outlets and sports personnel after Kopay came out, and what he found was that the Kopay story was being "systematically repressed."[14] Harrison revealed that a contact at the *Los Angeles Times* said the reason why the paper wasn't covering Kopay was that "it wouldn't be good for the game. It would be bad for the world of sports in general. It would destroy our culture."[15] Not all outlets ignored the story though; the *San Francisco Chronicle* interviewed Kopay, whom they deemed "the Jackie Robinson of sex."[16] The interview wasn't exactly friendly, as the reporter asked Kopay, "Since youth is a time of sexual confusion, do you think it's a good

idea to have homosexual coaches acting as role models for kids?"[17]
A question like that wouldn't have been controversial at the time
though, as only 27 percent of Americans supported a homosexual's
right to be a schoolteacher in 1977.[18] Even supportive journalists
were quick to point out that they were outliers, as Bill Dwyre from
the *Milwaukee Journal* said in his column, "Fans Not Ready for Gay
Athletes." Dwyre detailed the conversations he heard from average
fans that included an elderly Green Bay Packers fan talking about
how she hoped her son would rip up Kopay's autograph, business-
men making gay jokes, and a man saying, "I hope they never let the
jerk back into pro football."[19]

The public reaction to a gay athlete seemed to track with how the
public viewed gay rights in general. This was a time when 80 percent
of Americans thought that homosexuality was "always or almost
always wrong" and 57 percent felt that homosexuality should be il-
legal.[20] Despite the overall anti-gay climate, the reaction to Kopay's
coming out wasn't completely negative—Kopay received hundreds
of positive letters, and his book became the playbook for future gay
athletes who were dealing with coming out. Lesbian tennis legend
Billie Jean King told Kopay how much his book meant to her, and
openly gay former NFL defensive lineman Esera Tuaolo told Kopay
directly that the book saved his life. Kopay has embraced his role
as patriarch of the gay athletic movement. He spoke with Jason
Collins on the phone after his coming out and spent time advising
Michael Sam before he made his coming-out announcement. After
Sam's proclamation, Kopay penned an open letter to him that said
people will try to get in his way, but he needs to stay true to who he
is and continue doing what got him there in the first place.

Kopay's experience in the NFL showed that gay players can be
successful on a team, but the argument that openly gay players
disrupt the team dynamic continues to persist. After Esera Tuaolo
came out in 2002, NFL running back Garrison Hearst proclaimed,
"I don't want any faggots on my team."[21] Former standout wide

receiver Sterling Sharpe, who played with Tuaolo, implied that he and his teammates would have hurt Tuaolo during practice so he couldn't make it to the games. These types of comments have been repeated by other players, but in some cases anti-gay comments have turned out to be a productive educational opportunity. After former NBA center John Amaechi came out in 2006, fellow player Tim Hardaway told a Miami radio station, "I hate gay people,"[22] and years later, before the 2013 Super Bowl, San Francisco 49ers defensive back Chris Culliver said he would not welcome a gay teammate. But after both faced significant public backlash, they began volunteering with LGBTQ youth and are now vocal advocates of LGBTQ equality. While an active openly gay player may help speed this educational process for teammates who don't have much experience with LGBTQ people, the process itself is still part of the distraction argument.

Michael Sam

If anyone seemed destined to follow the barrier-breaking blueprint that Branch Rickey and Jackie Robinson established, it was Michael Sam. In January 2014, months before the NFL draft, Howard Bragman, a public relations expert known for helping celebrities own their own story when they come out as LGBTQ, met with two sports agents who had a client who wanted to come out. Following this meeting, Bragman texted Cyd Zeigler, who, along with Jim Buzinski, runs the groundbreaking site *Outsports*, the ultimate authority on the LGBTQ-sports intersection. The text said, "The Eagle has landed." Zeigler immediately knew what it meant—they were going to make history and finally put the question to rest of whether America was ready for the gay Jackie Robinson. Michael Sam was one of the best collegiate defensive ends in the country and was projected to be drafted in the third round of the NFL draft, but he wanted the team that drafted him to know he was gay. He had come out to his teammates at the University of Missouri the year before, and they continued to be one of the best teams in the country with no problems having a prominent gay player on their defense. "If we were choosing someone to be the first, we'd choose someone like Michael," Bragman said. "Smart, athletic, handsome. I don't think Central Casting could have come up with someone better."[23]

Bragman carefully sculpted each element of the process—hand selecting Chris Connelly at *ESPN* for the first TV interview, John Branch at the *New York Times* for the print story, and Zeigler at *Outsports* for the process story. They had planned to have Sam come out after Pro Day, so scouts could judge him purely on his merit before getting the extra information about who he was, but enough people knew what was going to happen that Sam was in danger of being outed by someone else. He wanted to be the one to tell the world about his story, so they moved the coming-out interviews up to February, and Michael Sam came out to the world four months before the NFL draft.

The idea was to come out once and then turn attention back to football. They wanted to limit the perception that this would be a distraction—something they were never able to achieve. An anonymous NFL assistant coach told *Sports Illustrated* that his team wouldn't draft Michael Sam because "there's nothing more sensitive than the heartbeat of the locker room. If you knowingly bring someone in there with that sexual orientation, how are the other guys going to deal with it? It's going to be a big distraction. That's the reality. It shouldn't be, but it will be."[24]

The 2014 NFL draft entered the seventh and last round, and still there was no Michael Sam. Prior to coming out, he was slated to be a third rounder, but now scouts said he was a "tweener," meaning he was too small to play defensive end and too inexperienced to play outside linebacker. This could have been true or could have been convenient cover for teams that didn't want to draft him for other reasons. LGBTQ sports fans and fans of equality still eagerly awaited his name to be called as the first openly gay player to be drafted into the NFL. The draft was nearing the end, and it looked like history would have to wait. Then at pick 249—the penultimate pick—the St. Louis Rams selected Michael Sam. Rams coach Jeff Fisher said he was proud to be a part of history as he noted that the Rams were also the first football team to sign a black player—Kenny Washington—a year before Jackie Robinson signed his Dodgers contract.

When Michael's name was called, the ESPN camera cut to his NFL draft party, where he enthusiastically kissed his boyfriend after hearing the news. It felt like we had made it. This is what equality was supposed to look like—a professional athlete being able to do his job and live as his authentic self at the same time. Michael Sam seemed to check all of the boxes that media and fans were craving for "the gay Jackie Robinson." He was coming out before entering professional sports, was going to be able to hold his own on the field, was tough and smart, and seemed to be built for this, the same way Robinson was so many years before.

He wasn't.

In many ways the Michael Sam story shows us what would have happened if Branch Rickey and Jackie Robinson would have been unsuccessful in breaking the color barrier. If Jackie had punched Pee Wee Reese or just quit because it was all too much to handle, the league's integration efforts would have been hindered measurably.

After the draft and the kiss, the Michael Sam story gradually trended toward ruin. Sports media had been salivating for a story like this for years—they covered his every move. Rams players were asked about him constantly, and any efforts to limit the distraction to the team completely failed. Sam didn't help things. Four days after being drafted, the Oprah Winfrey Network (OWN) announced a Michael Sam reality show, not exactly the move of someone who wanted to avoid media distractions. The show never happened, but the damage had already been done. Ultimately, Sam was cut from the Rams and picked up by the Dallas Cowboys practice squad. He was cut from the Cowboys a few months later and never played in an NFL regular season game.

The fallout continued to get worse, with rumors that the NFL pressured the Rams to draft Sam and the Cowboys to put him on their practice squad. Both accusations have been firmly denied by the teams and people involved, but the narrative continues. Sam then went on *Dancing with the Stars* and played in Canada before leaving in the middle of the season for personal reasons. If Sam hadn't come out before the draft, who knows if he would have been drafted earlier, made a team, and had an NFL career. We don't know what would have happened, but one thing is clear—the Michael Sam story sent a message to every closeted professional athlete that it is not worth it to come out. Part of the legacy of Jackie Robinson is that his barrier breaking was done in a way that allowed others to follow. Sam was handled in a way that pushed athletes farther into the closet.

I've never encountered anything that Jackie Robinson said on the record about LGBTQ people or issues. He spent his adult life fighting for racial equality and social justice, so I'd like to think that he would have been a firm ally of LGBTQ equality as well. Sure, part of his legacy in the LGBTQ community is that he set an unrealistic standard of excellence, but the bigger part of his legacy, for LGBTQ folks and everyone else, is that no space should be off limits because of who you are. Sports are supposed to be the ultimate meritocracy, where if you can play and contribute, nothing else matters. We have seen time and time again that barriers are still put up in the face of this meritocracy, but Jackie showed us all that the walls can eventually be brought down. All we want is for young queer and trans athletes to know that they don't need to divide themselves up in order to be themselves and have the career they desire. They can live an authentic life and still be out on the field. They can have a career in pro sports and get married and have children. No space should be out of reach because of who you are—that is what Jackie Robinson taught us.

AFTERWORD

The Legacy of Perfection

KEVIN MERIDA

During my forty years as a journalist, the last ten as a senior editor and executive, I have often marveled at just how extraordinary Jackie Robinson had to be. His example has inspired me, through the years, to challenge and chide my own industry to be better. As in: Stop hiding behind the excuse of dearth or lack of experience when it comes to hiring and promoting black talent. "The problem is everybody's looking for a Jackie Robinson," I've periodically suggested to media leaders. "By the time he becomes Jackie Robinson, you won't be able to get him. Everybody will want him."

The ideal of Jackie Robinson's perfection, the notion that he was a black unicorn specially manufactured for success, is etched into American history and American mythology. To be Jackie Robinson—in any field—is to not just be "the first" but to be a superhero, extra mortal, so phenomenal that you can't fail. This definition of black excellence—Jackie Robinson!—has amazingly and distressingly become the American norm. In his thoughtful essay in this volume, Adam Amel Rogers notes that Robinson's historic accomplishment of breaking baseball's color barrier is now commonly attached to any trailblazer in the LGBTQ community: "the gay Jackie Robinson."

It is a measure of pride that a black man is a stand-in for American exceptionalism. That is a legacy worthy of stadium-size standing ovations. But it comes with a cost. There seems to be an unwritten expectation in the country that running a *Fortune* 500 corporation or even a Hollywood writers room demands a remarkableness that black men don't have—unless you're lucky enough to be "Jackie Robinson."

The question is often raised, during Jackie Robinson Day observances and other moments of celebration, where do we go from here? It's a complicated question. Because of course we need more giants like Jackie Robinson, but also fewer. We need to normalize black success in the most segregated, exclusive corners of the job market, and to also not overweigh black failure.

To be the actual Jackie Robinson required enduring death threats, pitches thrown at your head, spikes to your legs, racist crowd taunts, the unrelenting oppression of segregation, isolation from fellow players . . . just to be acknowledged as one of the greatest players in the history of the sport. Rookie of the Year, and two years later the National League MVP and batting champ amid all of that racist nonsense? C'mon.

Not even Jackie Robinson subscribed to this magical construction of Jackie Robinson. And by the way, he did not believe in celebrating incremental progress. Once at an exhibition game, as Howard Bryant writes in his powerful essay about ownership, Robinson implored black fans to stop cheering because they had been permitted to sit in the grandstand instead of the usual "colored seats" in the bleachers. "Don't cheer, goddammit. Don't cheer. You're only getting what's yours!"

Were he alive today, Jack would invariably be disappointed in how white the entire decision-making infrastructure of sports remains—from the ownership and management of teams to the running of leagues and the executive ranks of sports media, and on and on. When Robinson retired in 1957, the year I was born, there were no black managers in Major League Baseball. As of this writing there was one: Dave Roberts, the skipper of the Los Angeles Dodgers.

On the eve of his death in 1972, Robinson had desperately wanted to see a black manager in the league he had pried open. He spoke out about his desire before game 2 of the World Series that year, just nine days before he suffered a fatal heart attack. "It is a shame baseball does not have a black manager," he said.[1] It didn't happen until two years after his death, when Frank Robinson was named to manage the Cleveland Indians. In 2018, the platform I oversee, *The Undefeated*, in collaboration with ESPN's Stats and Information Group, published a story based on the results of a four-month examination of this subject. Since Robinson's death in 1972, according to our research, there had been 469 managerial openings, with black men filling just 26 of those jobs.

What Jackie surely would've been impressed by is this generation of black professional athletes who are challenging convention, exerting their power, and carving out identities beyond their ability to steal bases or record triple-doubles. It's not a panacea, for sure. And it's not everyone. But kids growing up today see a growing number of athletes who are comfortable in their skin, unafraid to speak their mind or even protest for causes they believe in—LeBron James, Kristi Toliver, Adam Jones, Malcolm Jenkins, to name a few. Increasingly, it seems, athletes are using their influence to help better the communities they come from, and tackling issues as diverse as education, gender pay inequity, police abuse, mass incarceration, immigration, and even who should occupy the Oval Office.

While Robinson was not viewed as a militant in his day—he and Malcolm X engaged in a running feud after Robinson's playing days were over—he did believe in empowerment. His impatience with the speed of change aligned him with Malcolm in some ways.

"I disagreed with Malcolm vigorously in many areas during his earlier days," Robinson once observed, "but I certainly agreed with him when he said, 'Don't tell me about progress the black man has made. You don't stick a knife 10 inches in my back, pull it out three or four, then tell me I'm making progress.'"[2]

Some years ago, in a conversation with my colleague from *The Undefeated*, the legendary columnist Bill Rhoden, Rachel Robinson spoke of how dispirited her husband had become over all the sacrifices he had made for such limited advancements. He wondered, had it been worth it?

"He was so discouraged at the end of his life that change would not take place," she told Rhoden, "that it would not be permanent, that it would not be expansive."[3]

I believe Jackie Robinson deserves every statue that anybody wants to build for him. He is worthy of more schools and streets being named after him, more scholarships, more awards. Colleges should continue to fashion programs and lecture series to explore his legacy, and grade school children should be introduced to his story. Undoubtedly, more books will be written about number 42.

But if we want to go somewhere from here, let's change the way we think about black achievement and qualification. Jackie Robinson deserves to be remembered and assessed as the courageous, complex man he was. And not as a character from the Marvel Cinematic Universe.

ACKNOWLEDGMENTS

The contributors to this volume—Ken Burns, Sarah Burns, David McMahon, Howard Bryant, Randal Maurice Jelks, George Vecsey, Jonathan Eig, Mark Kurlansky, Chris Lamb, David Naze, Sridhar Pappu, Gerald Early, Yohuru Williams, Peter Dreier, Amira Rose Davis, Adam Amel Rogers, and Kevin Merida—deserve the deepest gratitude I can offer. They are all top-rated professionals with extraordinary demands on their busy schedules, and their willingness to make the time and expend the energy to contribute to this book testifies to their high esteem for Jackie Robinson. I could not be more pleased than I am to be part of this team.

I've dedicated our book to Rachel Robinson. Although she has not played a direct role in its writing or production, this book is possible only because of the remarkable generosity that she has shown in sharing her husband with us through the years. Jackie recognized that his legacy and Rachel's were inextricable, and those of us who study the Robinsons know that nothing about them could be truer. My hope is that a biography of Rachel will soon appear and that it will include a significant section on the legacy she has created through the Jackie Robinson Foundation and the Jackie Robinson Museum.

My gratitude also extends to the following individuals and institutions: my dear friend Sharon Herr, a grammarian with the eyes of an eagle; the National Baseball Hall of Fame Library and Museum;

the Jackie Robinson Foundation; the Manuscripts Division of the Library of Congress; New York University Press, especially editor Eric Zinner and editorial assistant Dolma Ombadykow; Lisha Nadkarni, formerly of New York University Press; and my wonderful family, Jackson, Nathaniel, and Karin.

And, of course, hats off to number 42—Jackie Robinson.

NOTES

Foreword

1 *Jackie Robinson*, episode 2, directed by Ken Burns, Sarah Burns, and David McMahon, produced by Florentine Films and WETA in Washington, DC, in association with Major League Baseball, 2016.

2 Ibid.

3 Bill Keefe, "Enemy of His Race," *New Orleans Times-Picayune*, July 18, 1956.

4 *Jackie Robinson*, episode 1, directed by Ken Burns, Sarah Burns, and David McMahon, produced by Florentine Films and WETA in Washington, DC, in association with Major League Baseball, 2016.

5 "Civil Rights Forces Lead Anti-Goldwater Demonstration in San Francisco," ABC News VideoSource, July 12, 1964.

Introduction

1 Jackie Robinson as told to Alfred Duckett, *I Never Had It Made: An Autobiography of Jackie Robinson* (1972; repr., New York: Ecco, 1995), 268.

2 Ibid., xxiv.

3 Jon Nordheimer, "Flag on July 4: Thrill to Some, Threat to Others," *New York Times*, July 4, 1969.

4 Steve Zeitchik, "Jackie Robinson's Widow Says '42' Hits Home," *Los Angeles Times*, April 5, 2013.

5 *Jackie Robinson*, episode 1, directed by Ken Burns, Sarah Burns, and David McMahon, produced by Florentine Films and WETA in Washington, DC, in association with Major League Baseball, 2016.

6 "Robinson's Legacy Examined," *Gainesville Sun*, April 4, 1997.

7 Robinson, *I Never Had It Made*, 269.

1. The Owner

1 Quoted in Jules Tygiel, *Baseball's Great Experiment: Jackie Robinson and His Legacy* (New York: Oxford University Press, 1997), 318.

2 Jackie Robinson as told to Alfred Duckett, *I Never Had It Made: An Autobiography of Jackie Robinson* (1972; repr., New York: Ecco, 1995), xxiv.

2. A Methodist Life

1 Charles Henry Phillips, *The History of the Colored Methodist Episcopal Church in America: Comprising Its Organization, Subsequent Development and Present Status*, 3rd ed. (Jackson, TN: Publishing House C.M.E. Church, 1925), 520, http://docsouth.unc.edu.; and "Negro Bishop to Speak of Africa," *Pasadena Star*, June 29, 1914.

2 Ann Scheid Lund, *Historic Pasadena: An Illustrated History* (San Antonio, TX: Historical Publishing Network, 2014), 49; J. W. Wood, *Pasadena, California: Historical and Personal* (Self-published, 1917), 325; and Arnold Rampersad, *Jackie Robinson: A Biography* (New York: Knopf, 1997), 21.

3 For a wider explanation of the social currents of the area, see Marne L. Campbell's *Making Black Los Angeles: Class, Gender, and Community, 1850–1917* (Chapel Hill: University of North Carolina Press, 2016).

4 Rampersad, *Jackie Robinson*, 25.

5 Michael G. Long and Chris Lamb, *Jackie Robinson: A Spiritual Biography* (Louisville, KY: Westminster John Knox, 2017).

6 For a critical evaluation of this preaching, see E. P. Thompson, *The Making of the English Working Class* (New York: Vintage, 1966).

7 "Methodist Church," http://bbc.co.uk, July 12, 2011.

8 Richard Watson, *The Religious Instruction of the Slaves in the West-India Colonies Advocated and Defended: A Sermon Preached before the Wesleyan Methodist Missionary Society*, 3rd ed. (London: Joseph Butterworth and Son, 1825), http://archive.org. See also Katharine Gerbner, *Christian Slavery: Conversion and Race in the Protestant Atlantic World* (Philadelphia: University of Pennsylvania Press, 2018).

9 James T. Campbell, *Songs of Zion: The African Methodist Episcopal Church in the United States and Africa*, rev. ed. (Chapel Hill: University of North Carolina Press, 1998).

10 Richard Allen, *The Life, Experience, and Gospel Labours of the Rt. Rev. Richard Allen* (Philadelphia: Martin & Boden, 1853), http://docsouth.unc.edu.

11 Janet Duitsman Cornelius, *Slave Missions and the Black Church in the Antebellum South* (Columbia: University of South Carolina Press, 1999); Albert J. Raboteau, *Slave Religion: The "Invisible Institution" in the Antebellum South* (New York: Oxford University Press, 2004).

12 Donald G. Mathews, *Slavery and Methodism: A Chapter in American Morality, 1780–1945* (Princeton: Princeton University Press, 1965).

13 E. Franklin Frazier, *The Negro Family in the United States* (Chicago: University of Chicago Press, 1939).

14 See Angela Gutting-Hornsby, *Black Manhood and Community Building in North Carolina, 1900–1932* (Gainesville: University of Florida Press, 2009).

15 Rampersad, *Jackie Robinson*, 52–53.

16 See Ralph Luker, *The Social Gospel in Black and White: American Racial Reform, 1885–1912* (Chapel Hill: University of North Carolina Press, 1998); and Randal Maurice Jelks, *Benjamin Elijah Mays, Schoolmaster of the Movement: A Biography* (Chapel Hill: University of North Carolina Press, 2012).

17 "Karl Everette Downs," http://findagrave.com.

18 Rampersad, *Jackie Robinson*, 53.

19 Richard S. Newman, *Freedom's Prophet: Bishop Richard Allen, the AME Church, and the Black Founding Fathers* (New York: New York University Press, 2009).

20 Daniel A. Payne, *Recollections of Seventy Years* (Nashville, TN: Publishing House of the A.M.E. Sunday School Union, 1888), http://docsouth.unc.edu; and Daniel A. Payne, *History of the African Methodist Episcopal Church* (Nashville, TN: Publishing House of the A.M.E. Sunday School Union, 1891), http://docsouth.unc.edu.

21 W. E. B. Du Bois, *The Negro Church* (Atlanta: Atlanta University Press, 1903), 123–31, http://docsouth.unc.edu.

22 "S. 53—Curt Flood Act of 1998," http://congress.gov.

23 The best discussion of Robinson's Republican politics is in Leah Wright Rigueur, *The Loneliness of the Black Republican: Pragmatic Politics and the Pursuit of Power* (Princeton: Princeton University Press, 2015).

24 Long and Lamb, *Jackie Robinson*, 34.

4. Telling It the Right Way

1 Rachel Robinson, interviewed by Jonathan Eig, September 2005. Subsequent quotations from Rachel Robinson are also drawn from this interview.

2 Jonathan Eig, *Opening Day: The Story of Jackie Robinson's First Season* (New York: Simon & Schuster, 2007), 77.

3 Martin Luther King Jr., "I Have Been to the Mountaintop" (Memphis, TN, April 3, 1968), http://kinginstitute.stanford.edu.

4 "Jackie Helps Dodgers Near Record Gate," *Pittsburgh Courier*, May 31, 1947.

5. A Champion of Nonviolence?

1 George Orwell, "Reflections on Gandhi," *Partisan Review*, January 1949, 85.

2 *Mahatma Gandhi: The Essential Writings*, ed. Judith M. Brown (New York: Oxford University Press, 2008), 61.

3 David Halberstam, "History's Man," in *Jackie Robinson: Between the Baselines*, ed. Dick Johnson and Glenn Stout (San Francisco: Woodford Press, 1997), 63.

4 Jackie Robinson as told to Alfred Duckett, *I Never Had It Made: An Autobiography of Jackie Robinson* (1972; repr., New York: Ecco Press, 1995), 28.

5 Ibid., 34.

6 Martin Luther King Jr., "Hall of Famer," *New York Amsterdam News*, August 4, 1963.

7 Quoted in Arnold Rampersad, *Jackie Robinson: A Biography* (New York: Knopf, 1997), 107.

8 Ibid., 177.

9 Giovanni Papini, *The Life of Jesus*, trans. Dorothy Canfield Fisher (New York: Harcourt Brace, 1923), 90.

10 Ibid., 104.

11 Ibid., 107.

12 Quoted in James R. Devine, "The Past as Moral Guide to the Present: The Parallel between Martin Luther King, Jr.'s Elements of a Nonviolent Civil Rights Campaign and Jackie Robinson's Entry into the Brooklyn Dodgers," *Jeffrey S. Moorad Sports Law Journal* 3, no. 2 (1996): 70, http://digitalcommons.law.villanova.edu.

13 Robinson, *I Never Had It Made*, 33.

14 Ibid., xxiii.

15 Ibid., 58.

16 Martin Luther King Jr., "Loving Your Enemies" (sermon, Detroit Council of Churches' Noon Lenten Services, March 7, 1961), http://kinginstitute. stanford.edu.

17 Robinson, *I Never Had It Made*, 60.

18 Ibid., 211.

19 Jackie Robinson, "Home Plate," *New York Amsterdam News*, July 13, 1963; Michael G. Long, ed., *Beyond Home Plate: Jackie Robinson on Life after Baseball* (New York: Syracuse University Press, 2013), 83.

20 Robinson, *I Never Had It Made*, 78.

21 Quoted in Maury Allen, *Jackie Robinson: A Life Remembered* (New York: Franklin Watts, 1987), 64.

22 Robinson, *I Never Had It Made*, 265.

23 Quoted in ibid., 143.

24 Quoted in Matt Welch, "When Jackie Robinson Fought Back," *Reason*, July 2013, http://reason.com.

25 Jackie Robinson, "Jackie Robinson," *New York Post*, April 25, 1960; Long, *Beyond Home Plate*, 71.

26 Jackie Robinson, "Home Plate," *New York Amsterdam News*, July 13, 1963; Long, *Beyond Home Plate*, 83.

27 Jackie Robinson letter to Barry Goldwater, n.d. [August 1964], Jackie Robinson Papers, box 5, folder 20, Library of Congress, Washington, DC; Michael G. Long, ed., *First Class Citizenship: The Civil Rights Letters of Jackie Robinson* (New York: Times Books, 2007), 199.

28 Jackie Robinson, column, *Chicago Defender*, March 1965, quoted in Justin Tinsley, "Jackie Robinson vs. Malcolm X," *TheUndefeated.com*, May 25, 2016.

29 Jackie Robinson, *Baseball Has Done It* (New York: Lippincott, 1964), 22.

30 Jackie Robinson, "Home Plate," *New York Amsterdam News*, May 5, 1962; Long, *First Class Citizenship*, 145.

6. The White Media Missed It

1 *New York Times*, October 24, 1945; Chris Lamb, *Blackout: The Untold Story of Jackie Robinson's First Spring Training* (Lincoln: University of Nebraska Press, 2004), 43.

2 *Sporting News*, November 1, 1945; Lamb, *Blackout*, 43.

3 *New York Times*, October 24, 1945; Lamb, *Blackout*, 44.

4 *Charleston News and Courier*, October 25, 1945; Lamb, *Blackout*, 46.

5 Lamb, *Blackout*, 44.

6 Jules Tygiel, *Baseball's Great Experiment: Jackie Robinson and His Legacy* (New York: Oxford University Press, 1997).

7 Tim Cohane, "A Branch Grows in Brooklyn," *Look*, March 19, 1946, 72.

8 Tygiel, *Baseball's Great Experiment*, 46; Chris Lamb, *Conspiracy of Silence: Sportswriters and the Long Campaign to Desegregate Baseball* (Lincoln: University of Nebraska Press, 2012), 60–61.

9 Lamb, *Conspiracy of Silence*, 23; Shirley Povich, interview by the author, July 8, 1996.

10 Lamb, *Conspiracy of Silence*, 3.

11 *New York World-Telegram*, February 6, 1933; Lamb, *Conspiracy of Silence*, 4.

12 *New York Daily News*, February 8, 1933; Lamb, *Conspiracy of Silence*, 5–8.

13 Chris Lamb and Glen Bleske, "Democracy on the Field: The Black Press Takes on White Baseball," *Journalism History* 24, no. 2 (Summer 1998): 51–59; Chris Lamb, ed., *From Jack Johnson to LeBron James: Sports, Media, and the Color Line* (Lincoln: University of Nebraska Press, 2016), 163; Lamb, *Conspiracy of Silence*, 18.

14 Lamb, *Conspiracy of Silence*, 133–55.

15 Ibid., 21, 89, 105.

16 Ibid., 93.

17 Ibid., 86–87, 95–96.

18 Ibid., 199–201, 203–4.

19 Ibid., 244–45.

20 Lee Lowenfish, *Branch Rickey: Baseball's Ferocious Gentleman* (Lincoln: University of Nebraska Press, 2009), 359; Lamb, *Conspiracy of Silence*, 244.

21 Tygiel, *Baseball's Great Experiment*, 44; Lamb, *Conspiracy of Silence*, 249–65.

22 Lamb, *Conspiracy of Silence*, 279.

23 *Chicago Defender*, November 3, 1945; *New York Amsterdam News*, November 10, 1945; *Sporting News*, November 1, 1945; Lamb, *Conspiracy of Silence*, 290–91.

24 *Pittsburgh Courier*, November 3, 1945; *Baltimore Afro-American*, November 10, 1945; *Daily Worker*, October 26, 1945; Lamb, *Conspiracy of Silence*, 290–91.

25 William Simons, "Jackie Robinson and the American Zeitgeist," in *Cooperstown Symposium on Baseball and American Culture*, ed. Peter Rutkoff (Jefferson, NC: McFarland, 2000), 79–80; Lamb, *Conspiracy of Silence*, 288.

26 Simons, "Jackie Robinson and the American Zeitgeist," 85; Lamb, *Conspiracy of Silence*, 286.

27 *Sporting News*, November 1, 1945; Lamb, *Conspiracy of Silence*, 296–97.

28 Simons, "Jackie Robinson and the American Zeitgeist," 94.

29 Ira Berkow, *Red: A Biography of Red Smith* (New York: Times Books, 1986), 109.

30 *New York Times*, February 4, 1946; Lamb, *Conspiracy of Silence*, 307–8.

31 *Pittsburgh Courier*, February 23, 1946; Murray Polmer, *Branch Rickey: A Biography* (New York: Signet, 1982), 186; Lamb, *Conspiracy of Silence*, 308–9.

32 Lamb, *Blackout*, 68–69; Lamb, *Conspiracy of Silence*, 309–10.

33 *New York Times*, March 5, 1946; Lamb, *Blackout*, 85–86.

34 Jackie Robinson as told to Alfred Duckett, *I Never Had It Made: An Autobiography of Jackie Robinson* (New York: Fawcett, Crest, 1974), 43.

35 Wendell Smith, untitled article, Wendell Smith Papers, National Baseball Hall of Fame, Cooperstown, NY.

36 Lamb, *Blackout*, 151–53.

37 Ibid., 135–42, 154–56.

38 William Simons, "Jackie Robinson and the American Mind: Journalistic Perceptions of the Reintegration of Baseball," *Journal of Sport History* 12, no. 1 (Spring 1985): 40.

39 Jonathan Eig, *Opening Day: The Story of Jackie Robinson's First Season* (New York: Simon & Schuster, 2007), 211.

40 Berkow, *Red*, 109.

41 Quoted in Lamb, *Conspiracy of Silence*, 199–201, 203–4.

42 Eig, *Opening Day*, 275.

7. On Retiring 42

1 Bob Nightengale, "Here's to You, Jackie: No. 42 Retired," *Los Angeles Times*, April 16, 1997.

2 Dayn Perry, "Mariano Rivera Reflects on Being the Final Baseball Hall of Fame Member to Wear Jackie Robinson's No. 42," *CBSSports.com*, January 22, 2019.

3 Jayson Stark, "An Oral History of the Night Baseball Stopped to Retire No. 42 Forever," *ESPN.com*, April 14, 2017.

4 Ibid.

5 Quoted in Arnold Rampersad, *Jackie Robinson: A Biography* (New York: Knopf, 1997), 459.

6 Hank Aaron, "When Baseball Mattered," *New York Times*, April 13, 1997.

7 Ross Newhan, "On Baseball: This Problem Is More Than Skin Deep," *Los Angeles Times*, April 25, 2004.

8 John Shea, "Big Leagues a Black Hole for African Americans," *San Francisco Chronicle*, April 18, 2004.

9 Terence Moore, "Where Are Braves' Black Americans?," *Atlanta Journal and Constitution*, April 15, 2004.

10 Cal Fussman, *After Jackie: Pride, Prejudice, and Baseball's Forgotten Heroes: An Oral History* (New York: ESPN Books, 2007), xi.

11 Ibid., 232.

12 Jeff Snider, "It's Time to Un-retire the Numbers," *Baseballessential.com*, May 14, 2015.

13 Ibid.

8. Before the World Failed Him

1 Arnold Rampersad, *Jackie Robinson: A Biography* (New York: Knopf, 1997), 431.

2 *Jackie Robinson*, episode 2, directed by Ken Burns, Sarah Burns, and David McMahon, produced by Florentine Films and WETA in Washington, DC, in association with Major League Baseball, 2016.

3 David Falkner, *Great Time Coming: The Life of Jackie Robinson from Baseball to Birmingham* (New York: Simon & Schuster, 1995), 253.

4 Rampersad, *Jackie Robinson*, 317.

5 Jackie Robinson, "Wilkins, Make Way for the Young Turks!," *New York Amsterdam News*, January 4, 1957.

6 Martin Luther King, Jr. "Address to the Southern Christian Leadership Conference Hall of Fame Dinner in Honor of Jackie Robinson," July 20, 1962, Jackie Robinson Papers, box 2, folder 7, Library of Congress, Washington, DC.

7 Quoted in Jackie Robinson, "Home Plate," *New York Amsterdam News*, November 30, 1963; Michael G. Long, ed., *First Class Citizenship: The Civil Rights Letters of Jackie Robinson* (New York: Times Books, 2007), 184.

8 *Jackie Robinson*, episode 2.

9 Ibid.

10 Jackie Robinson as told to Alfred Duckett, *I Never Had It Made: An Autobiography of Jackie Robinson* (1972; repr., New York: Ecco, 1995), 83.

11 Martin Luther King, Jr., "Beyond Vietnam" (speech, Riverside Baptist Church, New York, April 4, 1967), http://kinginstitute.stanford.edu.

12 Jackie Robinson, "Martin Luther King, Jr., Is Still My Leader," *New York Amsterdam News*, July 1, 1967.

13 *Jackie Robinson*, episode 2.

14 Bob Sales, "Robinson Renews Yawkey Bigot Rap," *Boston Globe*, October 25, 1967.

15 Rachel Robinson, interview by the author, January 26, 2012.

16 Jackie Robinson, "Mixed Emotions over Boycott of Olympics," *New York Amsterdam News*, December 16, 1967.

17 Lou House, *Black Journal*, episode 20, National Educational Television, New York, January 1970.

18 Long, *First Class Citizenship*, 184.

19 Robinson, *I Never Had It Made*, 83, 303.

20 Rachel Robinson, interview by the author, January 26, 2012.

9. The Dilemma of the Black Republican

1 Dewey W. Grantham Jr., "The Progressive Movement and the Negro," *South Atlantic Quarterly* 54 (1955): 465.

2 Donald J. Lisio, *Hoover, Blacks, & Lily-Whites: A Study of Southern Strategies* (Chapel Hill: University of North Carolina Press, 1985), 272.

3 Timothy N. Thurber, *Republicans and Race: The GOP's Frayed Relationship with African Americans, 1945–1974* (Lawrence: University Press of Kansas, 2013), 5.

4 Arnold Rampersad, *Jackie Robinson: A Biography* (New York: Knopf, 1997), 341.

5 Joan Hoff, *Nixon Reconsidered* (New York: Basic Books, 1994), 97.

10. "I've Got to Be Me"

1 Jackie Robinson quoted in David Falkner, *Great Time Coming: The Life of Jackie Robinson from Baseball to Birmingham* (New York: Simon & Schuster, 1995), 315.

2 Jackie Robinson, "An Open Letter to a Friend," *New York Amsterdam News*, March 30, 1963.

3 Malcolm X, letter to Jackie Robinson, *New York Amsterdam News*, November 30, 1963.

4 St. Clair Drake and Horace R. Cayton, *Black Metropolis: A Study of Negro Life in a Northern City* (1945; repr., Chicago: University of Chicago Press, 1993), 390.

5 W. E. B. Du Bois, *The Souls of Black Folk* (New York: Dover, 1903), 2–3.

6 Jackie Robinson as told to Alfred Duckett, *I Never Had It Made: An Autobiography of Jackie Robinson* (1972; repr., New York: Ecco, 2003), 168.

7 Peniel E. Joseph, "The Black Power Movement: A State of the Field," *Journal of American History* 96, no. 3 (December 2009): 753.

8 Murray Olderman, "What Makes Brown Negro Spokesman?," *Akron Beacon Journal*, September 29, 1964, 21.

9 Barack Obama, *The Audacity of Hope: Thoughts on Reclaiming the American Dream* (New York: Crown, 2006), 11.

10 Rachel Robinson quoted in Gary Libman, "Carrying On: Rachel Robinson Never Stops Hurting," *Tennessean*, July 6, 1975, 147.

11 "A Tribute to Jackie Robinson," John F. Kennedy Presidential Library, October 16, 2007, http://jfklibrary.org.

12 Ibid.

13 Rachel Robinson quoted in Libman, "Carrying On."

14 "Jackie Robinson: Man of the Year," *Hartford Courant*, October 24, 1964, 12.

15 Dick Gregory quoted in "Jackie Robinson Day," *Montreal Gazette*, September 10, 1966, 7.

16 Ibid., 7.

17 "Mixed Emotions over Boycott of Olympics," *Pittsburgh Courier*, December 16, 1967, 7.

18 Claire Smith, "A Grand Tribute to Robinson and His Moment," *New York Times*, April 16, 1997.

11. The First Famous Jock for Justice

1 Sean Gregory, "'You Have to Take a Stand': Soccer Phenom Alex Morgan Wants the Respect—and Money—Female Players Deserve," *Time*, May 23, 2019.

2 The criticism must have stung. Six years later he contributed $2,000 to Gantt's second unsuccessful effort to unseat Helms. And in 2000, like many NBA players, he publicly supported former New York Knicks star Bill Bradley's campaign for president. He later contributed $10,000 to Barack Obama's campaign for the U.S. Senate seat from Illinois. But labor activists tried and failed to enlist Jordan in their crusade to improve the sweatshop conditions in Nike's overseas factories.

3 L. Jon Wertheim, "The Ad That Launched a Thousand Hits. Tiger Woods Came under Fire for Failing to Take a Stand on Augusta National. After All, Hadn't He Volunteered for the Job?," *Sports Illustrated*, April 14, 2003.

4 Peter Dreier and Kelly Candaele, "Where Are the Jocks for Justice?," *Nation*, June 28, 2004.

5 Jonah Bromwich, "'To Me, It Was Racist': N.B.A. Players Respond to Laura Ingraham's Comments on LeBron James," *New York Times*, February 16, 2018.

6 There have been exceptions to this trend. The most obvious is Bill Veeck, who at different times owned the Indians (1946–49), the St. Louis Browns (1951–53), and the Chicago White Sox (1959–61 and 1975–81). In 1942, Veeck tried to buy the bankrupt Philadelphia Phillies so he could stock the team entirely with black ballplayers. When Commissioner Landis learned of his plans, he made sure another buyer got the Phillies. In the early

1950s, Veeck outraged the other owners by proposing the "socialistic" idea of sharing television revenue. Veeck's revenue-sharing idea eventually took hold in the 1990s, helping small-market teams remain competitive with bigger clubs and their lucrative television contracts. Veeck idolized Norman Thomas, the Socialist Party leader who ran for president six times (and for whom Veeck voted several times). Because of his radical views, Veeck's enemies kept him out of the Hall of Fame until 1991, five years after his death.

7 Brian Carroll, "'Jackie Robinson Says': Robinson's Surprising, Lengthy, and Multifaceted Career in Journalism," in *The Cooperstown Symposium on Baseball and American Culture 2017–2018*, ed. William Simons (Jefferson, NC: McFarland, 2019).

8 Arnold Rampersad, *Jackie Robinson: A Biography* (New York: Knopf, 1997), 91. See also Jules Tygiel, *Baseball's Great Experiment: Jackie Robinson and His Legacy* (New York: Oxford University Press, 1983), 61–62.

9 Jackie Robinson, *Baseball Has Done It* (Philadelphia: Lippincott, 1964).

10 Tygiel, *Baseball's Great Experiment*; Rampersad, *Jackie Robinson*; Chris Lamb, *Conspiracy of Silence: Sportswriters and the Long Campaign to Desegregate Baseball* (Lincoln: University of Nebraska Press, 2012); Irwin Silber, *Press Box Red: The Story of Lester Rodney, the Communist Who Helped Break the Color Line in American Sports* (Philadelphia: Temple University Press, 2003); Lee Lowenfish, *Branch Rickey: Baseball's Ferocious Gentleman* (Lincoln: University of Nebraska Press, 2009); Kelly Rusinack, "Baseball on the Radical Agenda: The Daily Worker and Sunday Worker Journalistic Campaign to Desegregate Major League Baseball, 1933–1947," in *Jackie Robinson: Race, Sports, and the American Dream*, ed. Joseph Dorinson and Joram Warmund (Armonk, NY: M.E. Sharpe, 1998); David K. Wiggins, "Wendell Smith, the *Pittsburgh Courier-Journal* and the Campaign to Include Blacks in Organized Baseball, 1933–1945," *Journal of Sport History* 10, no. 2 (Summer 1983): 5–29; Henry Fetter, "The Party Line and the Color Line: The American Communist Party, the 'Daily Worker,' and Jackie Robinson," *Journal of Sport History* 28, no. 3 (Fall 2001): 375–402.

11 Had Robinson lost his case and been dishonorably discharged, Rickey would certainly not have picked him to break Major League Baseball's color line.

12 Rampersad, *Jackie Robinson*, 172.

13 Tygiel, *Baseball's Great Experiment*, 188.

14 In 1947 and 1948, only one award was given. After that, each league had its own Rookie of the Year award.

15 This account of Robinson's congressional testimony draws on the following sources: Rampersad, *Jackie Robinson*; Martin Duberman, *Paul Robeson* (New York: Knopf, 1989); Howard Bryant, *The Heritage: Black*

Athletes, a Divided America, and the Politics of Patriotism (Boston: Beacon, 2018); Joseph Dorinson, "Paul Robeson and Jackie Robinson: Athletes and Activists at Armageddon," *Pennsylvania History* 66, no. 1 (Winter 1999): 16–26; Dan W. Dodson, "The Paul Robeson-Jackie Robinson Saga and a Political Collision," in *The Jackie Robinson Reader*, ed. Jules Tygiel (New York: Dutton, 1997); and Peter Dreier, "Half a Century before Colin Kaepernick, Jackie Robinson Said, 'I Cannot Stand and Sing the Anthem,'" *Nation*, July 18, 2019.

16 Born in 1898 to a former runaway slave, Robeson had starred in four sports at Rutgers, was twice named to the football All-America team, won Rutgers's oratory award four years in a row, was elected to Phi Beta Kappa, and was valedictorian of his 1919 graduating class. He played professional football to pay his tuition at Columbia University Law School but gave up practicing law to pursue a theater career. A highly successful film and stage actor, he could also sing opera, show tunes, Negro spirituals, and international songs in twenty-five languages. His concerts drew huge audiences. His recordings sold well. During World War II he entertained troops at the front and sang battle songs on the radio (Duberman, *Paul Robeson*).

17 Jackie Robinson as told to Alfred Duckett, *I Never Had It Made: An Autobiography of Jackie Robinson* (New York: Putnam, 1972).

18 The transcript of Robinson's testimony can be found at http://babel. hathitrust.org.

19 J. Christopher Schutz, *Jackie Robinson: An Integrated Life* (Lanham, MD: Rowman & Littlefield, 2016).

20 Carroll, "'Jackie Robinson Says.'"

21 Rampersad, *Jackie Robinson*, 302.

22 Ibid., 367.

23 Ibid., 344; and Schutz, *Jackie Robinson,* 120.

24 Johnny S. Moore, "Robinson Agonistes: The Curious Bromance and Breakup of Jackie Robinson and Richard Nixon," in Simons, *Cooperstown Symposium.*

25 Michael Beschloss, "Jackie Robinson and Nixon: Life and Death of a Political Friendship," *New York Times*, June 6, 2014.

26 Krishnadev Calamur, "Muhammad Ali and Vietnam," *Atlantic*, June 4, 2016.

27 Rampersad, *Jackie Robinson,* 415.

28 Tygiel, *Baseball's Great Experiment*, 341.

29 Ron Briley, "'Do Not Go Gently into That Good Night': Race, the Baseball Establishment, and the Retirements of Bob Feller and Jackie Robinson," in Dorinson and Warmund, *Jackie Robinson.*

30 Rampersad, *Jackie Robinson,* 459.

31 Robinson, *I Never Had It Made*, 268–269.

32 Ibid., 85–86.

33 Ibid., xxiv.

34 Damion L. Thomas, *Globetrotting: African American Athletes and Cold War Politics* (Urbana: University of Illinois Press, 2012).

35 Doug Merlino, "Bill Russell, Civil Rights Hero and Inventor of Airborne Basketball," *Bleacher Report*, April 29, 2011; Aram Goudsouzian, "Bill Russell and the Basketball Revolution," *American Studies* 47, nos. 3/4 (Fall/Winter 2006): 61–85.

36 Michael Wilson, "Brown: Sports Has Run Its Course," *Washington Post*, May 25, 1992.

37 Jack Davis, "Baseball's Reluctant Challenge; Desegregating Major League Spring Training Sites, 1961–64," *Journal of Sport History* 19, no. 2 (Summer 1992): 144–62.

38 Arthur Ashe, *Days of Grace: A Memoir* (New York: Knopf, 1993); Arthur Ashe, *A Hard Road to Glory: A History of the African-American Athlete* (New York: Amistad, 1993).

39 Thomas Hauser, *Muhammad Ali: His Life and Times* (New York: Simon & Schuster, 1991); David Remnick, *King of the World: Muhammad Ali and the Rise of an American Hero* (New York: Random House, 1998).

40 John Florio and Ouisie Shapiro, *One Nation under Baseball: How the 1960s Collided with the National Pastime* (Lincoln: University of Nebraska Press, 2017); Bill Shaiken, "1968: Dodgers Relent as Players Find Power to Precipitate Change," *Los Angeles Times*, July 19, 2018.

41 This account of Curt Flood draws on Brad Snyder, *A Well-Paid Slave: Curt Flood's Fight for Free Agency in Professional Sports* (New York: Viking, 2006).

42 John Carolos and Dave Zirin, *The John Carlos Story: The Sports Moment That Changed the World* (Chicago: Haymarket Books, 2011); Tommie Smith, *Silent Gesture: The Autobiography of Tommie Smith* (Philadelphia: Temple University Press, 2008).

43 Kareem Abdul-Jabbar, *Becoming Kareem: Growing Up on and off the Court* (New York: Little, Brown, 2017); Kareem Abdul-Jabbar, *Giant Steps: The Autobiography of Kareem Abdul-Jabbar* (New York: Bantam Books, 1983); John Smith, *The Sons of Westwood: John Wooden, UCLA, and the Dynasty That Changed College Basketball* (Urbana: University of Illinois Press, 2013).

44 Smith, *Sons of Westwood*.

45 Sam Farmer, "1968: Long Before Colin Kaepernick, David Meggyesy Began NFL National Anthem Protest," *Los Angeles Times*, July 18, 2018.

46 Dave Meggyesy, *Out of Their League* (New York: Paperback Library, 1971).

47 "Tom Seaver Says U.S. Should Leave Vietnam," *New York Times*, October 11, 1969.

48 Steve Travers, *The Last Icon: Tom Seaver and His Times* (Lanham, MD: Taylor Trade, 2011).

49 Jim Bouton, *Ball Four* (New York: World, 1970).

50 Christopher Lydon, "Celebrities Rally behind McGovern," *New York Times*, April 2, 1972; Jesse Bennett, *Pigskin Nation: How the NFL Remade American Politics* (Urbana: University of Illinois Press, 2018).

51 Ron Briley, "Baseball and Dissent: The Vietnam Experience," *NINE: A Journal of Baseball History and Culture* 17, no. 1 (Fall 2008): 54–69.

52 This account of Billie Jean King draws on Susan Ware, *Game, Set, Match: Billie Jean King and the Revolution in Women's Sports* (Chapel Hill: University of North Carolina Press, 2011); and Peter Dreier, "Billie Jean King and the Remarkable Success of Title IX," *Huffington Post*, June 24, 2012.

53 Dave Zirin, "Carlos Delgado on Deck," *Counterpunch*, July 9, 2004.

54 William C. Rhoden, "Delgado Makes a Stand by Taking a Seat," *New York Times*, July 21, 2004; Angel Flores-Rodriguez, "Baseball, 9/11, and Dissent: The Carlos Delgado Controversy," *OAH: Magazine of History* 25, no. 3 (2011): 55–56.

55 "Carlos Delgado: Colin Kaepernick's Actions Rooted in American Ideals," *ESPN.com*, September 26, 2016.

56 Dreier and Candaele, "Where Are the Jocks for Justice?"

57 This account of Foyle is based on Dreier and Candaele, "Where Are the Jocks for Justice?"

58 Tyler Kepner, "Off the Mound, Sean Doolittle Brings Relief to the Ostracized," *New York Times*, March 12, 2016.

59 Ted Berg, "A's Closer and Girlfriend Buying up Tickets to Team's LGBT Pride Night to Donate to LGBTQ Youth," *USA Today*, April 1, 2015.

60 whatwouldDOOdo, Twitter, January 28, 2017.

61 whatwouldDOOdo, Twitter, August 13, 2017.

62 Dylan Hernandez, "Dodgers' Adrian Gonzalez Chose Not to Stay in a Trump Hotel, but He Didn't Want It to Be News," *Los Angeles Times*, October 17, 2016.

63 Brandon McCarthy, Twitter, November 9, 2016.

64 Brandon McCarthy, Twitter, March 14, 2017.

65 Mark Saxon, "Dexter Fowler Unapologetic for Criticism of Trump's Travel Ban," *ESPN.com*, February 20, 2017.

66 Peter Dreier, "For NFL Players, Civil—and Visible—Disobedience Is the Only Option," *American Prospect*, May 29, 2018.

67 Bryan Graham, "Donald Trump Blasts NFL Anthem Protesters: 'Get That Son of a Bitch off the Field,'" *Guardian*, September 23, 2017.

68 Lindsay H. Jones, "Broncos' Brandon Marshall Calls President Trump's National Anthem Remarks 'Disgusting,'" *USA Today*, May 24, 2018.

69 Lorenzo Reyes, "Seahawks' Doug Baldwin: President Trump Is 'an Idiot, Plain and Simple,'" *USA Today*, May 24, 2018.

70 Joe Rodgers, "A's Rookie Bruce Maxwell First MLB Player to Take a Knee for the Anthem," *Sporting News*, September 25, 2017.

71 Peter Dreier and Kelly Candaele, "The Red Sox Should Not Visit the White House," *Nation*, October 30, 2018; and Michael Tackett, "Trump

Welcomes the Red Sox to the White House, but Not All of Them Are There," *New York Times*, May 9, 2019.

72 Marc Tracy and Alan Blinder, "Virginia Men's Basketball Will Not Go to the White House," *New York Times*, April 27, 2019.

73 Ali Krieger, Twitter, November 9, 2016.

74 "Hall of Fame Shut-Out: Baseball's Biggest Scandal," *Nation*, July 23, 2008.

75 Peter Dreier and Kelly Candaele, "Yankee Players Cross the Picket Line in Boston," *Nation*, October 10, 2018; and Peter Dreier and Kelly Candaele, "Are the Picket-Crossing Dodgers Cursed?," *Capital & Main*, October 26, 2018.

76 Sean Doolittle, "MLB Players Love Our Caps: The People Who Make Them for Us Deserve Fair Wages," *Washington Post*, February 28, 2019.

77 Jesse Dougherty, "Sean Doolittle on Declining White House Invite: 'I Don't Want to Hang Out with Somebody Who Talks Like That,'" *Washington Post*, November 2, 2019; and Peter Dreier, "The World Series Winners Should Not Visit the White House," *Nation*, November 1, 2019.

78 David Nakamura and Jesse Dougherty, "Nationals Embraced by Trump at White House, Where They Can't Escape Politics," *Washington Post*, November 4, 2019.

12. Supporting Black Women Athletes

1 Wilma Rudolph, *Wilma* (New York: Signet Books, 1977), 78–79.

2 Ibid., 78–79.

3 Jackie Robinson, "On Married Life," *New York Amsterdam News*, February 10, 1962.

4 Jackie Robinson, "Respect for Women," *New Journal and Guide*, May 21, 1966.

5 Quoted in Arnold Rampersad, *Jackie Robinson: A Biography* (New York: Knopf, 1997), 9, 29.

6 Quoted in ibid., 435.

7 *Our Sports*, June 1953, 9.

8 Ibid., 9.

9 Syd Pollock, press release, *Los Angeles Sentinel*, February 26, 1953; *Atlanta Daily News*, February 22, 1952.

10 For more on Stone, Morgan, and Johnson, see Amira Rose Davis, "No League of Their Own: Baseball, Black Women and the Politics of Representation," *Radical History Review* 2016, no. 125 (2016): 74–96.

11 Wendell Smith, "The Lady's Playing a Man's Game," *Pittsburgh Courier*, June 20, 1953; and Doc Young, "Should Girls Play Ball: No, Says Doc," *Chicago Defender*, August 28, 1954.

12 "Jackie Robinson and Althea Gibson Enter Golf Tourney Here," *Chicago Defender*, May 29, 1963.

13 "Althea Gibson Makes History; Joins Jackie as Trailblazer," *Philadelphia Tribune*, July 9, 1957.

14 "Portrait of a Girl with a Bat in Her Hand," *New York Amsterdam News*, November 8, 1947.

15 "Hank Aaron at Bat for Women," *Chicago Tribune*, September 25, 1977.

16 "Jackie Robinson's Daughter Steps in to Fill His Shoes," *Atlanta Daily World*, July 24, 1997.

13. The Challenges of a Gay Jackie Robinson

1 Dana Parsons, "Ellen's Gay, but Is Her Announcement Worth the Weight?," *Los Angeles Times*, April 18, 1997.

2 "Homosexual on Board Cites Role as Pioneer," *New York Times*, November 10, 1977.

3 Sarah Kaplan, "The Trials of Baseball's First Openly Gay Player, Glenn Burke, Four Decades Ago," *Washington Post*, August 17, 2015.

4 Ibid.

5 *OUT: The Glenn Burke Story*, produced by Comcast SportsNet, 2010.

6 Ron Dicker, "ESPN Actually Just Reported on Michael Sam's Showering Habits," *Huffington Post*, August 26, 2014.

7 Emma Margolin, "Major League Baseball Honors Gay Pioneer Glenn Burke," *MSNBC.com*, July 15, 2014.

8 Ibid.

9 Branch Rickey (speech, One Hundred Percent Wrong Club banquet, Atlanta, January 20, 1956), Branch Rickey Papers, Library of Congress, Washington, DC, http://loc.gov.

10 David Kopay and Perry Deane Young, *The David Kopay Story: An Extraordinary Self-Revelation* (New York: Arbor House, 1977), 8.

11 Jim Buzinski, "Moment #1: Dave Kopay Comes Out as Gay in Newspaper Interview," *Outsports*, October 4, 2011.

12 Kopay and Young, *David Kopay Story*, 6.

13 Ibid., 15.

14 Hugh Harrison, "The Cover-Up," *Newswest*, January 8, 1976.

15 Ibid.

16 Philip Nobile, "Ex-49er Is Candid—and Gay: I'm Proud of What I Am," *San Francisco Chronicle*, March 1, 1977.

17 Ibid.

18 Karlyn Bowman, "Gay Marriage and Public Opinion," *Forbes*, April 24, 2009.

19 Bill Dwyre, "Fans Not Ready for Gay Athletes," *Milwaukee Journal*, December 16, 1975.

20 Bowman, "Gay Marriage and Public Opinion."

21 L. Jon Wertheim, "Gays in Sports: A Poll," *Sports Illustrated*, April 18, 2005.

22 Edward Kian and Eric Anderson, "John Amaechi: Changing the Way Sport Reporters Examine Gay Athletes," *Journal of Homosexuality* 56, no. 7 (October 2009): 799–818.

23 Cyd Zeigler, "The Eagle Has Landed," *Outsports*, February 9, 2014.

24 Pete Thamel and Thayer Evans, "How Will News That Michael Sam Is Gay Affect NFL Draft Stock?," *Sports Illustrated*, February 9, 2014.

Afterword

1 Quoted in Rhiannon Walker, "Jackie Robinson's Last Stand: To See Blacks Break into the MLB Managerial Ranks," *TheUndefeated.com*, April 13, 2018.

2 Jackie Robinson as told to Alfred Duckett, *I Never Had It Made: An Autobiography of Jackie Robinson* (1972; repr., New York: Ecco, 1995), 76.

3 William C. Rhoden, "Baseball Has Yet to Deliver Greatest Tribute to Jackie Robinson," *New York Times*, April 14, 2016.

ABOUT THE CONTRIBUTORS

Howard Bryant is the author of nine books, including *Full Dissidence: Notes from an Uneven Playing Field*; *The Heritage: Black Athletes, a Divided America, and the Politics of Patriotism*; *The Last Hero: A Life of Henry Aaron*; and *Shut Out: A Story of Race and Baseball in Boston*. He is a former *Washington Post* reporter and is currently a senior writer for *ESPN.com* and *ESPN the Magazine*. He has also served as the sports correspondent for NPR's *Weekend Edition Saturday* since 2006. He was a finalist for the National Magazine Award in 2016 and 2018 and earned the 2016 Salute to Excellence Award from the National Association of Black Journalists. In addition, he has appeared in several documentaries, including *The Tenth Inning* and *Jackie Robinson*, both directed by Ken Burns.

Ken Burns, Sarah Burns, and **David McMahon** are the directors and producers of the film *Jackie Robinson*, a production of Florentine Films and WETA, Washington, DC, in association with Major League Baseball. Sarah Burns and David McMahon also wrote the text for the documentary.

Amira Rose Davis is Assistant Professor of History and African American Studies at Penn State University, where she specializes in twentieth-century American history with an emphasis on race, gender, sports, and politics. She is currently working on a book manuscript titled *"Can't Eat a Medal": The Lives and Labors of Black Women Athletes in the Age of Jim Crow*. Her work has appeared in scholarly journals such as *Radical History Review* and in edited collections, including the forthcoming *It's Our Movement Now: Black Women and the 1977 Women's Convention*. Additionally, she provides sports commentary and opinion writing for public venues such as NPR, ESPN, BBC, NBC, and others. She is also the cohost of the feminist sports podcast *Burn It All Down*.

Peter Dreier is the E.P. Clapp Distinguished Professor of Politics and chair of the Urban & Environmental Policy Department at Occidental College. He writes frequently for the *Nation*, *American Prospect*, the *Los Angeles Times*, and other publications. His books include *The 100 Greatest Americans of the 20th Century: A Social Justice Hall of Fame*; *Place Matters: Metropolitics for the 21st Century*; and *We Own the Future: Democratic Socialism—American Style*. His next book, *Baseball Rebels: The Reformers and Radicals Who Shook Up the Game on and off the Field*, coauthored with Robert Elias, is forthcoming.

Gerald Early is the Merle Kling Professor of Modern Letters in the African and African American Studies Department at Washington University in St. Louis, where he has taught since 1982. He is a noted essayist and American culture critic whose collections of essays include *The Culture of Bruising: Essays on Prizefighting, Literature, and Modern American Culture*, which won the 1994 National Book Critics Circle Award for Criticism; and *A Level Playing Field: African American Athletes and the Republic of Sports*. He is the author of *Daughters: On Family and Fatherhood* (1994), and he was twice nominated for Grammy Awards for writing album liner notes. Additionally, he is a prolific anthologist. He launched the *Best African American Essays 2010* with guest editor Randall Kennedy and *Best African American Fiction 2010* with guest editor Nikki Giovanni. His other anthologies include *The Cambridge Companion to Boxing* (2019); *The Muhammad Ali Reader* (1998); and *Body Language: Writers on Sport* (1998). He has served as a consultant on several Ken Burns films—*Baseball*; *Jazz*; *The Tenth Inning*; *Unforgivable Blackness: The Rise and Fall of Jack Johnson*; *The War*; *The Roosevelts: An Intimate History*; and *Jackie Robinson*.

Jonathan Eig is the author of five books, three of them *New York Times* best sellers, including *Opening Day: The Story of Jackie Robinson's First Season*. He was born in Brooklyn and graduated from Northwestern University's Medill School of Journalism. A former staff writer for the *Wall Street Journal*, he has also written for the *New York Times*, the *New Yorker* online, and the *Washington Post*. Prior to the *Wall Street Journal*, he worked as a feature writer for *Chicago* magazine and as a news reporter for the *Dallas Morning News* and the *New Orleans Times-Picayune*. His first book, *Luckiest Man: The Life and Death of Lou Gehrig*, won the Casey Award for best baseball book of the year, and *Ali* was named winner of the PEN/ESPN Award for Literary Sportswriting. He has appeared on *The Daily Show* with Jon Stewart, on *Fresh Air* with Terry Gross, and in two Ken Burns documentaries: *Prohibition* and *Jackie Robinson*. But what really impresses people is that he was part of a *Jeopardy* question in 2019. He is currently working with Burns and Florentine Films on a Muhammad Ali documentary. His next book will be a biography of Reverend Dr. Martin Luther King Jr.

Randal Maurice Jelks is Professor of African and African American Studies and American Studies at the University of Kansas. He is the author of three books: *African Americans in the Furniture City: The Struggle for Civil Rights Struggle in Grand Rapids*; *Benjamin Elijah Mays, Schoolmaster of the Movement: A Biography*; and *Faith and Struggle in the Lives of Four African Americans: Ethel Waters, Mary Lou Williams, Eldridge Cleaver and Muhammad Ali*.

Mark Kurlansky is the author of thirty-three books, fiction and non-fiction, including *Nonviolence: A History of a Dangerous Idea,* which won the Dayton Literary Peace Prize; *Hank Greenberg: The Hero Who Didn't Want to Be One*; and *The Eastern Stars: How Baseball Changed the Dominican Town of San Pedro de Macoris.* He is also the author of *Cod, Salt, Havana,* a novel, and three collections of short stories.

Chris Lamb, Professor of Journalism at Indiana University–Purdue University at Indianapolis, is the author of ten books, including *Blackout: The Untold Story of Jackie Robinson's First Spring Training*; *Conspiracy of Silence: The Long Campaign to Desegregate Baseball*; *From Jack Johnson to LeBron James: Essays on Race, Media, and the Color Line*; and *Jackie Robinson: A Spiritual Biography* (with Michael G. Long). His articles on baseball have appeared in the *New York Times*, the *Los Angeles Times*, and the *Wall Street Journal* and on *ESPN.com*.

Michael G. Long is the author or editor of numerous books on civil rights, LGBTQ rights, religion, and politics, including *Jackie Robinson: A Spiritual Biography, Beyond Home Plate: Jackie Robinson on Life after Baseball,* and *First Class Citizenship: The Civil Rights Letters of Jackie Robinson.* He appeared in Ken Burns's documentary about Jackie Robinson, and he has spoken at the Negro Leagues Baseball Museum, Fenway Park, the Central Intelligence Agency, the Library of Congress, the National Constitution Center, the National Museum of American History, the National Archives, and the Schomburg Center of the New York Public Library.

Kevin Merida is a Senior Vice President at ESPN and Editor in Chief of *The Undefeated.* He was formerly managing editor of the *Washington Post.* He is coauthor of *Supreme Discomfort: The Divided*

Soul of Clarence Thomas and editor of *Being a Black Man: At the Corner of Progress and Peril.*

David Naze is Vice President for Academic Affairs at Kankakee Community College in Kankakee, Illinois. He is the author of *Reclaiming 42: Public Memory and the Reframing of Jackie Robinson's Radical Legacy*, and his research focuses on the intersection of race, sport, politics, and rhetoric.

Sridhar Pappu is the award-winning author of *The Year of the Pitcher: Bob Gibson, Denny McLain and the End of Baseball's Golden Age.* A former columnist with the *New York Times* and the *New York Observer*, he also served as a staff writer with *Sports Illustrated* and the *Washington Post* and as a correspondent with the *Atlantic*. A native of Oxford, Ohio, and graduate of Northwestern University, he currently lives in Brooklyn, where he thinks about the Cincinnati Reds every single moment of every single day.

Adam Amel Rogers is based at the USC Annenberg Norman Lear Center and oversees research on how entertainment and media impact society. He has directed two conferences on sports and the LGBTQ experience, and he has conducted research on queer media representation and how sports fandom bridges political division. He has been a contributor to the NFL Network and *Huffington Post*, and his research has been featured in *Variety*, the *Hollywood Reporter*, and the *Los Angeles Times*. He previously wrote about social justice issues for *Change.org* and worked in communications for the Gay & Lesbian Alliance Against Defamation (GLAAD).

George Vecsey is a retired sports columnist at the *New York Times* who has written over a dozen books. He was raised a Brooklyn Dodger fan in New York City and met Jackie Robinson twice, once as a young fan and once as a young reporter.

Yohuru Williams is Professor of History, McQuinn Distinguished Chair, and Dean of the College of Arts and Sciences at the University of St. Thomas in Saint Paul, Minnesota. He received his PhD from Howard University and has held a variety of administrative posts both within and outside the university, including serving as Vice President for Public Education and Research at the Jackie Robinson Foundation in New York City and Chief Historian for the Jackie Robinson Foundation. He is the author of *Black Politics/ White Power: Civil Rights Black Power and Black Panthers in New Haven;* and *Rethinking the Black Freedom Movement.* He is also the editor or coeditor of *In Search of the Black Panther Party: New Perspectives on a Revolutionary Movement* and *Liberated Territory: Toward a Local History of the Black Panther Party.* He was featured in the Ken Burns film *Jackie Robinson* and the Stanley Nelson film *The Black Panthers.* He is also a regular contributor to *The Progressive.*

INDEX

Page numbers in *italics* indicate photographs.

Rickey, Branch, xii, 21, 140–41, 190–93;
for Brooklyn Dodgers, 23; legacy of,
24, 114, 142; Mack on, 66; with media,
58; politics of, 47–48, 54, 63–64, 145;
relationship with, 44–46, 49–51, 53,
67–68, 91, 118, 143, 216n11; segregation
for, 59–60
Rivera, Mariano, 72–73
Roberts, Dave, 202
Robeson, Paul, 2, 90–91, 121–22; career of,
217n16; relationship with, 143–46, 154
Robinson, David, 99, 167
Robinson, Frank (baseball player), 31, 78–
79, 153–54, 203
Robinson, Frank (brother), 11
Robinson, Jack, Jr., 4, 94
Robinson, Jack Roosevelt. *See specific
topics*
Robinson, Jerry, 20
Robinson, Mack, 11, 96
Robinson, Mallie, 11, 15–17
Robinson, Rachel (née Isum), 22; activ-
ism for, 98; discrimination for, 36–37;
history for, 37–38; Kaepernick for, 2–3;
legacy and, 36, 94–95, 127, 187–88;
with media, 75, 204; on MLB, 4, 77;
prejudice for, xiii; relationship with,
179; Robinson, S., and, 30, 76; as wife,
11, 22, 40–41, 69, 120–21
Robinson, Sharon, 3–4, 120–21; as family,
73–74; for MLB, 187–88; Robinson, R.,
and, 30, 76
Robinson, Willa Mae, 11
Robles, Víctor, 176
Rockefeller, Nelson, 94, 109, 115, 151
Rogers, Adam Amel, 201
Rookie of the Year, 114, 143, 202
Roosevelt, Eleanor, 104
Roosevelt, Franklin, 24, 100–106
Roosevelt, Theodore, 101
Rose, Pete, 31–32
Rosellini, Lynn, 195
Ross, Joe, 176

Rudolph, Wilma, 177–79, *178*, 188
Russell, Bill, 154–55, 161
Rustin, Bayard, 43, 47, 52
Rutgers University, 217n16
Ruth, Babe, 40

Sagmoen, Marc, 72
St. Louis Rams, 192, 199
Sam, Michael, 192, 196, 197–200
Schlafly, Phyllis, 106
Schoenke, Ray, 163
Scott, Isaiah Benjamin, 15–16
Seaver, Nancy, 163
Seaver, Tom, 163
segregation: *Black Metropolis*, 116–17; for
Brooklyn Dodgers, 29, 34; *Brown v.
Board of Education*, 108, 136; commu-
nism against, 149–50; in community,
20; for Democratic Party, 102–3; dis-
crimination and, 55–56; in education,
20; leadership against, 74–76; for me-
dia, 60–69, *67*, 73–74; in MLB, 12, 43,
93, 113–14, 153, 155–56; Negro Leagues
for, 30–31; in NFL, 10–11; politics of,
12, 39; for Rickey, 59–60; in sports, 13,
31–32; in US, 10, 121–22, 136, 141–42;
white people against, 45–46
Selig, Bud, 73–76, 126–27, 166–67, 187
Sharpe, Sterling, 197
Shea Stadium, 29
Shridharani, Krishnalal, 43
Simons, William, 65, 69
slavery, 18–19, 22, 99
Smith, Claire, 73
Smith, Red, 66, 69
Smith, Tommie, 96–97, 125, 153, 160
Smith, Wendell, 40, 61–62, 64, 67–68,
141–42
SNCC. *See* Student Nonviolent Coordi-
nating Committee
Snider, Jeff, 79–80
social justice, 134–37, 173
The Souls of Black Folk (Du Bois), 117